WHY WORK?

WHY WORK?

The Perceptions of a "Real Job"
and the Rhetoric of Work
through the Ages

Robin Patric Clair, Ph.D.
Megan McConnell, Stephanie Bell,
Kyle Hackbarth, and Stephanie Mathes

Purdue University Press / West Lafayette, Indiana

ISBN 978-1-55753-454-5

Library of Congress Cataloging-in-Publication Data

Why work? : the perceptions of "a real job" and the rhetoric of work through the ages /
Robin Patric Clair.
 p. cm.
Includes bibliographical references and index.
ISBN 978-1-55753-454-5 (alk. paper)
1. Work—Philosophy. 2. Work—History. 3. Labor—Philosophy. 4. Management—
History. 5. Rhetoric—Social aspects. I. Clair, Robin Patric. II. Title: Perceptions of
"a real job". III. Title: Rhetoric of work through the ages.
HD4904.W488 2008
331.01—dc22   2007001852

Acknowledgments

Although it may seem odd to acknowledge my coauthors, I do so because without their intellectual enthusiasm and youthful energy this book may not have reached completion. Megan McConnell, Stephanie Bell, Kyle Hackbarth, and Stephanie Mathes dedicated their energies and assisted me in conducting research, writing, and editing chapters in Part Two of this book. They demonstrated research and writing skills far above the average undergraduate student, and their youthful perspective allowed us to add interesting information that otherwise might not have been included. Although we were a diverse group, especially in our political views, that did not stop us from combining our efforts to complete a book that we feel is rich in information for anyone interested in the topic of work. I mention the disparities in our views only so that the reader understands why I provide the following disclaimer. My coauthors contributed significant amounts to Part Two of the book, but they should not be held accountable for any positions that I promote in Part One or Part Three of *Why Work: The Perceptions of a "Real Job" and the Rhetoric of Work through the Ages*. Before completing the acknowledgments, I would like to add one other disclaimer. The philosophers, rhetoricians, and activists whose lives and theories we have included in these chapters wrote from the time of antiquity to the end of the twentieth century. As a result their language is often sexist, laden with terms that are no longer acceptable. Nevertheless, we decided to let their words flow without interrupting their passages with the familiar *sic*. Please note that sexist language in the book is the result of relying on direct quotes from a time when scholars were not yet enlightened in this area. Any sexist language, then, should not reflect on the skills of Rebekah Fox, graduate student in the Department of Communication at Purdue University, whom I would like to thank for her insightful editorial advice. Ten blind reviewers also gave me advice during the early stage of this book's development. Thank you. In addition, Professor John Pomery of the Krannert School of Management at Purdue University generously agreed to read the first draft as well as a revised version of the manuscript and gave me excellent advice.

I would also like to thank Julia Ohaver. Most importantly, I would like to thank my husband Timothy Hack, my children Cory, Calle, and Shea, and my brothers and sisters for their support. I would also like to thank Margaret Hunt, managing editor, and Rebecca Corbin, marketing manager at Purdue University Press for their help. I am indebted to John Joerschke for assisting with editing in the final stages. Finally, I would like to thank Thomas Bacher, Director of Purdue University Press for his encouragement and patience.

Dedication

This book is dedicated to the memory of my parents. Although I would describe my parents as devout Republicans, they did not hesitate to give liberal advice when they saw fit. My mother taught me to support small business owners when malls began to take over the American landscape, and my father taught me never to cross a picket line. Both taught me to respect workers of every kind and to think critically about the world of work. May they rest in peace.

Contents

Preface

It is surprising that many college students are unaware of the philosophical and rhetorical traditions that underlie the organizational practices they encounter in every day life. Actually, American college students show an alarming lack of knowledge concerning prominent philosophers and theorists of work, labor, and organization. Specifically, only 26.6 percent of college freshmen at Texas A&M University "were able to identify Adam Smith" as the father of capitalism, and only "32.7 percent were able to identify Karl Marx" (Manton & English, 1988, p. 363). And these are not the only famous people that students have trouble identifying. In short, many students are unfamiliar with famous philosophers, practitioners, and activists who wrote and spoke on work-related issues. Clearly, an academic need exists to provide a general reference work that introduces the rhetorical and philosophical influences on the practice of work.

We wrote this book in order to provide professors and students with a comprehensive yet succinct reference book that introduces them to the lives and writings of those who have shaped the perceptions of work. Understanding the ontology of work, labor, and organization requires familiarity with the grand rhetorical arguments that have formed, sustained, challenged, or changed the meaning of work across time and across cultures. This book provides an overview of the discursive constructions of work, a brief history on work through the ages, and chapters highlighting prominent scholars and activists. It gives students a sorely needed background in how work has been addressed via the humanities, and it gives professors and instructors background information to guide their lectures. The goal of this book is to furnish interested individuals and especially professors and college students with an historical overview of the rhetorical arguments that helped to define and shape certain views of work, labor, and organization with a special focus on philosophers, practitioners, and activists who have contributed substantially to the meaning of work.

This book is not only *for* professors and students; it has been written *by* a professor and students. Four undergraduate honors students worked with me during the initial stages of the book project and became my coauthors. The first question we asked ourselves was which philosophers should be included in a book about the philosophy and rhetoric of work. Over 30 nominations were made. The students and I then explored these possibilities keeping in mind the criterion that the philosopher, practitioner or activist should have had a serious impact on the world of work or theories about work, labor, or organization. We divided these nominations among ourselves and did preliminary research about each individual's life and contributions to work.

During regular meetings, we also decided that we wanted a variety of theorists who held different views, as well as a respectable number of minority and female philosophers who have far too often been left out of the mix. We also wanted to be inclusive in the sense that theories are not always driven by scholars. Activists have certainly contributed to the changing meanings and practices of work. Once our list was narrowed to fifteen theorists, practitioners, or activists, we divided the research assignments. Each of us gathered more information about three selected historical figures and wrote reports to be shared with the group. The original list included Plato, Aristotle, St. Benedict, Adam Smith, Karl Marx, Mother Jones, Frederick Taylor, Emile Durkheim, Max Weber, Mary Parker Follett, Lillian Gilbreth, Chester Barnard, Ludwig Von Bertalanffy, Michel Foucault, and Jürgen Habermas. This list was later altered, as will be explained shortly.

We met regularly over the course of one semester (in which the students received independent study credit) to discuss research, biographical sketches, and contemporary articles that demonstrate the value of the perspective being discussed. All papers were shared, discussed, and improved upon by the group. By the end of the semester, we had collected information and written the first drafts for 11 of the 15 chapters. Not only did we do serious research concerning the life and philosophy of the scholar or activist, but we also challenged ourselves to find information that the average text or resource book does not include, information that would pique the interest of undergraduate students (e.g., Who would have guessed that Adam Smith had been kidnapped by gypsies at the age of three only to have his release negotiated within a few days?). Each report began with an introduction and was followed by a biographical sketch of the individual. The body of these reports described the philosophical perspective, theory, or practices of the individual's works or life activities. The historical figure's contributions were then related to contemporary research in a section that addressed how the philosophy is being used today.

However, at the end of the semester we noted that we had not done justice to the minority or female voice. With only three out of fifteen women and no minorities we decided that we needed to rethink our choices. All but one student graduated at the end of the year (one was a junior when we started, the others were seniors), so they were no longer actively involved in the project with the exception of Megan McConnell, who stayed and helped to proof some of the early drafts. I took it upon myself to add Confucius, Booker T. Washington, W. E. B.

Du Bois, and Emma Goldman to our list of historical figures. I then began arranging the book. Its length was unwieldy at this point, so I made the editorial decision to include only those scholars up to and including the twentieth century. Other books have taken up the twenty-first-century scholars such as Hannah Arendt and Michel Foucault (e.g., Schaff, 2001). We mention these individuals in sections on contemporary contributions to previous theories within the historical biography chapters.

In the case of ancient rhetoric, we had already chosen to discuss Aristotle's and Plato's lives and contributions within the same chapter in order to highlight their similarities and differences. I later did the same for the chapters on Confucius and St. Benedict, Booker T. Washington and W. E. B. Du Bois, as well as for Mother Jones and Emma Goldman. I sent the first draft of select chapters (including the historical overview and a few of the historical figure chapters) along with an outline to 10 professors who teach organizational communication. The book was also reviewed by Prof. John Pomery of the Krannert School of Management at Purdue University. These reviews encouraged the writing of an additional section, a conclusion. Thus, Part Three was written to act as a conclusion and commentary on why and how we work today.

Part One of this book provides two chapters: one chapter on the ontology of work and how discussions of work emerge in the classroom, and a second chapter on the history of work through the ages. Chapter One includes the story of how I have worked with my own students in the college classroom over the last twenty years to explain the history and relevance of work. Students write stories about the last time they encountered the expression *a real job*. The students then share those essays in class. The essays reveal that Adam Smith's rhetoric has had an impact on how we construct the meaning of valuable work. But it also becomes clear that there are people who challenge the status quo and sometimes evidence what Marx promoted in his writings. Issues of race, class, and gender are discussed. For example, we discuss the concept of class prejudice that surfaces in the stories, especially when students have inadvertently told someone with whom they work temporarily (perhaps over the summer) that they couldn't wait to get a real job, when the student's temporary job is the other person's real job. The conversations are eye-opening in a number of ways. Chapter Two provides a historical overview of how work has been organized throughout the ages. The chapter is limited culturally because it begins in the West, ancient Greece, and traces the European roots of work to a modern American understanding.

In Part Two of the book, chapters are provided on historical figures and their specific contributions. Max Weber suggested that "'historical individuals' are themselves values and in part determine what constitutes relevant or significant knowledge" (as cited in Wrong, 1970, p. 11). It is the humanities, he assured us, that recognize that values are subjective, created, and changing across time. Thus, the varied perspectives provide examples of how the concept of work has been conceived of and debated through the ages.

Turner (1998) suggests that a "distinctive rhetorical knowledge can be gained through historical perspectives" (p. 3). Gronbeck (1998) agrees and asserts "that the rhetorical study of history as something more than reports of the past has occupied the attention of significant theorists for a quarter of a millennium" (p. 48). Specifically, Gronbeck points to Adam Smith as an example of a rhetorician intrigued by historical accounts. Smith, according to Gronbeck, suggested that "some historians practiced what he called an *oratorical method*; he found that . . . historians used discussions of consequences and implications of actions in the past to deliver moral and political lessons to their audiences" (p. 47). Today, we note that history is constructed, whether the accounts are blatantly moralistic or covertly imbued with underlying meanings. The choice of whose rhetoric is to be presented, as well as how and what is presented, is telling in and of itself (Culpepper Clark & McKerrow, 1998; Turner, 1998; Zinn, 1995). Rhetoric, whether contemporary or historical, can "be regarded as a force that holds human societies together, shaping their social and political sensibilities and determining their direction and destiny" (Poulakos & Poulakos, 1999, p. ix). Rhetoric can also challenge social constructions of the world and offer possibilities for change. Revisiting the rhetoric of the past "counters a common presentist assumption that what happened had to happen—and it does so by directing attention to the roads not taken" (Zarefsky, 1998, p. 31). The rhetoric of the past is meaningful; the presentation (or lack thereof) of the rhetoric of the past is equally meaningful. With this in mind, we present the rhetoric of the past, some of which is commonly known, some of which is not, in order to gain a fuller, richer perspective on the meaning of work, the ways in which work is organized, and why people work.

Many of the key figures included in Part Two have been seriously neglected in the handbooks and textbooks used for organizational behavior, organizational communication, and industrial psychology classes, as well as business, management, leadership, and supervision classes. Sadly, Aristotle and Plato are not even mentioned in the leading organizational communication texts. Confucius has not been included in Western discussions of work. St. Benedict's contributions are nearly invisible. Women like Mother Jones, Emma Goldman, and Mary Parker Follett are rarely given the credit they are due. More often than not, critical theory surfaces half-way through the texts with a paragraph or less about Karl Marx. Neither Booker T. Washington, who founded Tuskegee Institute and the pragmatic approach to work, nor W. E. B Du Bois, who challenged the capitalist organization of work as exploitation on the grounds of imperialist racist practices, is anywhere in the undergraduate textbooks on work. This book includes those voices that have been silenced over the years. In addition, the chapters in Part Two extend beyond providing a profile of famous individuals and summaries of their work; it also provides a framework for positioning famous theorists and explaining their related contributions to the meaning and practice of work.

Following Part Two, the implications of these historical contributions are discussed in light of how and why we work in contemporary society. The different positions are portrayed as debates that emerge throughout history, an ongoing dialogue. Those positions give rise to questions that force individuals to consider the assumptions that undergird work. In Part Three, a conclusion is provided that addresses how these scholars' arguments present a debate related to how we define work, arrange work, and engage in work today.

Part One

The Ontology and History of Work

Chapter One

The Messy Business of Defining Work

We all work, in one way or another, depending of course, on how we define work. In *The Oxford Book of Work*, the editor notes that "*Work* is harder to define than one might think" (Thomas, 1999, p. xiii). Some 600 pages later the editor has not exhausted all the possible commentaries on work. Even the hardiest of readers is sure to be overwhelmed by the number of stories and poems, treatises and theories as well as quips and quotes about the meaning of work.

Extensive definitions of work, labor, toil, drudgery, employment, and job—as well as conceivable antonyms, such as leisure, unemployment, idleness, and play—have been discussed at length by various scholars for their similarities and differences (Ciulla, 2000; Levine, 2001; Muirhead, 2004; Okrent, 2001). Not to confuse the issue, but it's possible for some people to play at work and others to work at play. This notion upsets the dialectical and definitional applecart and makes distinctions between such terms as *work* and *play* ambiguous, paradoxical, and possibly even obsolete. In short, defining work is a messy business.

It is, however, worth the effort. In the search for the quintessential definition of work one is necessarily forced to grapple with the grander meaning of labor. Examining why we work, how we work, and under whose yoke we work forces us to assess our role in the world of work, our place in this social scheme of labor. In the novel *A Confederacy of Dunces*, Ignatius Reilly finds work to be a repugnant indignation unfairly served upon him, to be avoided or at the very least altered into some other more satisfactory state of reality (Toole, 1980). Each character realizes something different yet unique about work. Although each takes up one truth about work, the meaning and purpose of work are neither fixed nor uniform in any way. As Muirhead (2004) suggests, "There are as many experiences of work as there are workers, as many kinds of work as there are jobs" (p. 4).

3

Work is a slippery concept, and we should be grateful that it is so. Being slippery means that we are not limited to one view of work and that we can find or create alternative meanings and practices if a system is oppressive or, at the very least, improve upon a system of work that may seem less than satisfactory. We can relish some work and despise other work. We can find multiple meanings in one job or no meaning at all in another. But even though the concept may seem slippery, there are some fundamental aspects of work that seem to be shared within individual cultures or societies. As such, exploring how certain cultures have defined work in general throughout the ages may shed light on how contemporary workers come to their understanding and ways of practicing work.

The individual definitions of job, work, career, employment, etc., are important, but their importance takes on a specific significance when one considers how they are promoted through rhetorical arguments, philosophical discussions, and forms of organizing. The rhetorical or communicative creation of the meaning of work and the social organization of labor adds to the determination of what counts as valuable work as well as why we work the way we do. Thus, what counts as work may make a better question than what work is. Asking what counts as work suggests an ordering according to value that organizes how people approach work, undertake work, and judge others by their work. Indeed, how work organizes society and how societies organize work may tell us more about the working life than our continuing to struggle with individual definitions of work.

Kenneth Burke (1968) suggested that it is not the denotative or the connotative definition but rather the *dramatistic definition* that is crucial to defining who we are in relation to the world in which we live. Dramatistic definitions contain much more than denotative and connotative meanings. They are active and engaging; they frame the way we understand a phenomenon and contribute to how we act in the world in a cumulative way. Burke suggests that the dramatistic definition is laden with a *terministic screen*, which provides a way of seeing something, and once we see something a certain way, we are necessarily not seeing it in another way (Burke, 1935; see Clair, 1999a, for related discussion). Applying this philosophy to the concept of work, we find that once work is defined, its meaning created and constructed, we have a tendency to view it according to these parameters. Breaking free from a terministic screen requires critical and reflective thinking, which is not easy to do if we have been socialized to think of work, labor, jobs, etc., in a particular way. Why work? Most of us are quick to respond, "because we have to in order to survive." This is one frame surrounding our engagement in work.

The dramatistic definition could be discussed as the *narrative definition* or, more generally speaking, the discursive definition, allowing the definition to contain a rich history (White, 1980), a cultural aspect (Turner, 1980), a psychological sense (Schafer, 1980), a philosophical position (Derrida, 1967/1973; Foucault, 1966/1973; Nietzsche, 1872/1954), and perhaps a hidden purpose (Habermas,

1979, 1984). That is, the language that defines us and the work that we do contains the grand narratives of the past, as well as the everyday stories that we tell each other. These definitions are found in all forms of communication, including, for example, dialogue, conversation, stories, lectures, and speeches. They in turn frame our perceptions of work. In order to see beyond the present terministic screen we need to critique the current rhetoric and discourse surrounding work and explore those discursive or rhetorical constructions of work that have been marginalized. Doing so could provide a way to look beyond the immediate time and place in relation to definitions and arrangements of work.

Whereas socialization theorists focus on the individual contributors to our understanding of work, rhetorical scholars and philosophers focus on the discursive and material practices that surround work. For example, socialization scholars look to parental influence, part-time jobs, peer pressure, and media to explain how people attain their image and expectations of work (e.g., Jablin, 2001). Rhetorical scholars, on the other hand, look at a wide range of communicative practices, from the rhetoric of the past to the everyday discourse of today in order to understand how people attribute meaning to and engage with work. The rhetorical approach suggests that grand narratives (Lyotard, 1979/1984) of the past influence the ways that we think today (Clair, 1992, 1996). For example, Adam Smith devoted years to writing his book *An Inquiry into the Nature and Causes of the Wealth of Nations,* and within it the story of capitalism unfolds. Smith's rhetorical description of capitalism is just one rhetorical vision of work and socioeconomics. It is of course the dominant one in America today, and because capitalism has grown dependent on organizational success, scholars tend to place organizational work at the center of this socioeconomic story.

This was not always the case. Greek life, which will be given greater attention in the next chapter, promoted entrepreneurship. Working for someone else's profit was not a choice that would be made freely. In short, only slaves worked for another person's wealth. Today, working for an organization is the norm, not the exception. Its prevalence may contribute to the reason that so many researchers focus their attention on organizational life and so many college students focus on attaining organizational jobs. But it should be noted that this is a relatively recent development. Even Adam Smith wrote about a variety of jobs, including farming and being a soldier, when he discussed the hierarchy of job values. Yet today educational resources often place greater emphasis on corporate jobs, as if they were the *real jobs.* Farmers and soldiers are rarely mentioned in textbooks about work, organization, or business. Books exploring the societal focus on organizations or organizations' influence over society include Whyte's classic *The Organization Man* from the 1950s to more contemporary books, such as Cheney's (1991) *Rhetoric in an Organizational Society,* Deetz's (1992) *Democracy in an Age of Corporate Colonization,* or Ciulla's (2000) *The Working Life.* Drawing from Habermas (1984) and Giddens (1979), several of these scholars point out the hold corporations have on much of society today.

Each one of these scholars is seduced by the organizational aspect of the phenomenon of work. Its prevalence is undeniable. Yet although their work challenges corporate domination, it also seems absorbed by it. For example, even though Ciulla (2000) clearly states that not all work takes place in or at an organization, she nevertheless focuses on organizational work life, its shortcomings and its possibilities. Today we are seeing more researchers address alternative organizations as well as alternative forms of work, but the alternative approach is still in the minority. One of the first modern exceptions to defining work according to organizational jobs came in the form of a collection of interviews from working people.

Working is a book that questions the organizational frame that has constrained commentaries on work and expands what counts as work. Conceived by André Schiffren and written by Studs Terkel (1972), *Working* explores work from various angles. Based on interviews conducted by Terkel, the voices of people representing a wide array of jobs are heard. Ordinary people talk about their work lives in organizations and beyond. Terkel interviewed a factory worker and an executive, a prostitute and a former nun, a newspaper boy and a housewife. Some of these individuals' jobs were connected directly to organizational America; others could be linked indirectly to organizations; and some were outside the organizational purview altogether. Terkel's work defied the terministic screen and expanded the definition of what counts as work. Using this expanded approach, a child's newspaper route is not merely anticipatory socialization toward *real work* but rather embodies work itself; it counts as work.

For an expanded understanding of the meaning of work to be uncovered, the term *organization* must be expanded in yet one more way. That is, besides expanding the meaning of organization from business corporations or collectives to include nonprofit organizations, family businesses, and individual ventures (e.g., a newspaper route), an additional meaning of organization needs to be considered: organization as order. How does work bring order to society, and how does society organize work? A metalevel meaning of organization might open new vistas for researchers and provide new insights into the meaning of work. A metalevel perspective of organization refers to organization as arrangement or order. Using a metalevel perspective allows different questions to be asked: What forms of communication construct the concept and meaning of work? How do different modes of organizing labor vary with respect to the definition of work? How is work organized in society? How does the individual define work? How or when does work define the individual? Why and how are certain forms of work privileged over others? In other words, why has the lemonade stand been relegated to a prework status, and why has housework not counted as *real work* in the past? Why are certain philosophers' treatises on work praised and others quietly secreted away?

Once an expanded sense of organization exists, one can return to the topic of communication. It too must be viewed in its most expansive form if we are to understand the meaning of work. Communication includes the grand rhetorical arguments as well as everyday talk and everything in between. Communication has been called rhetoric, discourse, language, and symbolic interaction. Its forms are innumerable: narratives, metaphors, stories, arguments, talk, conversations, advice, proverbs, poems, dance, exchange, and so on. Covering every conceivable verbal and nonverbal form of expression, communication is expansive. By using expanded definitions of organization and communication, alternative ways of seeing work become possible; we can look with *new eyes* on the meaning of work.

I have been teaching organizational communication from an expanded rhetorical perspective for more than fifteen years. During that time, I have initiated the course with an exercise asking the students to write a true story about the last time or the most significant time that they heard the expression "a real job." It could have been someone's telling them to get *a real job* or their telling someone else. Or perhaps they overheard a conversation in which the expression was used. Whatever the case, I asked the students to write the story with as much detail as possible. The results have been intriguing to say the least (Clair, 1996, 1999a).

Sitting in a circle in the classroom, we share our stories about *a real job*; I usually start. The students' stories range from heartbreaking to humorous. They are poignant, touching, and personal. They often evidence an awakening on the part of the students about the construction of the meaning and value of work. Sometimes they make discoveries only after reading their own essay aloud.

One of the students described what he felt was a real job in a rather typical fashion: good pay, promotion potential, utilization of his education, and working in an office from nine to five. We discussed its implications and moved on to others' accounts. However, he suddenly interrupted and asked if he could speak again. "Sure," I nodded. And then he told us that he suddenly realized that what he had said wasn't what he thought *a real job* was at all. He paused; we waited. He said, "That was my dad talking."

On another occasion, as we went around the circle, upon reaching a young woman, the stories stopped. I asked her to tell us about her experience with the phrase *a real job*.

"I'm afraid to tell you all what I think *a real job* is," she said.

"Why?" I asked.

"I think people will make fun of me."

"We won't laugh, I promise," I said to her and looked around at the other students, who nodded in agreement. Then she told us what she wanted to do with her life.

"I want to be a mother and stay home with my children."

I smiled and told her that I thought being a mother is a very important job. The class began a lively discussion about the value of being a mother, stay-at-home moms versus moms who also hold paid jobs outside the home, feminism, and choice. We also talked about just how marginalized housework and mothering can be, especially when related to work (Clair & Thompson, 1996). The topic of stay-at-home dads was not raised as an option during this conversation but was discussed by another class (a graduate class, several years later).

Muirhead (2004) believes that Betty Friedan's (1963) book *The Feminine Mystique* not only discredited motherhood but mistakenly led white, middle-class women to believe that work outside the home promised enrichment and fulfillment. Muirhead suggested that Friedan didn't understand at the time that work made no such promise, not to blue-collar workers or to executives, not to hard-working lower-income workers, whether they are male or female, white or minority. He suggested that Friedan needed to be familiar with Whyte's (1956) *The Organization Man*. In short, few jobs hold the fulfillment, creativity, or expressiveness that Friedan sought, according to Muirhead. Muirhead offers an intriguing and debatable point that many scholars of the past and present have considered. Most recently, Medved and Kirby (2005) have explored the enabling and constraining aspects of current ways motherhood and work are framed. Specifically, they analyzed the discourse in several self-help books and Web sites that promoted the use of business jargon to define stay-at-home mothers. They found that the discourse created identities that encouraged a strong corporate ethic. These identities include: mothers as professionals (CEO Moms or Chief Home Officers—CHO), mothers as managers, mothers as productive citizens, and mothers as irreplaceable workers. The authors also provide a history that may explain the ideological struggle between feminist anti-motherhood of the 1960s and capitalist demands over the last century.

At any rate, the young woman in my class came away from the conversation feeling assured that she would not be wasting her education by becoming a mother and staying at home. Furthermore, an openness and supportiveness among the class members ensued. She was the only undergraduate student in the last twenty years to broach the topic of motherhood in my class; most students write and talk about working for organizations. More than 75 percent of the first group of narratives analyzed "alluded to working for organizations either explicitly (by name) or implicitly (e.g., wanting a bi-weekly pay check, advancement, or reporting to others)" (Clair, 1996, p. 263).

Although I did not lecture on any theories of work before the students provided their stories, I later explained to them that the vast majority of their accounts fit within Adam Smith's (1776/1937) description of valuable labor—producing goods and meeting other criteria. Moreover, their accounts tended to see working for an organization as a part of *a real job*. But there were exceptions. Some students reported facing prejudice because they held jobs that were not considered *real* by society's standards. Even the stories of work that did not fit the dominant image supported the dominant philosophy in the sense that these marginalized workers knew they represented the *black sheep* of the *real job market*. The following story demonstrates how certain philosophies influence people's perception of work.

A student who works as a ski instructor was told that he did not have *a real job* because his job was "seasonal," "recreational," "easy," "did not require much education," and most importantly it was "enjoyable" (see Clair, 1996, p. 256). Each of these attributes, according to Adam Smith's criteria, devalues the worth of a job. Although this individual felt he held *a real job*, he also reported that almost no one else saw it that way.

In a turnabout, another student in the class reported that he told his friend that he did not have *a real job* because even though his friend had a four-year degree he hadn't utilized it. He worked part-time as a snowplow driver, a job that did not require his education or skill. The student was annoyed because his friend was "capable of much more." Wasting one's education is a theme that can be linked to Adam Smith's philosophy because he argued that workers should be used to their fullest capacity. Although Smith was talking about manual laborers for the most part, the idea is transferable and explains in part why some people told the student who wanted to be a stay-at-home mother that she too would be wasting her education.

Most students wrote that a real job "pays well" (six figures was suggested), holds the possibility for "advancement," includes being a part of "management," allows for "independence" and "your own office," is "full-time," and is "40 hours" with "benefits" and with a "reputable company" (Clair, 1996, p. 257).

These attributes paint a picture that supports the image of an organizational society. But some students provided stories that showed their personal challenge to the organizationally driven society. One student majoring in business wrote that she had been struggling with exactly what she wanted to do after college. One day she heard a Peace Corps volunteer talk about volunteer experiences. She immediately knew what she wanted to do. She went to see her counselor and told her of her dream to join the Peace Corps. The counselor responded by saying:

> You've spent four long years of hard work to become a successful business-person out there in the corporate world. Why would you want to throw it all away to go live in Africa with a bunch of illiterate natives? You need to graduate and get a real job! (see Clair, 1996, p. 260)

Without a doubt the expression *a real job* is used to reinforce a particular meaning of work, which in turn directs certain people toward certain jobs and away from others. Outside the classroom, I interviewed a farmer and his wife. We met under casual circumstances, and they asked me politely, but with little interest, what I did at the university. When I told them I teach organizational communication and that recently I had been studying the students' perceptions of what it means to have *a real job*, the farmer became animated and involved in the conversation. He quickly and assertively responded by saying, "If they want to know what a real job is, I can tell them." We spent the rest of the time talking about his work as I followed him from the pigsty to the barn, where he and his wife threw bales of straw from the floor of the barn to the loft, a job that leaves one's arms badly pricked and sore and one's shoulders and back stiff the next morning.

Many of my students learned the hard way that their perceptions of *a real job* were not necessarily the same as everyone else's perception of *a real job*, as the following stories indicate.

> Some time ago when a friend of mine worked at a Sohio [gas] station she was asked why she couldn't get a real job. . . . she answered . . . "This job is as real as they come." [Although she] ignored the comment [at first], . . . she did think about changing her career expectations. She graduated from college and got a "real" job, she is currently not satisfied. She believes that a real job is an illusion mainly because there is so much more to life then [sic] a job. (Clair, 1996, p. 261)

Another student wrote that he was studying to be a pharmacist and could hardly wait until he got *a real job* but that he had to be careful whom he said this in front of at work. He worked as a clerk in a drugstore, and for many of the clerks, "this is their real job" (p. 263), he wrote. Other students said that they had felt guilty or embarrassed when they made reference to getting *a real job* when they worked in restaurants or at garden nurseries because, for many of their co-workers, these jobs *were* their *real jobs*. At a nursery another employee taunted the student, asking him when he was going to get *a real job*. The student wrote, "I guess he felt that I was in some way infringing on his job and he felt threatened by this" (p. 263). One student reported feeling terrible about asking her restaurant manager when he was going to get *a real job*. She later realized that she had insulted him because that was his *real job*. Tensions according to class difference certainly existed (Clair, 1996).

Students also wrote about being socialized to understand the meaning of *a real job*. According to the stories, fathers, more than mothers, fostered the spirit of working at *a real job*. For example, one student wrote:

> When I used to be a paper girl (ages 12–14), my father explained to me that soon I'd be getting a real Job, and for my age (15) I did in fast food. My jobs afterward progressed to waitressing, and again I discussed a real Job (when I'd graduate from college someday). (p. 260)

This story not only suggests that fathers help socialize their children to the concept of *a real job* but also that the concept of *a real job* changes over time. In the following story, a student points out how her father similarly set forth his expectations:

> My family and I were eating dinner in a restaurant, talking about school, graduation, future plans. My sister has her life mapped out to the letter. . . . She is in computers. . . . Then there is me, a Liberal Arts major, a senior, graduating soon with no clear plans. My father after listening to my sister says [to me] "When are you going to limit down your career goals and decide on a real job?" (p. 260)

More recent research has revealed that mothers, like fathers, give a good deal of "memorable" job advice and that both male and female college students are encouraged to place their families first and their jobs second (Medved, Brogan, McClanahan, Morris, & Shepherd, 2006).

Only on rare occasions did I hear students consider their studies *a real job*. When questioned later in discussion, students most often explained that being a student did not count as *a real job* because they did not get paid. Again, there have been a few exceptions over the years, students who believe they work hard and that being a student is in itself *a real job*.

Even if students held *reputable* jobs they felt their specific workplace was diminished by other factors, such as the quality of management. Numerous stories spoke to the abilities of managers. If students worked for poorly managed organizations, then they quickly responded with comments like, "I can't wait until I get *a real job*."

Not only did students judge management and bring it into the *real job* equation, but they found themselves being judged by others according to their jobs. Students both judged and were judged by their occupations. One student wrote about a personal relationship and the concept of *a real job:* "We had gotten rather close and all was well until one day she asked me when I was going to get a real job" (p. 260). The interpersonal relationship became a victim of *job judgment*. Valuing or devaluing a friend, a lover, or a significant other according to job status (due to any one of several criteria) categorizes the individual according to the tasks performed (the organization worked for, the money paid, etc.) rather than to the person performing the tasks.

Only two of the first thirty-four students[1] to write stories discussed work as a *calling*, something that was "at the core of the work ethic" but is disappearing in the secular, credit-oriented era of capitalism, according to Muirhead (2004, p. 10). One student wrote that she wanted to be "happy" and have a job "that I can deem as God's will for me, where I am helping others, because I tend to look upon those in need and want desperately to make a change." The student was working at a home for disabled children, and she felt that "few appreciate" the work, "(even the kids!), few understand, and even fewer could give a shit (excuse me) by their Real Job standards. Down comes my self worth again. My Real Job doesn't measure up" (Clair, 1996, p. 258). She continued:

> ... I've neglected myself and my Real Job goal. Discouraged and lost, I don't know how long it will be before I achieve it, but when I do, perhaps I should add to my criteria ... even though others may not agree ... one that takes more than a degree, one that says, It's O.K. to be me. (p. 263)

The dynamic and dialectical nature, the tensions between labor and management, college-educated or not, between job and calling, between socializers and socialized, all demonstrated the powerful effect that a colloquialism, a small part of everyday language, can have on people. The expression helps to encapsulate ideologies, promote certain ways of organizing the world of work, and yet can be used in defiance to challenge that working world, as well. The stories represented the grand arguments of Adam Smith, for the most part, but made room for other philosophies. The everyday talk reinforced the grand rhetorical arguments, and the grand rhetorical arguments reinforced the use of this everyday expression—*a real job*. That is to say they "co-produced" each other (Giddens, 1979; see R. Smith, 1990/1993, 1993 for a discussion of this co-production in relation to organizational communication), generally supporting the dominant view of reality but also always leaving room for resistance.

Following this classroom exercise, I provide an overview of the history of work through the ages, pointing out how conceptions of work, as well as organization, have changed. The students point to philosophies and practices that seemed to appear in their stories. Then I link the meaning and value of a job with the rhetoric or discursive practices that create and sustain the meanings of work. For example, one of several criteria that Adam Smith uses to ascertain the value of work is whether the person performs it as a full-time source of income rather than part-time or for enjoyment—a farmer's job versus a person's caring for a garden in his or her backyard. Both individuals are growing crops, tending the plants, hoping for a good harvest. Although the gardener is working, capitalism credits this activity with little value. It's not *a real job* in our society by most people's standards. And if it's not *real work*, then why do we do it? Our reasons surely go beyond self-sustenance. Our discussions move to the topic of how the rhetoric of the past influences how people think and behave today, how people engage in work, and how people judge work and other people in relation to it.

Furthermore, how we talk today can reinforce or challenge the rhetoric of the past. For example, the student who told his friend to get *a real job* because he only wanted to play music is reinforcing Adam Smith's philosophy of work. But the student who said she did not care what other people said about her work is challenging the generally accepted meaning of work. Likewise, textbooks that begin studies of work with organizations and or with philosophers like Adam Smith or management theorists like Frederick Taylor encourage a certain terministic screen, one that reinforces a capitalist meaning of work. An expanded rhetorical approach encourages looking at the dominant ideology as well as the marginalized. A rhetorical approach suggests that there is nothing wrong with studying the philosophy of Adam Smith or the theories proposed by Frederick Taylor. But the expanded approach encourages us to look also at the philosophies of Aristotle, Plato, Karl Marx, Booker T. Washington, W. E. B. Du Bois, Emma Goldman, Mother Jones, and a host of other philosophers, theorists, and activists. By doing so we open new vistas and provide more than one way of seeing the world of work. Whether it is through lectures, textbooks, or everyday talk, our communication sustains, maintains, or challenges certain work perspectives and practices. How we talk about work may answer the question, why work?

Today's emphasis on organizations and organizational theories did not emerge accidentally. To the contrary, the fact that so many textbooks begin with scientific management is based on a terministic screen and a specific choice.[2] Making Taylorism prominent keeps organizations, technological advancements, and a functional perspective within the parameters of the status quo, suggesting that there are no other theories or other ways of organizing theories (Clair, 1999b). Understanding the rhetoric of the past positions the theories of today in a whole new light. Sexism and racism are not separate topics related to work; they are part and parcel of the ordering of society. Class distinctions and work stereotypes are not superfluous issues; rather, they are at the heart of sustaining a certain system. When certain philosophers, rhetoricians, and activists are marginalized, alternative voices are not heard with the same intensity as the dominant voice. Consequently, one view permeates our everyday lives. Thus, we can find whole ideologies encapsulated in a single phrase like "a real job" or "hard work."[3] People become stereotyped by the jobs they hold, and a hierarchy of work status prevails. Many of the students faced their own prejudices when they shared their "real job" stories. Even more said that they had to question how they thought of other people and other jobs after I read the following story to them.

The story comes from Studs Terkel's book *Working* and is entitled "Who Built the Pyramids." A factory worker laments the monotony, the hardship, and the incessant supervision of his job and describes the resulting frustration from holding such a job.

> I put on my hard hat, change into my safety shoes, put on my safety glasses, go to the bonderizer . . . rake the metal, . . . wash it, . . . dip it in a paint solution and . . . take it off. Put it on, take it off, put it on, take it off, put it on, take it off . . .
>
> . . . . I say hello to everybody but my boss. At seven it starts. My arms get tired about the first half-hour. After that, they don't get tired any more until maybe the last half-hour at the end of the day. I work from seven to three-thirty. My arms are tired at seven thirty and they're tired at three o'clock. . . . I always want my arms to be tired at seven thirty and three o'clock. (Laughs.) 'Cause that's when I know that there's a beginning and an end. That I'm not brainwashed. In between, I don't even try to think. (p. 5)

Mike LeFevre, the factory worker, does indeed think. He considers issues of racism and says:

> I can't really hate the colored fella that's working with me all day. The black intellectual I got no respect for. The white intellectual I got no use for. I got no use for the black militant who's gonna scream three hundred years of slavery to me while I'm busting my ass. . . . I have one answer for that guy: go see Rockefeller. (p. 6)

The factory worker realizes that it is capitalism that perpetuates the current system. Furthermore, he recognizes that communism is no different. Communism is "the intellectual's utopia, not mine" (p. 6). Mike LeFevre may have been aware that Taylorism and time management studies were just as quickly put into effect in Russia as they were in the United States. Communists are pictured as if

> They're singing about how they love the factory . . . I cannot picture myself singing to a tractor, I just can't. (Laughs.) Or singing to steel. (Singsongs.) Oh Whoop-dee-doo, I'm at the bonderizer, oh how I love this heavy steel. No thanks. Never happen. (p. 6)

And with respect to hierarchy and the roles of supervisor and subordinate, the factory worker is quick to set the record straight.

> I would rather work my ass off for eight hours a day with nobody watching me than five minutes with a guy watching me. Who you gonna sock? . . . You can't sock a system. . . . all day I wanted to tell my foreman to go fuck himself, but I can't. So I find a guy in a tavern. To tell him that. And he tells me too. I've been in brawls . . . [in the tavern] all that'll happen is the bartender will bar us from the tavern. But at work, you lose your job. (pp. 2–3)

Could there be more to work? Of course, after all:

> It's not just the work. Somebody built the pyramids. Somebody's going to build something. Pyramids, Empire State Building—these things just don't happen. There's hard work behind it. I would like to see a building, say, the Empire State, I would like to see on one side of it a foot-wide strip from top to bottom with the name of every bricklayer, the name of every electrician, with all the names. So when a guy walked by, he could take his son and say, "See that's me over there on the forty-fifth floor. I put the steel beam in." Picasso can point to a painting. What can I point to? A writer can point to a book. Everybody should have something to point to. (p. 2)

Mike LeFevre is also aware that

> The twenty-hour work week is a possibility today. . . . What do you think would happen in this country if, for one year they experimented and gave everybody a twenty-hour week? . . . The intellectuals, they always say there are potential Lord Byrons, Walt Whitmans, Roosevelts, Picassos working in construction or steel mills or factories. But I don't think they believe it. I think what they're afraid of are the potential Hitlers and Stalins that are there too. The people in power fear the leisure man. (p. 4, order changed slightly)

One way to resist the mind-numbing, alienating aspect of factory work is to find a way to put your signature on it. As Mike LeFevre says:

I want my signature on 'em, too. Sometimes, out of pure meanness, when I make something, I put a little dent in it. I like to do something to make it really unique. I deliberately fuck it up to see if it'll get by, just so I can say I did it. (pp. 9–10)

This is a way to be immortalized. The factory worker speaks of one other way to be immortalized: through his children. Mike LeFevre wants to see his children graduate from college. He says:

This is gonna sound square, but my kid is my imprint. He's my freedom. There's a line in one of Hemingway's books. I think it's from *For Whom the Bell Tolls*. They're behind enemy lines, somewhere in Spain, and she's pregnant. She wants to stay with him. He tells her no. He says, "if you die, I die," knowing he's gonna die. But if you go, I go. Know what I mean? This is why I work. Every time I see a young guy walk by with a shirt and tie and dressed up real sharp, I'm lookin' at my kid, you know? That's it. (p. 10)

I cannot tell you how many students have asked if they can borrow my copy of Studs Terkel's book after I read this story to them. Several young students have had tears in their eyes as they reach for the book saying, "That's my dad." Some of them call home that very night. Others have bought their own copy of the book to mail home, saying thank-you to parents whose sacrifices have all too often, until then, gone unrecognized. This generates a conversation between students and parents that continues throughout the semester. Parents call, asking their son or daughter, "What else are you reading?" And sons and daughters call home, asking their parents for their opinion on some other reading that I have assigned, most often Ben Hamper's (1986) *Rivethead*.

Others have admitted to presuming that factory workers were limited to unskilled jobs because they were not smart enough to work elsewhere. They are humbled that Mike LeFevre, a factory worker, knows more about economics, philosophy, and literature than they do. And they are moved by the fact that he works in order to make sure his children have a better life. The reasons why LeFevre works may not be the same as why others work. His reasons certainly move beyond the basic instinct of survival. His reasons may not speak for all people, but they do speak of concern for his children and an interest in the future.

The questions regarding why we work are no easier to answer than the question of why certain work is more valued than other work. But like exploring the definition of work, investigating why we work also deserves our time and attention. After providing a history of work through the ages and the multiple voices of philosophers, rhetoricians, and activists, I provide a concluding chapter as well as an epilogue. I discuss how we have come to accept certain meanings of what counts as *a real job*, how we might view work from different perspectives, and what questions might be asked in the future about work.

Notes

1. It should be noted that these students came from two different universities: an urban university where the average age of the undergraduate was, at the time, twenty-eight years, and the other a land-grant institution that specialized in engineering, where the students were younger.

2. Several exceptional textbooks on organizational communication include alternative perspectives (e.g., see Cheney, Christensen, Zorn, & Ganesh, 2004; Conrad & Poole, 2005; Eisenberg, Goodall, Jr., & Trethewey 1997; Miller, 2003).

3. Both of these everyday phrases reached the zenith of ideological display when they were used during the 2004 U.S. presidential campaign. Seemingly struck by an epiphany, George W. Bush told the American public in 2004 that it's "hard work" being president of the United States of America. On an equally incredible note, the opponent's wife, Theresa Heinz Kerry, asserted that First Lady Laura Bush had never held "a real job." Meant as an insult, the barb was quickly turned around on the Democrats, who were reminded that Laura Bush had been a librarian, a teacher, and a mother, all of which represent *real jobs*. An apology was quickly issued. Of course it hasn't always been the case that jobs such as librarian, teacher, or mother were spoken of with respect, and it still isn't the case in many circles, especially those that privilege organizational (i.e., corporation-type) jobs.

Chapter Two

Philosophy and Rhetoric of Work

Throughout history, philosophers, activists, and practitioners have espoused theoretical positions about the meaning and value of work. At times, these philosophical and rhetorical arguments have held such powerful sway that they have influenced entire cultures and changed the face of how people live and work. At other times, unforeseen events, sometimes in the vein of natural disasters or catastrophic wars, have altered the course of labor's history and the meaning of work.

The very idea that the meaning of work is relative, dynamic, and changing is new. In the past, scholars and philosophers both thought that their views of work espoused the truth of the matter. And they often argued vehemently for their positions. These classical and modern scholars, philosophers, rhetoricians, and practitioners asserted that they could supply a true definition of what constitutes work and labor. Today, postmodernists believe that the meanings of work are created through discursive practices. That is to say, different cultures, at different times, have created the meaning of work, and people have acted accordingly. If this is the case, then the true meaning of work is elusive and subject to change; its ontology is relative. With this in mind, in order to understand contemporary conceptualizations of work, it would be necessary to review how past societies through rhetorical argument and discursive practices have defined work and influenced modern perceptions and practices, especially if Derrida (1967/1973; 1967/1976) is correct in his assessment that "traces" of the distant discourse persist and perhaps, to some degree, influence the present.

Ancient Greek Meanings and Practices of Work

Ancient Greeks demonstrated a lively commerce rooted in "agriculture, handicrafts, trades, wholesales and retail business, and daily labor" (Van Hook, 1923, p. 97). Some jobs were held in higher or lower esteem than others, but in general work was valued. Slaves and freed slaves labored at the most tedious and loathsome jobs. Women of the upper-class were primarily sequestered in the homes. They conducted the domestic affairs, especially caring for children. Women of the lower class worked as weavers and wool-makers, as nurses, physicians, wet-nurses, and midwifes, as dress makers, hairdressers, seamstresses, and stenographers. They were also vendors who bought and sold salt and other groceries in the market (Lefkowitz & Fant, 1982). Citizens of Greece—that is, the white male ruling class—worked at a variety of activities including such notable professions as senators and philosophers. In ancient Greece only one form of labor stood out as deplorable. It is described in an anecdote written down by Xenophon, a student of Socrates:

> Eutherus, who has lost his overseas estates as a result of the war, has been reduced to earning his living by manual labor. Socrates asks what he will do when his bodily strength fails and suggests that he find a job as a rich man's bailiff. Eutherus is horrified at the suggestion. "I could not endure to be a slave. . . . I absolutely refuse to be at any man's beck and call." (Jones, 1957, p. 11)

"What the Athenian thete [a member of the lowest working, property class] objected to was not hard work . . . but being another man's servant" (Jones, 1957, p. 11). To work for another's profit was considered degrading by most Athenians. Eutherus would have preferred slavery to working for another man's profit of his own free will. To choose to work for someone else's profit was a foreign concept to ancient Greeks. Yet, Socrates encouraged Eutherus to take the job and explained to him that men work at the accountability of other men no matter what their occupation. Nevertheless, the repugnance associated with working for someone else's profit remained all the way into the nineteenth century. The expression *slave wages* was applied to the concept of low-paid labor during the early days of the industrial revolution. In England, "early factories had to rely on criminals and paupers to do the work" because it was considered unnatural and deplorable to work for the benefit of others (Perrow, 1986, p. 49).

Today, working for others is commonplace. Many college students look forward to landing a job with IBM, General Motors, Intel, or Exxon. They rarely view working for others as repugnant. Rather, working for someone else's profit is at the heart of the capitalist system. In order to find out why and how modern day socioeconomic systems of work took such a dramatic turn away from the ancient Greek meaning of work, an exploration beyond the ancient Greeks is in order.

Early European Changes in the Meaning and Practices of Work

Greek images of work remained intact throughout Roman rule. The Roman Empire borrowed heavily from Greek tradition in many areas, including religion and education. The practice of slavery was continued by ancient Romans, as well. However, the invasion of the Roman Empire by Vandals and Visigoths resulted in alternative work practices. During the Middle Ages two distinct socioeconomic systems emerged with very different views of labor (Burke, 1985).

Both monastic and feudal systems were grounded in protectionist practices. Monasteries and convents became the refuge of elite Roman nobles escaping the terrorism of the northern Vandals and Visigoths. Men who did not seek refuge in the monasteries became feudal lords. These medieval kings entered into contracts, often oppressive, with serfs seeking protection from the violence.

Monasticism

Medieval monasteries flourished under the philosophy of hard work, self-sufficiency, and spirituality. The monks regarded labor as a holy activity, whereas some holy activities, or rather devoting too much time to holy activities, such as prayer, were met with less enthusiasm by the abbots. Persuading the monks to work was not always easy. Many young men who went to the monasteries had come from the class of Roman freemen, who considered much manual labor, including agriculture, to be slave work, "beneath their dignity" (Sorg, 1953, p. 61). Some monks who shirked manual labor claimed that their energies were better put to use through prayer and contemplation. This justification was subverted by *St. Benedict's Rule*, which defined acceptable labor as "that labor done by the hands, which is productive of a livelihood" (Sorg, 1953, p. 32). Pursuits of a capitalist nature (i.e., business, banking, or merchandising) were forbidden to monks as early as the fifth century because occupations devoted to the making of profit were not founded on one's own labor. Consequently, any excess wealth that resulted from the monk's manual labor was distributed to the poor (Sorg, 1953). However, "the Church itself, through the monastic discipline, became a network of interconnecting points of trade and distribution criss-crossing Europe," resulting in wealth and power (Clegg, 1989, p. 244).

As the Catholic Church grew in its power to control the distribution of goods and information, it became a powerful influence in the everyday lives of the peasantry. Opposed to the practice of slavery, the Catholic Church had a marked impact on its decline during the Middle Ages (Blake, 1860).

Feudalism

Feudalism, spanning several centuries (Gibbs, 1953), crossed a widespread geographical terrain altering somewhat from culture to culture. Feudalism was practiced in Africa, Constantinople, Europe, India, Ireland, Japan, Jerusalem, Pakistan, Russia and elsewhere (Critchley, 1978). Although much of the labor during the feudal era was similar to that in ancient Greece (e.g., crafts or agriculture), the sociopolitical arrangement was quite different.

The early distinguishing features of feudalism included "a form of divided or shared ownership" unlike any seen before (Critchley, 1978, p. 11) and a system of contractual exchange for service. Although exceptions existed, generally a lord gave land to a vassal in exchange for military service. The joint ownership was evident in that most contracts allowed for the land to be inherited by the sons of the vassal, yet ownership could revert back to the lord if abuse of the land occurred or if military services were not rendered. Furthermore, if no sons were born to a fief holder, then the land was returned to the lord. Additional payment was also collected through tax monies and agricultural products or other services. Military service was a definite requirement for holding land.

Although the feudal system was based on "co-existent property rights" (Critchley, 1978, p. 21) these opportunities existed only for the bravest of soldiers. The lord maintained his superior status through the loyalty and capabilities of his finest knights or samurais; in turn, the finest of soldiers were drawn to lords who held reputations of great valor. The lord was expected to fulfill certain responsibilities referred to as the *patron-client obligation* (Critchley, 1978). The lord *wined and dined* large numbers of people, including his knights and their entourages, which not only ensured loyalty but acted as a means to draw new knights to the wealthy kingdom (Dyer, 1983). Festivals and feasts encouraged the development of cooking and entertainment as occupations, if not as industries.

The patron-client obligation filtered down through the hierarchical system, which shed some light on how certain occupations were valued. For example, professionals and skilled laborers were treated with great respect by the fief holders, who often gave them gifts and invited them to the feasts. Conversely, unskilled laborers and peasants received minimal appropriations. Serfs could be treated well, relatively speaking, or abused as the patron saw fit. In the strictest sense of the term, slavery, for the most part, disappeared during the Middle Ages; however, it was resurrected in later years following the Renaissance. Nevertheless, medieval laborers did not live an easy life. When change to their status came, it did so at a catastrophic price.

The black plague, among other factors, can be credited with changing the medieval status of labor and laborers (Burke, 1985; Clegg, 1989). It has been estimated that the bubonic plague killed nearly one half of the European population. Due to the system of inheritance via feudal arrangements, the rich became richer and the poor became poorer, but the rich and poor had something in common. All had suffered greatly due to the plague. Most were ready to build a new Europe. The people longed to put the horror behind them by celebrating life. Grand cathedrals and libraries were planned. Artists were commissioned by wealthy patrons. Scientists and philosophers were supported by the Catholic Church (as long as they did not challenge Catholic doctrine). People believed that a new Europe would surely flourish. A revival of the classical Greek antiquity was planned and executed through a renaissance. However, one obstacle blocked the path to this rebirth of society.

Because the workers were few in number, their services were in high demand; subsequently, they began to command higher wages, revolt against the oppressive practices of the aristocrats, and break their feudal contracts. The formation of guilds strengthened the solidarity of craft workers, who participated in social criticism of the elites through popular plays and literature (Gibbs, 1953; Shepherd, 1983). In short, the workers refused to labor under the then current system. An alternative social order loomed on the horizon.

The growth of urban centers (Clegg, 1989) plus the mingling of new religious views with a weakened feudalistic system further contributed to a new philosophy of work. The Catholic Church was unable to control the workers as it had in the past, in part due to the development of the printing press, which gave the peasantry a new way to spread and gather information. The protestant reformation also loosened the hold of the Catholic Church (Burke, 1985). Furthermore, expanding colonization gave way to the practice of export-emphasized trade, which in turn grew into a new system of economic exchange. Finally, new systems of banking, including the concept and practice of charging interest and the focus on gold and silver gave business a new ideological home—mercantilism. Thus, due to a variety of forces, the existing order of production was challenged and with it the ideological and ontological status of work.

Mercantilism and the Meaning of Work

Mercantilism incorporated old and new ways of organizing labor. The new methods included the practice of charging interest on loans. The Catholic Church condemned this previously unheard of practice. Catholics were not allowed to charge interest on a loan because it was considered an act of greed. Jews, on the other hand, who had suffered a long history of oppression, found interest and banking a source of relief from their financial suffering, if not their social suffering. Jews were obliged to wear yellow circles on their jackets to denote their status as business people who charged interest, and although charging interest was frowned upon, it was not long before Christians joined their Hebrew contemporaries in this lucrative practice (Burke, 1985). With respect to Islamic economic jurisprudence, interest (*riba*) is still considered unacceptable today because it "is forbidden by the Qur'an" (Riba, 2007, n.p.).

In addition to this new practice, an old practice was resurrected during this period—slavery. Although Europeans attempted to enslave the native people of the "New World," they died at such a dramatic rate under the oppressive conditions that the Europeans had to embark upon a new plan that would make slavery a good business investment (Josephy, 1994). Stolen from their motherland, Africans were shipped under the most inhumane conditions to the American colonies (Blake, 1860). Exploitation, colonization, and greed were the practices of the day. The focus was on exporting goods in exchange for silver and gold, the conquering of foreign lands, and the exploiting and dehumanizing of people as slaves, all in the name of the sovereign state. This material excess contributed to Adam Smith's critique of mercantilism.

Capitalism and Communism and the Meaning of Work

Although the previously discussed ideologies provided unique sets of beliefs concerning work and the individual's position within the workforce, little formal rhetoric advanced notions of the ontology of labor itself. The philosophies of capitalism and communism, however, offer richly developed formal rhetorical arguments on the ontology of labor.

Capitalism

Two philosophical movements paved the way for capitalism. The first, physiocracy, was introduced by François Quesnay. He and a few other French intellectuals developed their thoughts on economics. Quesnay, in particular, argued in *Tableau Économique* (1766/1970) that a natural order of economics existed and could be observed. His observations led him to propose a system of classifications that organized labor into three categories: the productive class (those who produce in terms of agriculture, mining, or fishing), the proprietors (the ruling class), and the artisans (the skilled workers). The productive class, according to Quesnay, is the only class that can produce surplus; thus, it is the only class that can truly contribute to the wealth of a nation. Manufacturers, or artisans in this case, reshape what has been produced, but they do not contribute new wealth. The physiocrats argued that the sovereign's mandates regarding regulation of production, trade, or income, whether through taxation, tariff, or law, had little to do with generating wealth.

This critique of mercantilism set the stage for Adam Smith (1776/1937) to expand these ideas and lay out the tenets for modern capitalism.[1] He agreed with the physiocrats with regard to the natural order of economics and the ills of state or sovereign intervention, but he disagreed with the physiocrats with respect to the notion that productivity was limited to one class. Furthermore, Smith challenged the accepted view that the value of a commodity is related to the amount of gold or silver for which it could be exchanged. Instead, he suggested that labor is the real measure of the value of a commodity. He argued that labor had value and that different types of labor hold varying degrees of value for a society. This notion is crucial to understanding how contemporary capitalism affected the perceptions of work.

In his now famous book, *An Inquiry into the Nature and Causes of the Wealth of Nations*, Adam Smith (1776/1937) discusses labor as the core of production:

The value of any commodity, therefore, to the person who possesses it, and who means not to use or consume it himself, but to exchange it for other commodities, is equal to the quantity of labour which it enables him to purchase or command. Labour, therefore, is the real measure of the exchangeable value of all commodities. (p. 30)

Subsequently, labor in its various forms could be considered in terms of how valuable it is to society. Smith purported that *unproductive labor* (i.e., labor that does not produce a good) under certain circumstances can be useful to society, but it is without tangible value. For example, the following occupations are not considered productive: "menial servants, public servants, clergy, lawyers, physicians, professors, buffoons, musicians, singers, dancers, actors, and orators" (see Smith, 1776/1937, p. 314, for a complete list). However, they may be somewhat useful to society.

The value of labor is affected by the principles of exchange and the laws of supply and demand, as well as the "inequalities arising from the nature of the employments themselves" (see Smith, 1776/1937, pp. 100–118). Five circumstances contribute to the inequality of employment. They are (1) the agreeableness/disagreeableness of the work (e.g., management/labor), (2) the ease/difficulty with which the labor is learned or the expense incurred in order to learn the trade (e.g., unskilled labor/skilled labor), (3) the inconsistency/stability of the employment (e.g., temporary/tenured), (4) the amount of trust that is required on the part of those who benefit from the product or service (e.g., patient to physician/consumer to retailer), and the (5) improbability/probability of successfully attaining the position (e.g., poet laureate/editorial assistant). According to Smith, agreeable jobs, unskilled jobs, temporary jobs, jobs that require little trust, or jobs that have a low probability of success are of less value to a capitalist system.

Three other criteria affect the credibility of the job, according to Smith (1776/1937). They are (1) how long the trade or association has been established, (2) whether the job is conducted in its natural time (e.g., a soldier during war-time or peace-time), and (3) whether the work is the primary employment. Later in *The Wealth of Nations*, Smith adds another criterion to determining the status of a job, the utilization of the worker in terms of duration and intensity. Finally, in a separate section, Smith speaks of the reputation of the employer or employing company as having some bearing on the value of the job (e.g., today the position of a clerk at Saks Fifth Avenue may hold more prestige than the position of a clerk at K-Mart).

Defining the value of different forms of labor was one small part of Smith's contribution to the rhetoric and philosophy of capitalism. He also provides a theoretical account of work behavior and market, including concepts like the laws of supply and demand, stock ownership, trade, laissez-faire government, the invisible hand, capital, the role of the state, and much more. Furthermore, he addressed ethics and morals in his book *The Theory of Moral Sentiments*. His philosophical treatise contributed to providing a welcome home for the advancing industrial revolution.

As machines and mechanical power (e.g., the steam engine) developed in the late 1800s, industry became revolutionized beyond what had been imagined possible only a century earlier. This allowed for capital ownership in a way that had not existed previously. In the past, a person might work at a trade—being a seamstress, for example. The seamstress as an entrepreneur owned her business, so to speak, and she might take on an apprentice or two, but she did not own a factory where hundreds of workers produced a multitude of garments. The industrial revolution allowed for a new form of work arrangement where one person could own a garment factory, buy sewing machines, and hire seamstresses. This kind of private ownership was promoted by Adam Smith and became the primary characteristic of capitalism. Furthermore, consumers—not government rulers—were considered sovereign. That is to say, consumers could choose to spend their money in whatever ways that they felt satisfied their wants and needs. Consumer sovereignty, as the theory purports, should force the capital owners to produce according to the consumers' demands, which should result in competition among owners. Furthermore, the role of government, according to early capitalists, is to protect private property and the practices of capitalism.

Capitalist activities flourished in England, the United States, and Germany. The United States may have had a unique advantage in that it no longer suffered the restraints of a sovereign ruler or tyrannical government. Nevertheless, in each of these countries, capitalism and the industrial revolution gave rise to capitalists, a new class of people who were not necessarily born of the wealthy class. In addition, the division of labor became so pronounced that instead of having three classes in society as described by the physiocrats, two classes emerged: the working class (proletariat) and the owner class (bourgeoisie).

Wealth did not filter down to the working class. Deplorable factory conditions existed that were intolerable to the point that workers, often children, were chained to their stations at night to keep them from running away. The work days were long, from sunrise to sunset, and work weeks were without even one day off (Perrow, 1986). These conditions spurred activists to speak out on behalf of the working class.

Communism

Just as Adam Smith's name has become synonymous with capitalism, Karl Marx's name has become synonymous with communism, and like capitalism more than one force was at work in the advancement of communism. Hardly a novel idea, discussions of communism, as communal living, were first advanced in Plato's *Republic*, and communes as utopian communities were prevalent in the 1800s although most failed after a short time. Nevertheless, the more familiar connotation of the term *communism* is that associated with the mode of organization developed primarily by Karl Marx with the assistance of Friedrich Engels.

Kamenka (1983) states that "Marx recognized more clearly than others the birth of modern society and the tensions and conflicts involved in its internal dynamic. . . . His predictions have proved at least partly false; his presentation of the issues may now seem far too simple; but he saw where the issues lay, not only of his time but of ours. The study of modern society still begins with the work of Karl Marx" (p. xii).

In order to appreciate Marx's philosophical position and why he made the predictions that he did, it is necessary to understand what the world was like at the time that Marx lived and wrote. Europeans had little freedom from tyrannical governments. Poverty persisted, indentured servitude remained a norm in Europe, and slavery continued in the United States of America. Paupers and prisoners were being put to work in the new factories, which promoted an entirely different method of production, one that concerned Marx.

Marx's early writings were devoted to his ideas of labor and alienation. He wrote:

> . . . man produces even when he is free from physical need and produces truly, indeed, only in freedom from such need. . . . man produces the whole of nature. . . . steps out freely to confront his product. . . . knows how to produce according to the standard of every species and always knows how to apply the intrinsic standard to the object. Man, therefore, creates according to the laws of beauty. (Marx, 1844/1983, pp. 139–140)

Marx's views on human nature suggest that human fulfillment is achieved through meaningful activity:

> the object of labor is, therefore, the objectification of man's species-life, for he no longer reproduces himself merely intellectually, as in consciousness, but active and in a real sense, and he sees his own reflection in a world which he has constructed. (Marx, 1844/1983, p. 140)

According to Marx (1844/1983), living labor, a fulfilling activity of social and self expression, is oppressed and alienated through capitalism. For capital labor

> appropriates nature by means of his labor, this appropriation appears as alienation; the worker's spontaneous activity appears as activity for another and as the activity of another, living appears as a sacrifice of life, production of the object as loss of the object to an alien power, to an alien person. (p. 146)

Marx wrote about two important concepts: *praxis* and *product*. Praxis refers to the active process of creating our material goods. Praxis, according to Marx, is a rewarding experience that involves creative thinking as well as skillful physical engagement with the world around us. The product, of course, is the outcome of the praxis. When factories take away the experience of creating products, they alienate people from themselves, from their creative activities, and from the products that are made. Marx saw the onset of the industrial revolution as a means of controlling workers and turning them into cogs of the capitalist machinery.

Thus, he believed the loss of both praxis and product through the division of labor would destroy the creative reality of work itself. The seamstress no longer creates a beautiful coat; she merely sews one seam. She sews a single seam, one after another, over and over, ad infinitum. She loses not only the product but also the living fulfilling activity; hence, "the *loss of reality* of the worker" (Marx, 1844/1983, p. 132). Labor or work, for Marx, meant the expression of self, the creation of reality.

Marx viewed capitalism as a form of production that pitted workers against each other in a competitive way. Wealthy factory owners exploited the workers by always paying them less than their labor was worth. Only if they paid the workers less than what they were worth could the owners make a profit. As Kamenka (1983) points out:

> With the rise of the industrial system the attack on property gained a new impetus. It was helped by the concentration of the propertyless in the new industrial towns and barracks, but it rested, above all, on the perception that ownership, now of capital and machines, had, in these new conditions, vast social ramifications. (Kamenka, 1983, p. xxxi)

Some European scholars looked to the newly formed democracy of the United States for a more humane and moral social organization. However, it must be noted that even the United States lacked the moral integrity that Marx was seeking. Slavery persisted, "Indian" massacres continued, reservations were instituted, child labor existed, women were refused enfranchisement, and inhumane factory and mining conditions prevailed. Struggle for freedom, then, was not limited to freedom from the monarchs and totalitarian regimes of Europe. For Marx, all of history could be explained according to conflict and class struggle, which persisted around the world:

> The introduction of tools, the division of labor, and the rise of private property divide men into social classes, primarily into the class of exploiters, who own and administer the means of production, and the class or classes of the exploited, who actually work and produce. (Kamenka, 1983, p. xxxiv)

This system was bound to failure, according to Marx, for it only protected the ruling class, not the people in general.

Marx predicted the fall of capitalism. Capitalism would meet its inevitable demise because of its reliance on competition, he argued. Competition, he predicted, would escalate to the point that workers would be paid the lowest possible wages. Machines would eventually squeeze out middle managers, and the owners would produce more than society could consume. Ever fewer people would control the vast majority of the wealth, while the majority of the people, the poor, would reach the point of literally having nothing to lose. Marx believed the exploitation of the workers would eventually end in revolution that would bring about yet another mode of production. This new mode of production would be grounded in principles of communal living rather than competition. It would be a rational, organized society that would expect people to work according to their abilities and would supply to people according to their needs. A central government would be charged with dispensing housing, education, medicine, and other necessities to the people. The people would own the means of production and govern according to a system of egalitarian rule.

A series of upheavals culminated in the Russian revolution of 1917, which brought the violent birth of communism to an impoverished country. The form of communism that took hold in Russia did not meet the philosophical tenets of communism as laid out by Marx and Engels. Although Marx's rhetoric motivated the revolution and contributed to Russia's communism in theory, in practice serious distinctions emerged. The new communist state enacted censorship, of which Marx had been an opponent; it imprisoned its political enemies, killed traitors, and moved to build a military and industrialized nation-state.

However, some of the basic characteristics of communism flourished in Russia in the form of worker-owned industries and gender equality. Other communist tenets arose in European countries in the form of socialist reforms, such as socialized medicine. Communist parties developed and spread throughout European countries, such as Italy, France, and Hungary. Even the United States undertook socialist reform by advancing public schools and public libraries. Communism had reached China by 1921 and has held all legal power in the People's Republic of China since 1949. In studies of the expression *a real job*, mainland Chinese students were the only ones to state that they did not know what this phrase meant. When I took them aside and explained it, they told me that, indeed, they did know what I meant but that in a communist society it is inappropriate to mention that anyone's job might be of less value than any other person's job. Once they had provided that disclaimer, they felt free to describe the inequities among jobs in their homeland.

Today, the modes of production in relation to political systems are in dynamic flux. Globalization, the information age, ecosystem sustainability, political challenges, and cultural concerns may be just some of the contributing factors. Whatever the causes, the world of work is changing.

Work through the Ages

Work has a dynamic history. Its definition and the ways in which it has been practiced have varied over time, suggesting its *ontological relativity*. In short,

"Work, it seems, has no single definition or essence, good or bad—only a history of various and unique experiences" (Muirhead, 2004, p. 4). What constituted *a real job* in ancient Greece does not necessarily constitute *a real job* in modern America (see Clair, 1996). Nor are the ways of organizing labor in society stagnant and immutable. Several different modes of organizing labor have been discussed, including slave societies, feudalism, monasticism, mercantilism, capitalism, and communism. And these are not the only modes of organizing. For instance, various religions claim to have either a unique economic system (e.g., Islamic economics) or a distinct way of viewing work (e.g., the Buddhist concept of temporality). However, it is beyond the scope of this chapter to detail every mode of economic practice. Suffice it to say, the way in which labor is organized has an impact on how it is defined, valued, and viewed. In short, these philosophical underpinnings in turn affect the ways in which we work and the reasons why we work.

Philosophers through the ages have argued for what counts as work and how people should work. Most argued as if they possessed the truth. More recently, scholars have suggested that philosophers like Adam Smith and Karl Marx did not provide the ultimate answer concerning the meaning of labor but instead provided rhetorical arguments so persuasive that they have been embraced by whole nations of people. That is to say, these grand rhetorical narratives are not Truth but rather arguments about truth (Lyotard, 1979/1984). Furthermore, these grand arguments can be found embedded within our everyday discourse (e.g., *a real job*), and our everyday discourse can reinforce the grand narratives (Clair, 1996). In addition, Foucault (1966/1973, 1977/1979, 1976/1990) pointed out that these discourses about work *normalize* people so that they behave according to the dominant ideology. For the most part, people *discipline* themselves and act according to the interests of the powerful. However, both de Certeau (1984) and Foucault suggested that people also resist. Resistance comes from multiple directions, often from the bottom up. People have the opportunity to challenge their current state of affairs; they have agency. They can name different activities as valuable or not and engage in them accordingly. They can alter their terministic screen and view the world from a different perspective. Means of resistance are within easy reach as people use whatever is available to them in their everyday settings to disrupt the hegemonic control of the grand narratives. That would explain, in part, how the meaning and value of work changes. In other words, a student who recognizes that factory work is valuable and a farmer who sees the relevance of college may just be looking at the world in new ways. Students who question what they hitherto perceived to be the only way challenge the taken-for-granted social system. The student who wants to be an artist and the student who wants to be a mother are not so different from the factory worker who wants to put his name on what he makes. They are all asking *why work* is treated the way it is in society.

Part One of this book has presented an argument that work holds no pure essence, no ontologically determined status, but rather has a relative nature, changing according to the practices and philosophical and rhetorical arguments of the day. Chapter one specifically noted that multiple meanings of work exist, that different values are assigned to different kinds of work by different people, and that those definitions can effect the way we behave and the way we work. The meaning of work changes over time, whether we are talking about the papergirl who moves on to fast-food service as discussed in chapter one or over historical epics as discussed in chapter two. This changing nature of work calls for an exploration of the voices from the past, the philosophers, rhetoricians, and activists who have set forth arguments on the meaning of work.

The following chapters of this book provide specific overviews of some of the most famous, as well as the lesser known, philosophers, activists, and practitioners who wrote or spoke on the topic of work. Within each chapter, a brief biography of the individuals, an overview of their philosophy, and a summary of the way their philosophy is being enacted today, is presented. Parts One and Two of this book discuss the historical background as well as the philosophical treatises and rhetorical voices that have added to the changing meanings and arrangements of work through the ages. Part Three addresses the implications of sharing the voices from the past on the current understandings of work.

Note

1. Anthony (1977) argues that "we can hardly credit Adam Smith with an ideology of work" primarily because his theory is simply not sophisticated enough to explain complex systems of power in an industrialized society. Nevertheless, Anthony does suggest that ideologists drew from certain passages of Smith's work to support more fully developed conceptualizations of labor and market, which were grounded in dehumanizing practices and limited ethics. Chief among those who drew from Smith to create an ideology of work, which can be considered the "apotheosis or the spirit of capitalism," was Saint-Simon (see Anthony, 1977, p. 92). Whether credit for the ideological development of capitalism rests with Saint-Simon or Adam Smith (or Ricardo, Ure, or Smiles for that matter) remains an issue of debate. For the purposes of this section it is more important to focus on the characteristics of capitalism.

Part Two

Philosophers, Rhetoricians, and Activists

Chapter Three

Plato and Aristotle

Philosophies of Labor

Introduction

Although it may seem politically incorrect to begin studies of the philosophy and rhetoric of work in ancient Greece, as if it were the center of world thought, it can also be argued that some of the earliest and most enduring theories about the organization of work drew their first breath during antiquity. Two of the most influential philosophers of ancient Greece, Aristotle and Plato, each contributed opinions, if not complete theories, about the organization and meaning of labor. Although their understanding of labor and its role in society is somewhat different from our contemporary view, both Aristotle and Plato provide philosophies of work that have played an instrumental part in the foundation and advancement of labor theories throughout the ages. Before discussing these philosophers' ideas, brief biographical sketches, first of Plato and then of Aristotle, are provided.

Biographies

Plato, born in 427 BCE to affluent parents in Athens, began his academic career under the tutelage of Socrates (Hare, 1996). Socrates, the outspoken philosopher whose ideas were judged dangerous to society, was eventually condemned to death for his teachings. Plato was only twenty-nine years old when he witnessed his mentor drink the deadly hemlock (Gaarder, 1991/1996). Following Socrates' death, Plato decided to continue his teacher's work. First, he utilized Socrates' dialogic examinations, and second, he incorporated both his own and Socrates' philosophical positions. More simply put, Plato wrote about philosophy through dialogues.

33

In those dialogues, Plato often featured Socrates as the main character. Two of the most famous dialogues are *The Republic* and *The Apology* (Hooker, 1996).

One concept for which Plato is perhaps best known is his idea of "forms." According to Plato, the world in which we live consists of both "visible and intelligible things" (Hooker, 1996). The visible things are those that can be seen, heard, and touched, whereas the intelligible things include the eternal "forms," which are unchangeable. For example, the form of a desk applies to all desks, even though desks in the visible world vary in shape, size, and structure. The form of a desk will always remain the same, although a visible desk may be destroyed (e.g., if it were burned). Plato used this theory to examine and define knowledge and the ultimate good (Hooker, 1996). He also considered it when he explored the idea of a perfect or ideal society versus the society that condemned his mentor to death (Gaarder, 1991/1996). In addition to his written contributions, Plato established his own school in 385 BCE, which he called the Academy. This school produced many astute philosophers, its most famous being Aristotle (Hare, 1996).

Aristotle was born in 384 BCE to upper-class parents. His father was a well-respected physician who could afford to provide tuition for his son's education. During his teenage years, Aristotle traveled to Athens to study at Plato's Academy. Following Plato's death in 347 BCE, Aristotle served as the tutor for Alexander the Great. However, he eventually returned to Athens, where he continued his studies for twelve years (Taylor, 1955). Aristotle "founded his own school, the Lyceum" (Singer & Ammarman, 1962, p. 381) and authored numerous works, "including the *Organon, Physics, Metaphysics, Nicomachean Ethics, Politics, Rhetoric,* and *On the Heavens*" (p. 381).

Whereas Plato viewed the world conceptually, Aristotle preferred to think in more concrete, scientific terms. That is to say, Aristotle rejected Plato's notion of the ideal form. Instead, he believed that the idea of a thing arises from its characteristics. This premise allowed Aristotle to define phenomena according to certain characteristics, which in turn could be grouped into typologies or genres. Aristotle studied a wide variety of subjects, crossing both the physical sciences and the humanities. Some knowledge, Aristotle asserted, is always true, such as that of mathematics and science, whereas other knowledge is imprecise and often varies, such as that of human interaction (Hooker, 1996). Furthermore, Aristotle understood the constant presence of change, an idea first developed by Heraclitus (ca. 535–475 BCE), and spent much of his life studying the causes of change related to various phenomena. As Hooker (1996) states, "Aristotle was the first major thinker to base his thought and science entirely on the idea that everything that moves or changes is caused to move or change by some other thing" (n.p.). Aristotle's contributions were extensive and influential.

Plato's and Aristotle's contributions to philosophy are beyond measure. The brief biographies supplied in this chapter barely skim the surface of their philosophical treatises. In order to do some justice to their work, in the following sections, we elaborate on each philosopher's thoughts concerning labor and the organization of society.

Philosophy and Rhetoric of Work

Beginning with Plato and moving on to Aristotle, the next few sections explain each philosopher's key concepts and specific positions concerning work. For both Aristotle and Plato, these include discussions of slavery, class, gender, and the general organization of society.

Plato's Philosophy of Slavery

Plato's vision of any society included a belief in the necessity of slavery. This is an important issue to explore; it gives a better understanding of the rationale that guided Plato's attitude toward labor. According to Morrow (1939), Plato held that

> a) The slave is a possession, b) but also a person subject to the arbitrary will of another person, his master, and c) subject also, independently of his master, to law . . . d) He is protected against certain forms of abuse by religious laws and e) in his public capacity at least, by the laws of the state. But f) he possesses no rights of action, except in his public capacity, and *a fortiori* no political rights. (p. 188)

Although it may be argued that Plato's attitude toward slavery was simply the reflection of the Greek culture at the time, Morrow (1939) makes a strong argument against any such assumptions. "It is significant that Plato does not say . . . that in the best state there will be no slavery. And though he refers to various opinions about slavery he does not mention the doctrine that slavery is contrary to nature" (p. 194). Therefore, it can be supposed that Plato did, indeed, deem slavery to be a fundamental aspect of any society.

Plato's Division of Labor

The very fact that Plato allowed slavery in a society gives insight into his ideas concerning the necessity of social classes. However, before he assigns individuals to social classes, he first establishes the need for the division of labor as an efficient means of production (Hill, 1996). Plato believed that each individual in a society was best suited for a particular occupation in that state. In addition, he asserted that in order for a state to function properly these individuals must pursue the occupation for which they are best suited. He wrote,

> each of us is born somewhat different from others, one more apt for one task, one for another. . . . Both production and quality are improved in each case, and easier, if each man does one thing which is congenial to him, does it at the right time, and is free of other pursuits." (*Republic,* 370a–c)

After establishing the proposition that each individual in society is best suited for a particular task, Plato suggested that these individuals could be grouped according to classes—first between those who are rich and those who remain poor, and second among the various types of work needed in a society (Hill, 1996).

Plato identified several occupations that he deemed to be necessary in any society. He includes farmers, builders, weavers, cobblers, carpenters, metal workers, merchants, retailers, and what he calls wage-earners. According to Plato, these wage-earners are "not worth admitting into our society for their intelligence, but they have sufficient physical strength for heavy labour. These sell the use of their strength; their reward for this is a wage" (*Republic*, 371e). Plato realized, however, that these occupations do not constitute the full requirements for a good city. He then added those individuals who pursue the arts—"painters, actors and musicians" (*Republic*, 373a–b). In addition, Plato identified the need for guardians, or those individuals who are responsible for the protection of society and the creation and enforcement of laws.

Plato's Guardian Class

Plato's guardians hold what he believed to be the most important position in a society. Therefore, he commits a large portion of the *Republic* to a discussion of their selection, training, and duties. Plato makes it exceedingly clear that the guardians are not to participate in menial labor but should instead be focused on the development of their physical and mental abilities. This strong focus on the guardian class seems to imply that Plato did not hold manual labor in high regard, as it did nothing to further the pursuit of knowledge. As a result, Plato reserved manual labor for those individuals who were naturally less intelligent and incapable of achieving the "good life." These people included the slaves of a society.

Plato further divides the guardian class into those who protect and those who govern. Those who govern are to be the best and noblest of the guardians (*Republic*, 412c). This class, although the smallest, would be the most capable of acquiring wisdom and would therefore be the most qualified to rule. Plato asserts,

> Then a whole city which is established according to nature would be wise because of the smallest group or part of itself, the commanding or ruling group. This group seems to be the smallest by nature and to it belongs a share in that knowledge which, alone of them all, must be called wisdom. (Republic, 428e)

For Plato, the ultimate goal of any society should be the happiness of the society as a whole. Such happiness, said Plato, can be achieved when each individual carries out his or her occupation to the best of his or her ability. According to Plato,

> We must compel and persuade the auxiliaries and the guardians to be excellent performers of their own task, and so with all the others. As the

whole city grows and is well governed, we must leave it to nature to provide each group with its share of happiness. (*Republic,* 421c)

However, Plato believed both poverty and wealth to be barriers to achieving such
happiness. On one hand, if poverty exists then an individual will not have the
tools necessary to make a quality product. On the other hand, if extreme wealth
exists then the worker will no longer see the need to produce a quality product
and will therefore lower his or her work standards. This decrease in production
standards, Plato concludes, will lead to unhappiness and discontent among all
members of society.

Plato's Communal-Based Society

Plato introduced the idea of a communal-based society in order to solve the
problems that he hypothesized would result from either extreme poverty or
extreme wealth. His ideal society would not suffer from such economic imbal-
ance. He wrote,

> if you approach them as many and give the possessions of one to the other,
> their wealth, their power, and even their persons, you will have many allies
> and few enemies. As long as your city is governed with moderation as we
> have just established it, it will itself have greatness. (*Republic,* 423a)

However, Plato discusses this communal way of life only in respect to the guardians themselves. As a result, it is unclear whether the laborers of a society should
also distribute everything equally. In any case, this idea of distributing wealth
among all citizens in a society should extend into every aspect of the guardians'
lives, said Plato. Therefore, a wife should not belong to one man, but should
instead be seen as a communal person. Furthermore, children should not be
designated as belonging to a certain mother or father but should be seen as the
property of the state itself. Patriarchy went unquestioned; it was an accepted assumption. Specifically, Plato suggested that

> All these women shall be wives in common to all the men, and not one of
> them shall live privately with any man; the children too should be held in
> common so that no parent shall know which is his own offspring, and no
> child shall know his parent. (*Republic,* 457d)

From this discussion, we can conclude that Plato believed that manual
labor was of low importance in a society and should therefore be reserved for
slaves and those individuals who were not designed to pursue knowledge. Furthermore, the citizens of a society who were by nature capable of becoming
guardians should be allowed to focus solely on the training and education necessary to fulfill their roles to the very best of their ability, thereby exempting
them from any manual labor. Finally, Plato believed the most honorable position in a society should be given to the most noble and wisest of the guardians.

These individuals were to be responsible for ruling the city and were to refrain from any kind of manual labor.

Aristotle, Slavery, and Social Classes

For Aristotle, slavery was a natural part of humanity as well. In his treatise *Politics,* he asserts that "It is thus clear that, just as some are by nature free, so others are by nature slaves, and for these latter the condition of slavery is both beneficial and just" (*Politics,* 1255a). This strong support for slavery in any society led Aristotle to emphasize the need for slaves to carry out much of the manual labor in a society. He believed, in fact, that slaves were naturally suited for manual labor. He writes,

> But it is nature's intention also to erect a physical difference between the body of the freeman and that of the slave, giving the latter strength for the menial duties of life, but making the former upright in carriage and (though useless for physical labour) useful for the various purposes of civic life—a life which tends, as it develops, to be divided into military service and the occupations of peace. (*Politics,* 1254b)

Although Aristotle did not reserve all manual labor for slaves, he made it clear that manual labor was not something to be held in high regard. As Anthony (1977) writes, "Aristotle regarded work not only as inferior but as debased and debasing" (p. 17). It is difficult to contest such a statement when Aristotle seems to make it abundantly clear that manual labor inhibits citizens (defined as men of the ruling class) from seeking goodness. As he states,

> a state which has for its members men who are absolutely just . . . cannot have its citizens living the life of mechanics or shopkeepers, which is ignoble and inimical to goodness. Nor can it have them engaged in farming: leisure is a necessity, both for growth in goodness and for the pursuit of political activities. (*Politics,* 1328b–1329a)

Here it is interesting to note, however, that Aristotle did not regard all manual labor as degrading. In fact, he made it clear that labor could be done by citizens as long as it was done properly. The point seems to be that the ruling class can only undertake its intellectual tasks if freed from manual labor.

Aristotle and the Proper and Improper Use of Things

Aristotle drew many of his thoughts concerning work from his theory of the proper and improper use of things. According to Aristotle, there is for every object both a proper and an improper use. He offers as an example the use of a shoe. In Aristotle's mind, the proper use of a shoe is to be worn, while the improper use resides in its being sold for a profit. Aristotle then extended this idea to the concept of work. He believed that to work for oneself was proper; however, to work for another or for the accumulation of wealth was dishonorable. Aristotle made it clear that to work for a profit was against nature and did not lead to a just state. Instead, wealth should only be obtained through good management of the household.

Household management was, for Aristotle, a key part in the development of a good society. He did not advocate the communal concepts of his mentor, Plato. Instead, according to Aristotle, each household was, in a way, a small state in and of itself. Therefore, the tactics utilized in household management should be extended to the management of a larger society. However, Aristotle believed not that single households could stand alone but that people are naturally born to live within a larger society. As a result, he believed it was important to establish a society that is just and honorable.

Aristotle and Plato on the Role of Women

The creation of such a society stems from the goodness of its people, according to Aristotle. When addressing the good individual, Aristotle once again makes a distinction between the slave and the ruler. Although he understands that all participants in a society must possess some type of temperance and justice, Aristotle claims that slaves, women, and children have a different kind of goodness than the leaders possess. He insists,

> The conclusion which clearly emerges is that both classes [the ruled as well as the ruler] must share in goodness, but that there must be different kinds of goodness [one for the ruler and one for the ruled]—just as there are also different kinds among different classes of the ruled. (*Politics*, 1260a)

Here, as in many parts of his *Politics*, Aristotle groups women and children with the slaves because he held women and children to be inferior to men. "Again, the relation of male to female is naturally that of the superior to the inferior—of the ruling to the ruled" (*Politics*, 1254b). As such, women should act the part of the inferior, said Aristotle. Furthermore, Aristotle embraced the writings of Sophocles, who stated, "A modest silence is a woman's crown" (*Politics*, 1260a). With such strong distinctions among the varying classes and genders, Aristotle asserts that the goodness that is attained by rulers is truly the highest type of goodness. "The ruler, accordingly, must possess moral goodness in its full and perfect form" (*Politics*, 1260a).

Aristotle's view of women's roles in society greatly differed from that of Plato. Whereas Aristotle strongly resisted the idea that women could perform the same tasks as men, Plato believed women should be able to partake in similar occupations as men. In the *Republic* he wrote,

> Therefore, the nature of man and woman is the same as regards guarding the city, except in so far as she is physically weaker, and the man's nature stronger. . . . Such women must then be chosen along with such men to live with them and share their guardianship, since they are qualified and akin to them by nature. (*Republic*, 456a–b)

Plato added that women should also receive the same education and physical training as men and that each should take on the task for which he or she is best suited.

Aristotle and the Ownership of Private Property

Not only did Aristotle and Plato differ in their opinions concerning the capabilities of women; they also varied greatly in their discussions of communal sharing. Whereas Plato proposed a communal system at least among the guardian class, Aristotle argued for private ownership of property. According to Aristotle, the very fact that each and every man and woman is, by nature, different from other men and women compelled him to resist the idea that a community should be seen as a singular unit. Rather, Aristotle believed that "the 'good' of each thing is what preserves it in being" (*Politics,* 1261b) and that "the higher degree of self-sufficiency is the more desirable thing, the lesser degree of unity is the more desirable than the greater" (*Politics,* 1261b). In these passages, Aristotle voices his concern for a sense of unity that is so strong it drowns out the individuality of every citizen and causes confusion and quarreling. Additionally, Aristotle asserted that individuals will care more for things that are their own than things that belong to a community. Therefore, Aristotle believed that citizens should be able to retain certain things as their own.

One issue that Aristotle addressed very specifically is Plato's idea of sharing wives and children. According to Aristotle, it is essential that women and children are not the property of a community but are instead part of a single household. He noted,

> If it be understood in the first sense, the object which Socrates desires to realize may perhaps be realized in a greater degree: each and all separately will then say "My wife" (or "My son") of one and the same person; and each and all separately will speak in the same way of property, and of every other concern. But it is not in the sense of "each separately" that all who have children and wives in common will actually speak of them. They will all call them "Mine"; but they will do so collectively, and not individually. . . . It is therefore clear that there is a certain fallacy in the use of the term "all." It is a term which . . . is liable by its ambiguity [to produce quarrels in actual life, and] equally to breed captious arguments in reasoning. (*Politics,* 1261b)

Aristotle continues his argument by asserting that the communal sharing of women and children will also cause increased criminal acts and will, overall, lead to the weakening of a society. Therefore, Aristotle believed that it is important for men and women to feel a sense of kinship and identity rather than ambiguity and community in the matters of family.

In regard to private property, Aristotle held that individuals should be allowed to own property but that they should reserve part of that property to be used by the community at large. Aristotle continued his argument by writing,

> It is clear from what has been said that the better system is that under which property is privately owned but is put to common use; and the function proper to the legislator is to make men so disposed that they will treat property in this way. (*Politics,* 1263a)

Such an allowance of the private ownership of property starkly contrasts with Plato's view that all property should be owned and used by all.

Differences in philosophical opinions concerning private property and communal ownership have continued to plague philosophers throughout history. The grand arguments of Adam Smith and Karl Marx, to be discussed in detail later, would refine those thoughts that Plato and Aristotle had only begun to mention, and each of these philosophers' thoughts would shape contemporary thinking on the topic and lead to the development of socioeconomic practices that span the globe.

Aristotle and Citizenship

Just as in the issues discussed previously, Aristotle makes a strong distinction between citizens and noncitizens. He begins by providing a definition of a citizen: "The citizen . . . is best defined by one criterion, 'a man who shares in the administration of justice and in the holding of office'" (*Politics,* 1274b). Therefore, Aristotle is excluding from the rights of citizenship manual laborers, as well as slaves, women, and children. This distinction serves, once again, to broaden the gap between the ruler and the laborer, the master and the slave, the man and the woman, the adult and the child.

Later in his discussion of citizenship, Aristotle suggests that there is no need for citizens to pursue those occupations that are held by the ruled.

> Here it is not necessary for the ruler to know how to do [what he requires the ruled to do], but only to know how to use [the capabilities of the ruled]: indeed the former kind of knowledge (by which we mean an ability to do menial services personally) has a servile character. . . . The occupations pursued by men who are subject to the rule of the sort just mentioned [i.e., the rule of a master or an employer over persons in servile positions] need never be studied by the good man, or by the statesman, or by the good citizen. . . . (*Politics,* 1277a–b)

These passages deal with the issues surrounding the ruler and the slave. However, Aristotle suggested different guidelines for those rulers who rule over persons who are born free. He calls this type of ruling *political rule* and asserts that it is necessary for any ruler to first be ruled by some other before obtaining the position of ruler. "The fact remains," he suggests, "that the good citizen must possess the knowledge and the capacity requisite for ruling as well as for being ruled" (*Politics,* 1277b). Aristotle's view of society and the roles of its individuals is based largely on his system of class.

This system of class leads Aristotle to continue his discussion of the requirements for citizenship: "The best form of state . . . will not make the mechanic a citizen" (*Politics*, 1278a). Aristotle then explained his rationale for this statement with regard to what would happen if a state were to admit mechanics and laborers as citizens.

> In states where mechanics *are* admitted to citizenship we shall have to say that the citizen of excellence of which we have spoken [that of the good citizen who has experience of ruling as well as of being ruled] cannot be attained by every citizen, or by all who are simply free men, but can only be achieved by those who are free from menial duties . . . for a man who lives the life of a mechanic or labourer cannot pursue the things which belong to excellence. (*Politics*, 1278a)

In this passage, Aristotle's distinction between the manual laborers and the philosophers and rulers becomes exceedingly clear. The former are incapable of pursuing those things that bring about goodness and the pursuit of excellence, and the latter are best suited for the ruling positions and for the pursuit of knowledge and wisdom, which are the most worthy pursuits.

For Aristotle, the ultimate goal of any society is, indeed, to "produce cultivated gentlemen—men who combine the aristocratic mentality with love of learning and the arts" (Russell, as cited in Anthony, 1977, p. 19). These gentlemen were to be the wisest and most honorable men in any society and were to achieve true goodness. This goodness, however, could be achieved only if these men were allowed to focus on their training in the arts and were given extensive leisure time. Therefore, in order to produce such leisure time, others in society, namely the slaves and laborers, must perform the less honorable duties. This proposition leads back to the concept previously stated—that Aristotle held manual labor in low regard and believed it needed to be reserved for those individuals who were not, by nature, able to achieve the highest form of goodness.

Basic Concepts of Aristotle's Philosophy of Labor

As Anthony (1977) explains, Aristotle believed that "leisure is more valuable than work and that the existence of a leisured class was incompatible with the general spread of education and leisure," and therefore Aristotle "wanted the citizens to become aristocrats but their existence was to depend upon slaves" (p. 20). Second, Aristotle believed these citizens should be allowed to own private property rather than participate in the communal sharing of all goods. He asserted that the ownership of property gave these citizens a sense of pride and individuality. Third, Aristotle supported the belief that women are inferior to men and should therefore not be allowed to participate in the same occupations as men or be allowed to become citizens of a society. Each of these aspects of Aristotle's philosophy is based heavily upon his belief that classes are not only a natural but an essential part of any society, and that in order for the highest classes to achieve true goodness, the lower classes must be made to carry out those occupations that, while necessary, inhibit anyone from pursuing excellence or nobility (Anthony, 1977).

Although it is evident that Plato and Aristotle varied somewhat in their philosophies of work, it is equally obvious that they shared many similarities. Both philosophers embraced slavery as a natural and necessary part of a society. Furthermore, both philosophers based much of their arguments on the idea that some men are, by nature, more suited for manual labor, and others are more suited for a life of leisure, for the pursuit of knowledge and goodness, and the role of the ruler.

Contemporary Scholarship

Although the concept of strict class division may seem somewhat outdated, hints of it are still embedded in some modern organizational behavior. In a study of blue-collar workers at a medium-sized manufacturing corporation, Gibson and Papa (2000) found that many of the workers believed they were naturally predisposed to participate in that type of labor. According to some of the workers, they were "a tough breed of worker, uniquely geared to the rigors of life at *Industry International*, including long work weeks, adverse working conditions, and tedious job tasks including working with molten plastic metals and large machinery" (Gibson & Papa, 2000, p. 74). This seems to imply, according to these workers, that only a particular type of individual can perform the labor-intensive work that they perform.

In addition, Gibson and Papa (2000) found that the workers described themselves as being "naturally fitted to the job." The authors continued to explain that the workers saw this "as if only they are suited to this type of work. They readily identified how other people would be excluded from such work on the basis of their inability to handle the toll that physical labor places on an individual" (p. 75). Through this belief that they are naturally suited for manual labor, the workers formed a sense of community and camaraderie among themselves. This sense of solidarity is then often transferred to the workers' children—the majority of whom end up working for the same organization where their parents are employed.

Although contradictory examples could also be given (recall the discussion of Mike LeFevre from chapter one), this example suggests that the kind of thinking advanced by Plato and Aristotle—that some people are naturally predisposed to certain classes and tasks, still exists in today's workplace. These remnants include the idea that certain individuals in a society are naturally suited for manual labor and others are not. Therefore, despite the immense cultural differences between ancient Greece and modern society, certain underlying principles continue to have an impact on contemporary views of labor. Furthermore, debates surrounding race, class, and gender with respect to the organization of society can be traced to ancient Greek philosophers (see

Mahowald,1983, for a more detailed discussion of ancient Greek rhetoric and the "place" of women.)

Because of the widespread attention both Plato and Aristotle have received throughout history, their philosophies concerning labor and the organization of a society were considered relevant to this project. Issues that were addressed in this chapter include slavery, the division of labor, social classes, and the private or communal ownership of property. Although both Plato and Aristotle are strong proponents of slavery and social classes, many of their thoughts concerning private property and the roles of women in society differ greatly.[1] Despite these differences, both of these philosophers have been recognized for their contributions to the philosophical understanding of work, and each has left a formidable legacy.

Note

1.   Plato's more generous view of women's capabilities might be traced to the influence of Aspasia on his mentor Socrates. A more detailed discussion of this proposition appears in Chapter 13 (see pages 156–157). It is also possible that Aspasia may have been the influence for the *Socratic method.*

Chapter Four

Confucius and St. Benedict

Spiritual Leaders

Introduction

Spiritual leaders from the past to the present and representing a wide array of cultural and religious beliefs have influenced the theory and practice of work. Two such leaders from distinct cultural backgrounds who provide a picture of similarities and differences across time and space are Confucius and St. Benedict. These two spiritual leaders represent extremes with respect to being from Eastern and Western origins; yet they represent similarities in that each provided work-related philosophies for his followers. Each also relied on the rule "teach by example" to promote his respective theory of work among his followers; in short, *they practiced what they preached*. Although Confucius has been compared to Socrates and lived during the same era (Riegel, 2002), the juxtaposition of Confucius to Benedict of Nursia makes sense because each of these spiritual philosophers provided detailed guidelines for his followers regarding decorum, social relations, and rituals concerning work. For these leaders, there was little question as to what counted as work and how work was to be performed.

Biographies

Much like Plato's and Aristotle's, Confucius's and Benedict's life stories have been gathered from secondhand accounts. Some debate surrounds the factual reliability of the biographies of both Confucius and Benedict. Nevertheless, it is the narratives that have been handed down that impact society today.

Confucius's life story was not written until the second century BCE, even though it is believed that he was born around 551 BCE. Sima Qian, a historian who is believed to have lived between the years 145 and 85 BCE, wrote in the "well-known and often quoted Records of the Historian (Shiji)" that Confucius's ancestors were from the Royal State of Song and were forced to leave for Lu (southeastern Shandong) when turmoil erupted (Riegel, 2002, p.1). Other scholars have suggested that Confucius was born in answer to his parents' prayers (Kong, his surname, means *thankfulness when prayers have been answered*) and that he did not come from a royal lineage. In either case, scholars agree that Confucius lived a childhood of poverty and as a young man took jobs considered "petty," such as accounting and caring for livestock (Riegel, p. 1). Further, there is agreement that Confucius studied with the Daoist master Lao Dan and later found himself surrounded by disciples. He devoted much of his adult life to political issues and education (Riegel).

By the time Confucius turned fifty, the ruler of Lu recognized his talents and named Confucius minister of public works. Later Confucius became minister of crime. However, this relationship and his privileged position did not last long because political turmoil surfaced. Confucius, who disagreed with the ruler's political position, was exiled for his views. He left the province with his disciples and traveled the country seeking a ruler who might appreciate his perspective. This period in Confucius's life is remarkably similar to the circumstances portrayed in heroic poems of the *Book of Songs*. Written before Confucius was born, the *Book of Songs* is a collection of poems that come from folklore as well as from nobles. The poems can be sung. The topics range from everyday situations about work and love to epics about heroic resistance. From across three provinces and covering a span of time from the eleventh to the sixth century BCE, the *Book of Songs* provides one of the earliest pictures of culture and history. Some scholars have suggested that the themes of exile, alienation, and suffering are used to strengthen the image of Confucius as heroic (Riegel, 2002). In other words, Confucius's life may have been portrayed with some exaggeration in keeping with folklore. Confucius is believed to have ended his exile by returning to Lu in 484 BCE and accepting a position at court that allowed him to organize the *Book of Songs* and the *Book of Documents*, a history of the Lu province stretching from the eighth century to the fifth century BCE, and to edit the *Spring and Autumn Annals*.

Another debate surrounding Confucius continues today concerning the authorship of an ancient work called the *Analects*. Similar to the relationship between Socrates and Plato, it is believed that Confucius's disciples took notes on their mentor's philosophy and included his wisdom along with discussions about his philosophy within the *Analects*. Some scholars suggest that the original *Analects* may have been written as a prescription for how a good person should behave and was later revised to describe specifically how Confucius behaved. In either case, as prescriptive rules or as a role model, the *Analects* as a representation of Confucius's life provides a template for proper conduct. Many Chinese individuals aspired to emulate these prescriptive behaviors in order to become perfect citizens within Chinese society (Riegel, 2002).

Stories of Benedict's life are subject to skepticism as well because most were collected after his life. Benedict was a celebrated and revered man in his own time; he was considered a miracle worker who offered both spiritual and physical security to the people. Stories of his deeds spread across Europe and across time. Following Benedict's death, Pope Gregory I, also known as Gregory the Great, collected the stories of Benedict's life from bishops, monks, elders, disciples, neighbors, villagers, and guild workers. Pope Gregory had met Benedict on at least one occasion, and thus he included his own firsthand accounts as well. He called this collection of stories the *Dialogues* (Chapman, 1971).

According to the stories, Benedict was born around 480 AD in the village of Nursia, which lies about sixty miles north of Rome. His life coincided with the violent years that followed the fall of the Roman Empire. Italy had been ravaged by the Justinian and Ostrogothic wars in the fifth century and was further torn apart by the Lombard invasion in the sixth century (Chamberlin, 1982). This was a time of upheaval, and individuals sought safety and security both spiritually and physically. Benedict of Nursia offered this twofold security through his spiritual leadership and his management of a monastery.

Benedict's legitimacy with regard to spiritual leadership dates back to his childhood. The first miracle that Benedict performed occurred when he was a boy; it may seem simple, but the villagers took it as a sign of his spiritual prowess. On his way through the village, he miraculously repaired a broken sieve. The witnesses took the sieve and hung it in the church. The villagers praised the child beyond what his humility could tolerate. Subsequently, the monk Romanus took the embarrassed boy to a cave and proceeded to teach and guide him in monastic ways. During this time, Benedict overcame temptations of the flesh "by rolling in thorns" and devoting himself to God (Chapman, 1971, p. 10). After being discovered by local shepherds, his name spread throughout Italy.

Benedict, at the request of the monks of Vicovaro, gave up his reclusive life-style and became their leader. These monks espoused a strict Eastern form of monasticism, which, according to Benedict, they failed to achieve fully. Two forms of Eastern monasticism existed at the time. The first began with Palladius, a monk from Palenstine who ventured to Egypt in 388 A.D. and developed a form of asceticism that included having the monks live in isolated huts. These monks led individualistic lives and only met on Saturday and Sunday. The second form of Eastern monasticism was developed by Pachomius (290–346 A.D.). Pachomius converted to Christianity upon his arrival in Alexandria, Egypt. Pachomius's form of monasticism brought the monks together under one roof and stipulated rules about working and living together. His philosophy is believed to have had a considerable influence on Benedict of Nursia. As the new leader of the Vicovaroan monks, Benedict set out to guide them on a path toward perfection, but his relentless discipline led the monks to revolt. Benedict nearly lost his life at the hands of these monks, but he gained valuable wisdom about organizing and ruling individuals. He left his severely austere ways behind and began to develop what would come to be known as the Benedictine Rule (Benedictine Monks of St. Meinrad's Abbey, 1937).

Following another period of solitude, Benedict moved to Montecassino and became the abbot for a handful of monks. Under his guidance, the monastery grew, as did his reputation for moderation, as opposed to his earlier austerity. Benedict opened twelve monasteries, each with twelve monks, and named a *pater* to oversee the monasteries. Within a few years he had more than 150 monks under his guidance. Word of his miracles and his approach to monasticism spread to Rome. "Religious nobles (*nobiles et religiosi*) from Rome now came in numbers to visit him and offered their sons as monks" (Chapman, 1971, p. 10). The Benedictine way spread across Europe.

Benedict copied early manuscripts that had been derived from Greek sources and translated by Jerome into Latin. These included "the *Rule* of Pachomius, Rufinus, the *Rule* of Basil, Augustine of Hippo's Epistle 211, and the writings of Cassian who taught in the monastic centers of southern France in the fifth century" (Chamberlin, 1982, pp. 2–3). Pachomius's works date back to 250–350 A.D., prior to the Gothic sack of Rome in 410 A.D., whereas St. Augustine of Hippo's writings on monasticism were written between 354 and 430 A.D., just prior to Attila's invasion of Italy and the Vandals' sacking of Rome (Skrabec, 2003). In addition, Benedict drew from the *Regula Magistri* before he finalized his own organizational treatise, entitled the Rule of Benedict, *Regula Benedicti*.

Philosophy and Rhetoric of Work

Beginning with Confucius and moving on to Benedict, the following sections will explain the philosophies of each, especially in light of their relation to work. For both Confucius and Benedict, the idea that instituting an organized system of rules surrounding work and relationships as well as decorum promised to bring order to chaos.

Confucius on Work and Relationships

Like Socrates, Confucius's conversations with his disciples have been used as the basis of his philosophical treatises. He spoke to his disciples about a natural force and a supernatural force. The natural force included the cycles of nature, as well as a kind of fate. The supernatural force included a supreme being and a heaven. In short, according to Confucius, although people's lives may be predetermined in many ways through fate, they do indeed have free choice and a heaven for which to strive. Thus, they should comport themselves accordingly, which can be described as the Confucian way. The Confucian way includes compassion (*ren*), righteousness (*yi*), faithfulness (*zhong*), altruism (*shu*), and honor (*li*)—especially through commitment to rituals and respect to ancestors, and virtuousness (*de*).

Compassion (*ren*) is key to Confucian thinking. Loving others meant that an individual would not be given to self-aggrandizement. Boastfulness was frowned upon for the sake of others, but false humility was considered inappropriate as well. *Ren* also meant that one must find a balance in speech that neither deprecates others nor falsely compliments them, according to Confucius. Taking comportment a step further, Confucius told his disciples that it is also their duty to help others achieve what they desire: "Since you yourself desire standing then help others achieve it, since you yourself desire success then help others attain it" (Lunyu, 12.2, 6.30 as cited in Riegel, 2002, p. 4). This form of compassion is promoted through concern for others and through self-discipline.

The second concept, righteousness (*yi*) has an opposite (*li*), which must also be considered in explanations of the proper type of behavior (Lin, 2003). *Yi* refers to the concept of righteousness, and *li* refers to profit. Confucius explained that acting in a way that demonstrates what one ought to do exemplifies *yi*. For example, if one's friend were in need of money, then one would lend it to him or her. On the other hand, if one made friends with wealthy individuals in the hope of attaining money, then one would be demonstrating *li*, acting in a way as to profit from the relationship. Thus, *yi* can also refer to having a sense of shame for not doing what is righteous (*li*; Lin, 2003). Confucius encouraged *yi*.

The practices of faithfulness (*zhong*) and altruism (*shu*) are equally important in the Confucian philosophy (Chai & Chai, 1965). "*Zhong* requires one to do to others what one wishes [for] oneself, while *shu* suggests that one should not do to others what one does not wish for oneself" (Lin, 2003, p. 16). The first requires a sense of faithfulness to one's ideals and the second requires a generosity of spirit.

Respecting rituals (*li*—spelled the same, but pronounced differently from the word *li* that means profit-making for selfish purposes; see Lin, 2003) is one way that individuals can develop self-restraint and discipline. Rituals are enacted to show respect to others (e.g., ancestors, family members, fellow workers) and to give order to society. Confucius thought that rituals should be maintained and never desecrated. Further, he suggested that if people engaged in superficial displays of ritual without true compassion (*ren*), then their actions should be questioned, for rituals without sincerity are empty acts. "I consider not being present at the sacrifice as though there were no sacrifice," Confucius said (Lunyu, 3.12, as cited in Riegel, 2002, p. 4). Both the presence of self (mentally, physically, and spiritually) and the undertaking of the ritual act create a sense of order for society and for the culture (Riegel, 2002).

Order, for Confucius, was also dependent on the right kind of governance and leadership. Virtue (*de*) is what gives a ruler true power, for a moral leader will draw followers through good actions and deeds rather than through force or threat. Good actions or deeds were best exemplified through ritual practice, paying homage to the ancients through sacrifice, participating in ritual gift exchange (a complex system of obligation and indebtedness), and following rules and practices of politeness and decorum (Riegel, 2002).

Titles and their associated behavior also represented an important part of Confucian thinking. The hierarchical ordering of relationships and the responsibility as well as respect arising from one's various roles is crucial to the overall Confucian way of thinking. This concept is called the *rectification of names*. As Confucius wrote, "Good government consists of the ruler being a ruler, the minister being a minister, the father being a father, and the son being the son" (Lunyu, 12.11 as cited in Riegel, 2002, p. 5). Respect and responsibility in relationships are expected with regard to the five relationships that govern society (*wu lun*): "(a) Father-son (the relationship of love); (b) Emperor-subject (the relation of righteousness); (c) Husband-wife (the relation of chaste conduct); (D) Elder-younger (the relation of order); and (e) Friend-friend (the relation of faithfulness)" (Lin, 2003, p. 76).

In addition to concern about relationships, Confucius placed emphasis on education. He believed that studying was at the heart of learning, but he did not dismiss reflective meditative thinking: "He who learns but does not think is lost. He who thinks but does not learn is in great danger" (Lunyu, 2.15 as cited in Riegel, 2002, p. 6). The proverb extols the virtue of serious study and also promotes critical thinking. Confucius is credited with having taught more than three thousand students, but only seventy were considered disciples who had mastered the Confucian way. He taught "morality, proper speech, government and refined arts, while he also emphasized the '*Six Arts*'—ritual, music, archery, chariot-riding, calligraphy, and computation" (Riegel, 2002, p. 6).

Like Socrates, Confucius engaged his students with questions and provided them with analogies and passages from the classics. He argued that long lectures did not precipitate the students' exploration. Speaking of how the good teacher should comport himself and speaking of his own ways of teaching, Confucius concluded that tedious lectures should be omitted. "Instead he [the good teacher] poses questions, cites passages from the classics, or uses apt analogies, and waits for his students to arrive at the right answers. *I only instruct the eager and enlighten the fervent: If I hold up one corner and the student cannot come back to me with the other three, I do not go on with the lesson*" (Lunyu, 7.8, as cited in Riegel, 2002, p. 6).

The truthfulness and value of language were important to Confucius, who criticized the use of false flattery and sycophantic behavior as an effrontery to a moral society. Furthermore, those who did not live up to their names or titles damaged the credibility of language and the honor of the word. The possibility for false rhetoric to flourish was as much a concern to Confucius as it had been to critics of the Sophists.

Confucius extolled virtues that he considered crucial to the organization of a harmonious (*Ho*) society, but even more importantly he lived by his own rules.

Saint Benedict's Rule for Work and Relationships

Like the Confucian way, the Rule of St. Benedict was more than a philosophy. Although it did indeed profess a utopian or ideal way of organizing, it went beyond most philosophies by being put into practice. Furthermore, Benedict's Rule was tested under the most extreme conditions during the Dark Ages.

The actual text of *Regula Benedicti* contradicts the image one might expect based on its title. St. Benedict's Rule is not one rule but, rather, several rules. Today, the "text of the Rule itself is about sixty pages in typical typescript. It consists of seventy-three *chapters*, which average from three to five paragraphs" (Skrabec, 2003, p. 2). Numerous medieval copies of the manuscript exist, which is not surprising because copying manuscripts was common work for monks (Chamberlin, 1982). Eventually, the manuscript was translated from Latin to other languages, including German and English. "The earliest surviving text (known as Codex 914) can today be found in the monastic library of St. Gall in Switzerland, and dates to 900 A.D. It was from this text, that Charlemagne commissioned a copy to be made for use across the Holy Roman Empire" (Skrabec, 2003, p. 2).

The first chapter of the Benedictine Rule clarifies the definition of "monk" and admonishes those men who claim to be monks but do not follow God's word; these include Sarabaites , monks who followed their own path but later became known as fallen-away monks or degenerate monks and vagabonds. In addition, clergy who became hermits were also excluded from St. Benedict's definition of "monk," even though they had tested themselves and obtained the spiritual strength necessary to meet God's demand. Their exclusion might be explained on the grounds that hermits do not live in communities; communal living was of paramount importance to Benedict because his rule(s) were meant to organize monastic communities.

The second chapter explains the role of the abbot as the father and symbol of Christ who should teach and govern by word and by deed. Further, it instructs the abbot to treat the monks with fairness and equality: "Let not one of noble birth be raised above a slave" (*Regula Benedicti,* as cited in Benedictine Monks, 1937, p. 9). If a monk failed in his duties, the abbot was instructed to use "gentleness with severity" by acting like a father who rebukes disobedience and praises obedience. Benedict recommended using words before resorting to corporal punishment. Finally, Benedict asserted that the abbot must always remember the responsibility that has been entrusted to him.

Chapter 3 addresses the decision-making role of the community. The abbot was instructed to call all of the members together, gather their advice, and "weigh it within himself" (*Regula Benedicti,* as cited in Benedictine Monks, 1937, p. 12). St. Benedict ordered that "all are to be called to counsel because it is often to the younger that the Lord reveals what is better" (p. 12). Each monk is reminded to give his opinion humbly and to allow the final decision to be the abbot's choice. Counsel is critical to decision making, and obedience to the decision is mandatory.

Chapter 4 reminds the monks to follow the Ten Commandments and adds that the monks should fast, care for the poor and sick, control their tempers, not give in to vice or evil, not speak too much, and believe in the mercy of the Lord. These general statements are detailed in seventy-two specific statements, called *the instruments of good works.*

Chapters 5 through 22 deal with comportment, from how to pray to how to sleep. Specifically, chapter 5 calls for obedience without delay, which demonstrates humility. To pause, stop, or question a command is to assert one's knowledge or self as superior. Chapter 6 praises silence because silence honors God. Chapter 7 draws from Luke 14:11: "Everyone that exalts himself will be humbled, and he that humbles himself shall be exalted" (*Regula Benedicti*, as cited in Benedictine Monks, 1937, p. 19). Chapters 9 through 21 address specific details on what, when, and how to pray. Chapter 22 interestingly describes how the monks are to sleep. The monks were instructed to sleep in separate beds with a light burning all night. They also were instructed to sleep with their clothes on but not to have knives at their sides for fear that they might wound themselves in their sleep; they were to be always ready to do the work of the Lord (Benedictine Monks, 1937). This last rule reminds us that survival depended on both physical readiness against further invasions by enemies and physical readiness to work in the fields.

Chapters 23 through 30 address punishment for failure to follow the rules. The most severe was excommunication, but abbots were instructed to give private warnings first and to give public rebuke second before resorting to excommunication. Even those who chose not to change their errant ways and were excommunicated could be taken back by the abbot if they repented.

Chapter 31 explains the need for a cellarer, one who cares for "the sick, the young, the guests, and the poor" (*Regula Benedicti*, as cited in Benedictine Monks, 1937, p. 45) as well as "the vessels and goods of the monastery" (p. 45). This should be a man of "humility" and neither "covetous" nor "wasteful" (p. 45).

Chapter 32 discusses the appointment of a brother to take charge of tools and clothing. This monk should be prepared to answer to the abbot for deviations in the inventory, which should be kept in writing. Although in chapter 33 Benedict notes that no monk should claim ownership of any article, in chapter 34 he also advises that distribution of articles, tools, and clothing should be based on need. Citing Acts 4:35, Benedict writes: "Distribution was made to each one according as he has need" (p. 47); special consideration should be given to those with "infirmities" (p. 47).

In chapter 35, Benedict lays out a work plan based on rotation. Especially kitchen duties are described as having to be shared. The only exception is given to the cellarer (or another having duties beyond those of the other monks).

The next two chapters detail how to care for the sick, elderly, or weak. Chapters 38, 39, 40, and 41 discuss proper ways of sharing a meal, including the times at which to eat. Silence is the custom at dinner. As one monk reads from Scripture, another carefully measures food and drink according to specific guidelines. Rules concerning silence and tardiness are discussed in chapters 42 and 43, followed by three chapters on the punishments for those breaking these rules. Chapter 47 addresses the proper time for the work of God. Prayers, meals, and labor were kept to a strict schedule.

Perhaps the most famous of Benedict's rules appears in chapter 48. Here Benedict lays out his treatise on labor. "Idleness is the enemy of the soul" (*Regula Benedicti*, as cited in Benedictine Monks, 1937, p. 61). Monks should balance their time between manual labor and reading. "They are truly monks if they live by the labor of their hands as did our Fathers and Apostles. Let all things, however, be done in moderation on account of the weak" (p. 61).

The next four chapters deal with how to follow the Benedictine way when traveling outside of the monastery. In turn, chapter 53 addresses how the monks at the monastery should receive a traveler "as Christ himself" (Benedictine Monks, 1937, p. 65). Chapters 57 through 61 explain the etiquette of receiving and or dealing with other members of the community who are not monks. Admonishing privilege is discussed in chapters 62 and 63. First, when selecting one of the monks to lead Mass, it is important to choose someone who is humble. That person will officiate Mass but then immediately return to his status as a monk. In community decisions, "let not age determine the rank nor have any bearing on it: for Samuel and Daniel even when children judged the elders" (Benedictine Monks, 1937, p. 79). Most importantly, the appointment of the abbot must be made by the "entire community," and they "shall choose unanimously" (p. 81). And of the abbot, Benedict says, "let him seek rather to be loved than to be feared" and to assign tasks in a "moderate" fashion (p. 82). It is also noted in chapter 65 that no prior (second in command) should be named to a monastery, for the prior, who is too often given to being "puffed up by the evil spirit of pride," exacerbates jealousies and "causes dissension in the community" (p. 83). But a porter (gatekeeper) may be named. This person should be mature and capable of responding to the requests of those who come knocking at the abbey's gate. The monastery should be self-sufficient so no brethren need to leave and the needs of those who come can be satisfied. However, should a monk be sent on a journey, then, according to chapter 67, when he returns he should prostrate himself in case he heard some evil and he should not repeat what he heard or speak of what he saw outside the monastery.

Some basic guidelines on how a monk should act if he is asked to do the impossible are given in chapter 68. Although challenging tasks can be good, impossible tasks cannot move the monk toward God. In chapter 69 monks are told never to defend another monk within the monastery. This rule is based on the notion that one is coming to the defense of a relative and that this will give rise to other problems. However, Benedict also reminds us in the next chapter that there should be no reason to have to come to someone's aid because a monk should not "excommunicate or strike any of his brethren, unless he be given authority to do so" (*Regula Benedicti*, as cited in Benedictine Monks, 1937, p. 88). This is further instantiated by the rule that the brethren should obey one another. Their obedience can be expected because, as chapter 72 suggests, the monks should approach each other with "zeal" to do good, to honor each other, and to be patient with each other, "to surpass one another in the practice of mutual obedience" (pp. 89–90).

In the final chapter, Benedict explains that this Rule has been written in order to guide the monks, so that they "may give proof of our having attained at least some degree of virtue and made a commencement of religious life" (*Regula Benedicti*, as cited in Benedictine Monks, 1937, p. 90).

Contemporary Scholarship

The Benedictine Rule was originally created to bring order to monastic communities that existed during turbulent times. Quentin R. Skrabec (2003) claims that Benedict's rules, modified slightly, can bring success to businesses today. Of course Skrabec does not feel that we can follow Benedict's edicts to the letter, but with minor modification, many of Benedict's insights can be or have already been applied within contemporary business organizations.

First and foremost, Benedict's concept of community is crucial to organizational success. Skrabec (2003) argues that whereas we have seen the popularity of teams and quality circles ebb and flow, the idea of community is stable. Skrabec led a team of workers at LVT Steel Corporation to win the first *USA Today* National Quality Cup award. Through "camaraderie, communal welfare, and stability" (p. 15), the members of the community share goals and much more. Skrabec suggests that even little activities, from eating together to troubleshooting small problems, will have an effect on the success of a business.

Skrabec (2003) believes one of the most important aspects of Benedictine philosophy is that work and reading Scripture were given equal attention; study and learning were considered crucial. Skrabec associates these dimensions of work and study with the contemporary characteristics of *learning organizations*. Learning organizations are those businesses that continually seek out information from their environment so that they might adapt accordingly (see Shockley-Zalabak, 2006, for a discussion of Argryis & Schön's 1990 introduction of the concept; see also Senge's 1990 and Morgan's 1997 contributions to the topic). Benedict divided the day into labor periods and study periods. Benedict's "motto—*Ora et Labora* (to work is to pray)—became a standard of the Rule" (Skrabec, p. 30). Skrabec (2003) believes that in this day and age it would be negligent not to incorporate a learning component into a working day. This aspect of the Benedictine community is easier to emulate than either the lifelong covenant or the joint appointment of the leader by all members of the community.

Security and egalitarianism are also characteristic of the monasteries. Security through lifelong tenure is rarely given in the United States, but that does not mean it would not make business sense (Skrabec, 2003). It has worked for universities. It is also rare to find an organization that allows its employees to choose the CEO, but Skrabec suggests that in universities, where a chair is elected by the department faculty members, such a practice has and does occur with some efficiency and effectiveness.

The key to achieving such goals as education, security, and egalitarianism might be found in another aspect of Benedict's philosophy—leadership. For example, Benedict saw humility and obedience as the cornerstones of the monastery's success. Nobles had to give up their arrogance, and slaves had to give up their resistance. Each needed to demonstrate humility and obedience to the other. A tradition of hierarchical thinking in contemporary Western organizations means that this will be another hurdle for most of these organizations to overcome. According to Skrabec (2003), recent discussions of *servant leadership* and *stewardship* are examples of the Benedictine philosophy's making its way into contemporary organizational management practices. This focus on obedience, serving, and humility is meant to bring about harmony and stability (Skrabec, 2003).

Other contributing factors include involvement, commitment, and training. Involvement in the monastery includes a morning meeting where all decisions of any relevance are brought to the entire community for their advice. Employee participation of this sort is not common in U.S. organizations, which might well benefit from increased employee input, according to Skrabec. Commitment or organizational loyalty leads to increased quality, but in a society that is marked by massive so-called downsizings, it will be difficult to convince workers to commit to their jobs with the same zeal that a Benedictine monk would commit to his order. Training is associated with socialization, and Benedict gave it careful thought. Skrabec (2003) suggests that mentoring was a common practice in the monastery and should be so in modern organizations, as well.

Unlike the application of St. Benedict's philosophy to modern organizations, scholars studying Confucianism are less likely to call for incorporating it into organizations and are more likely to investigate how it continues to exist today. The most prominent contemporary studies focus on how Confucianism impacts the Chinese workplace as well as on how Chinese managers differ from American managers. Scholars have explored such topics as conflict management styles, decision making, and leadership approaches in these intercultural studies. For example, Fu and Yukl (2000) found that American managers were more likely to give higher effectiveness ratings to rational persuasion and exchange, whereas Chinese managers were more likely to give higher ratings to people who employed coalition building, appeals to authority, and gift-giving—Confucian ideals. Although some scholars think that Chinese workers eschew conflict and use avoidance strategies in order to keep harmony, Tjosvold et al. (as cited in

Lin, 2003) find that Chinese workers ask questions (Tjosvold, Hui, & Sun, 2000), choose disagreement (Tjosvold, Nibler & Wan, 2001), and explore opposing views (Tjosvold & Sun, 2003) in order to reach a true harmony. Scholars have also looked at how Confucianism's principles of shame and education influence workplace practices (see Krone, Garret, & Chen, 1992; Krone, Chen, & Xia, 1997).

Since the time that the majority of these studies were conducted in the 1990s, Lin (2003) has questioned how lingering influence from Confucianism is intermingled with the more contemporary influence of Chinese communism through the philosophy of Mao Zedong. Lin's study shows a clear influence from communism on workplace practices, which should be included in future intercultural organizational studies (also see Lin & Clair, 2007). With capitalism making its mark on China today, future studies might explore how these three disparate philosophies—Confucianism, communism, and capitalism—conjoin or clash, at both the micro- and macrolevels of socioeconomic practice.

Both Confucius and Benedict have been credited with providing philosophical paths meant to establish order in eras of despotic leadership or violent times. Confucius promoted the idea of the moral leader and the perfection of people through compassion for one another. Balancing responsibility with respect seems to be another shared concern for Confucius and Benedict. However, Confucius extended his commentaries on the subject to include family relations, organization, and government, whereas Benedict limited his concerns to the monasteries. Both men promoted discipline, albeit to different rituals, and both advocated education. Each man left his mark.

St. Benedict was considered a visionary for his time. He was what the community called a wonder worker. Benedict probably died between 533 and 535, following a famine that struck Italy (Chapman, 1971). He was canonized and named patron saint of Europe in 1964 by Pope Paul VI (Skrabec, 2003). Confucius was also considered a visionary for his times. He is believed to have died in 479 BCE at the age of seventy-two, which is considered a magical number "with far reaching significance in early Chinese literature" (Riegel, 2002, p. 1). Each man's story is grounded in suffering, exile, and a return to help the people. Confucius lived during a time of political upheavals; Benedict lived through the chaos of the Dark Ages. Both men attempted to bring order and harmony to the society in which they lived.

Chapter Five

Adam Smith

The Father of Capitalism

Introduction

The philosophy of Adam Smith, the father of capitalism, had a dramatic and sweeping effect on the world. Although he was not alone in his critiques of economics and politics, his works provided the most detailed and voluminous challenge to the thinking of the mercantilist period. The 1700s ushered in an era of curiosity and concern grounded in the principles of the Enlightenment, especially rational empiricism, which encouraged Smith to explore the state of political and economic expansionism by Europeans and organize a treatise on how nations accumulated wealth. Mercantilism and the colonization of America as well as the exploitation of Africa, brought about a series of philosophical treatises on the topic of wealth and politics. These early commentaries on mercantilism may seem mild when compared to the radical critique that Karl Marx leveled against capitalism a hundred years or so later. Nonetheless, Smith's eighteenth-century works were instrumental in changing the philosophical face of economics and politics. This chapter provides a biography of Adam Smith, examines one of the most famous books on the subject of economics—*An Inquiry into the Nature and Causes of the Wealth of Nations*—and covers concepts that Smith advanced, including *laissez-faire economics, the division of labor, self-interest, the equity of jobs,* and *the invisible hand.*

Biography

Adam Smith was born in 1723 in Kirkcaldy, Scotland. His father, who died six months before his birth, had been a customs agent. His mother, Margaret

Douglas, who was from a family of property owners, raised him by herself. His life was considered somewhat uneventful, with the exception that at the age of three he "was carried off by a band of gypsies and only with difficulty restored to his family" (Lerner, 1937, p. vi). In 1737, at the age of fourteen, Adam Smith attended Glasgow University to study moral philosophy. At that time, Glasgow was at the center of the "Scottish Enlightenment" (Henderson, 2002, p.1). Smith's theories would become part of the Enlightenment, a philosophical movement that praised reason.

Later, at the age of seventeen, he attended Oxford's Balliol College. It was there "that he read Hume's *A Treatise of Human Nature*. Smith's interest in Hume's work [soon] brought him into conflict with the authorities at Oxford" (Landry, 2002, p. 2). He left Oxford in 1740 and returned home to his mother. After giving two well-received lectures, one on logic (1751) and one on moral philosophy (1752), he was named chair of both departments at Glasgow University, and in 1759 he published the book *Theory of Moral Sentiments*.

In 1764 he left the world of academics to tutor a young man by the name of Henry Scott, the third duke of Buccleuch. As a result of his tutoring position, and more specifically the generosity of the duke, Smith was able to travel throughout Europe over the next two years. During the course of his travels, he met Voltaire, Rousseau, and several other philosophers of the Enlightenment, who eventually became his academic colleagues. Smith, who was already "steeped in history and philosophy, [was] exposed to both the English and French political-economic systems of the day" during his travels (Landry, 2002, p. 5). His exposure to varied economic systems, his studies, and his acquaintances with some of the most influential European thinkers allowed Smith to develop his own thoughts on the moral, ethical, economic, and political situation in the Western world. After retiring from the employment of the duke, Smith returned home to write *The Wealth of Nations*, which was published the same year as the signing of the American Declaration of Independence, 1776.

"Throughout his life Smith treasured his library and was continually absorbed in abstractions" (Landry, 2002, p. 3). In 1778, he took a position with the government and worked as the commissioner of customs in Scotland. Overall, "Smith lead a quiet and sheltered life; he lived with his mother and remained a bachelor all his life" (Landry, p. 3). In 1790, Smith became ill and died. He was buried in Scotland. Adam Smith's contributions have stood the test of time; although written centuries ago, the principles of capitalism are practiced in numerous countries today and act as a powerful force in the contemporary global economy.

Philosophy and Rhetoric of Work

Throughout his life, Adam Smith was a tireless worker and prolific writer. His countless lectures have been published on topics including moral rights, justice, and domestic law. Smith's most noted publications are *An Inquiry into the Nature and Causes of the Wealth of Nations* (1776) and *Theory of Moral Sentiments* (1759).

Smith followed a linear form of thinking that was made up of three parts, morality, justice, and economics, with the parts following a natural progression. Kerr (2002) explains this progression: Smith "based his economic theories upon his theories of jurisprudence, and those in turn were based on his moral theories" (p. 397). The basis for his treatise was one of complete moral belief. His moral beliefs were grounded in theories of rights, including the right to self-interest.

Self-Interest and Moral Sentiments

The prosperity of a nation can best be advanced, according to Smith (1776/2003), "by allowing each individual to pursue his own interests as he sees them." And "it is not from the benevolence of the butcher, the brewer, or the baker that we expect our dinner, but from their regard to their own interest" (pp. 23–24). Specifically, Smith felt that if individuals could pursue their self-interests the prosperity that followed would expand beyond the initial individual. In short, Adam Smith determined "self-interest as the basis of the economic order and as the main psychological factor in industrial prosperity" (Morrow, 1927, p. 326).

According to Smith, self-interest supports the economy. Through self-interest people spend and save capital depending on their wants and needs, and through this practice they not only support their self-interests but those of others. Morrow (1927) explicates the matter in the following way:

> The condition [of self-interest] is that in which a man who intends to benefit only himself in a particular way may, in the act of procuring that benefit, produce a benefit of a different kind for everyone including himself. A merchant who instead of engaging in foreign trade engages in domestic trade—where his capital is more secure and no less profitable—contributes to the defense of the nation [and] all citizens. (p. 443)

Self-interest establishes the wealth of the individual as well as the nation and satisfies a moral necessity. "For the self-seeking of men could increase the wealth of the nation . . . a contribution that is in the public interest" (Morrow, 1927, p. 444). This unintentional outcome of self-interest is called the *invisible hand*. The invisible hand "reflects our admiration for the elegant and smooth functioning of the market system as a coordination of autonomous individual choice in an interdependent world" (Evensky, 1993, p. 197). Smith believed that the economy would run itself through a natural process if individuals were left unrestrained by rules and regulations and allowed to pursue their financial desires. As Rothschild (1994) explains:

> In *The Theory of Moral Sentiments* Smith is describing some particularly unpleasant rich proprietors who are quite unconcerned with humanity or justice but who in their natural selfishness and rapacity pursue only their own vain and insatiable desires. They do however employ thousands

of poor workers to produce luxury commodities: They are led by an invisible hand to . . . without intending it, without knowing it, advance the interest of society." (p. 319)

The invisible hand is theoretically the controlling factor that influences all decisions, personal and organizational. It stems from self-interest, which Smith believed was a moral right. Following his theories of moral sentiments, Smith details how the natural process, guided by the invisible hand, demonstrates a valuable form of economics. For example, the invisible hand theoretically controls a company's decision to use the division of labor, as it complements self-interest. And the use of the division of labor will further promote the wealth of a nation, so long as government interference does not attempt to stop the invisible hand. Thus, laissez-faire economics should be controlled by unseen forces and not through government interference and regulation. This was a new doctrine for the times, a challenge for an old Europe emerging from feudalism and monarchic control as well as mercantilism. Nevertheless, *The Wealth of Nations* is considered more of an explanation of existing economic situations at the time than the call for a new order (Lerner, 1937).

An Inquiry into the Nature and Causes of the Wealth of Nations

As mentioned earlier, the first edition of the book *An Inquiry into the Nature and Causes of the Wealth of Nations* was published in 1776 and is comprised of over one thousand pages of text. It contains five sections, or books. The chapters within the various books are based upon Adam Smith's lectures. The first book opens with a discussion of the division of labor, which is followed by discussions of the origin of money, the concept of commodities, the inequalities of labor and employment, the rent of land, the value of gold and silver, and the effects of progress. Book 2 discusses the nature of accumulation and stock. Book 3 delves into the concept of wealth as it varies across nations. Book 4 addresses the political aspects of economy, especially with regard to the unreasonableness of government restraints on commercial practices. Book 5 deals with the commonwealth and public works. Rather than detail each of the five books, the following sections focus on those points most directly related to economics and a theory of work.

Economics and the Division of Labor

The Wealth of Nations begins with a discussion of the division of labor as a reasonable and logical means to create wealth and satisfy self-interest. Smith uses the example of pin manufacturing to show how labor division increases productivity in the factory. He states, "the greatest improvement in the productive power of labour, and the greater part of the skill, dexterity, and judgment with which it is anywhere directed, or applied, seem to have been the effects of the division of labour" (Smith, 1776/2003, p. 9). Smith believed that the only way that we are able to maximize productivity is to split or divide the labor into many different parts:

> One man draws out the wire, another straightens it, a third cuts it, a fourth
> points it; a fifth grinds it at the top for receiving the head; to make the head
> requires two or three distinct operations; to put it on, is a peculiar busi-
> ness, to whiten the pins is another; it is even a trade by itself to put them in
> the paper; and the important business of making a pin is, in this manner
> divided into about eighteen distinct operations . . . [the workers could],
> when they exerted themselves, make among them about twelve pounds
> of pins in a day. There are in a pound upwards of four thousand pins of a
> middling size. Those [workers] then could make among them upwards of
> forty-eight thousand pins in a day. But if they had all wrought separately
> and independently, and without any of them having been educated to this
> peculiar business, they certainly could not each of them have made twenty,
> perhaps no one pin in a day. (Smith, 1776/2003, p. 11)

Through the division of labor, in Smith's example, the workers are able to create
thousands of pins in a single day.

Division of labor results in additional advantages. They are "the improvement of dexterity, saving of time, and the invention of machinery, which facilitate
and abridge labour" (Smith, 1776/2003, p. 14). Improvement to dexterity means
that when workers complete only one simple task, they are able to complete the
task very quickly. In addition, through muscle memory workers are able to complete the task without much thought. The development of dexterity and muscle
memory means that workers do not have to stop and think about their jobs, as
long as those jobs are simple and repetitive, which saves time and thus money.
In addition, according to Smith, because the jobs are boring at best and use
machinery, workers will be driven to invent more efficient means of machinery
in order to free themselves even more quickly from this drudgery. Specifically,
workers are going to improve the machines they work with in order to make
their jobs easier. For example:

> in the first [steam engines] a boy was constantly employed to open and
> shut alternately the communication between the boiler and the cylinder,
> according to the position of the piston either ascending or descending. One
> of these boys observed that by tying a string from the handle of the valve,
> which opened the communication, to another part of the machine, that
> valve would open and shut without his assistance, and leave him at liberty to
> divert himself. One of the greatest improvements that has been made upon
> this machine, since it was first invented, was in this manner the discovery
> of a boy who wanted to save his own [labor]. (Smith, 1776/2003, p. 17)

So the direct effects of the division of labor are not only the saving of time
for the worker but also the improvement of manufacturing equipment for the
factory. The division of labor and self-interest work hand in hand. In short, Smith
surmised that not only will the division of labor improve the ability of the workers to complete their tasks, but self-interest will also improve the way in which

the tasks are completed. Labor and its organization were a crucial concern to Smith. As he further detailed his theories concerning the wealth of nations, he found it necessary to redefine the exchange process and labor.

Money, Commodities, and Labor

Adam Smith concluded that the division of labor, even in its most primitive form, would lead to difficulties in the barter system. These difficulties could only be resolved by making particular commodities act as money. In ancient Greece, Homer spoke of oxen as the measure of money, whereas in Abyssinia it was salt (see Smith 1776/1937, p. 23). Eventually silver and gold reigned supreme. In time, metal pieces were shaped and stamped to assure the quality of the metal and to standardize the exchange. But what rules determined the value of the exchange was still not clear, and what was meant by value could be defined in terms of the use or the exchange in the mercantilist system. However, Smith suggested that the real measure of the commodity did not exist in the exchange or the use but in the labor involved. Labor became central to Smith's theory, and the value of labor needed to be assessed and measured. Thus, Smith carefully considered what would make some forms of labor or employment unequal to other forms.

First, Smith felt that productive labor was certainly more valuable than that which did not produce a commodity or a product. For example, the farmer who grows produce has a commodity to sell, but the teacher who guides a student has no product to take to market. Thus, Smith concluded that occupations that did not produce goods were generally less valuable to society. For example, professors, buffoons, orators, musicians, menial servants, lawyers, and government servants are people who hold occupations that do not produce a commodity. Nevertheless, Smith realized that society needs people to fill these occupations as well. Therefore, he included them in his definition of labor, but not without suggesting that they are less valuable to society than are people who have occupations or perform labor that results in a product.

Second, Smith felt that the level of skill, stability, enjoyment, and trust and the probability of success associated with the occupation or labor played a part in determining its value to society and to the exchange process. Furthermore, whether a job was performed in its natural time or not (e.g., a soldier during wartime is providing a more valuable form of labor or service than a soldier during peacetime) affected its value, as did whether the job utilized the skills and dexterity of the worker. For whom the work was performed could also have bearing on the inequalities of labor (e.g., performing somewhat similar duties for a more reputable organization increases its value over labor for a less reputable organization—being a clerk at a prestigious store versus being a clerk at a less prestigious store).

Employment, as opposed to individual entrepreneurship, occurs when one person has accumulated enough stock to require another's assistance and the person with the stock wishes to expand his/her holdings. The owner must, of course, pay for both supplies and labor but can also expect "profit" for taking on the risk of this "adventure" (Smith, 1776/1937, p. 48). But wages and materials are only two parts of the equation in the exchange process. Because land is privately owned, one cannot simply gather from the land, but must pay rent to whoever owns the land, and because some form of labor is required to obtain and maintain the private ownership of the land, labor once again becomes central. Smith (1776/1937) concludes, "Labour, therefore, is the real measure of the exchangeable value of all commodities" (p. 30).

Division of Labor, Stock, and the Circulation of Capital

In book 2, Smith attempts to untangle the relationship between the onset of the division of labor and the necessity of stock. He tells us that a person must have a certain amount of stock stored up in order to specialize in one area. "A weaver cannot apply himself entirely to his peculiar business, unless there is beforehand stored up somewhere, . . . a stock sufficient to maintain him" (Smith 1776/1937, p. 259). Otherwise, s/he would also have to farm, care for the animals, etc. But by stocking extra, the weaver can expand his or her business and acquire money to pay others to farm, etc. Thus, accumulation enters into the capitalist equation. Accumulation, according to Smith, will lead to further investment and production. An individual may directly place his or her holdings into new ventures or may lend the money/stocks/profit to others to invest in capital ventures. Thus, stock is divided.

The division of stock should lead to capital improvements. That is to say, the first order of capital is the owner's profit, but as the owner lends the stock for other projects, a second order of capital is produced for society through the development of improved machinery and buildings. As the capital circulates, industry grows. However, not all capital can circulate. A certain amount of capital must be fixed. Fixed capital assures the maintenance of the original business and plays a part in the success of capitalism. Circulating capital helps a nation to grow; thus, the people of a nation must feel secure enough to circulate their money.

Security plays an important role in the success of balancing the circulating and fixed capital. In countries where violence and threats of disaster loom large, people tend to conceal or safeguard their holdings. This kind of fear is detrimental because both fixed and circulating capital, via banking (i.e., saving and investing), are crucial to capitalism (Smith 1776/1937). Banks, according to Smith, are fundamental to the system because they foster exchange of money both within and between nations.

In Smith's day, the greater part of the gold and silver sent to other nations via banks was exchanged for materials (e.g., silk, jewels, coffee, salt). Smith wrote, "I have heard it asserted, that the trade of the city of Glasgow doubled in about fifteen years after the first erection of banks there; and that the trade of Scotland has more than quadrupled since the first erection of two public banks at Edinburgh" (Smith, 1776/1937, p. 281).

In addition, the industriousness of the people and their willingness to participate in the circulation of capital contributes to the overall wealth of a nation. A nation with idle and unproductive people will fail to meet the success of a nation with a stronger working class. "The uniform, constant, and uninterrupted effort of every man to better his condition, . . . is frequently powerful enough to maintain the natural progress in spite of extravagance of government, and the greatest errors of administration" (Smith, 1776/1937, p. 326). Welfare is a last resort for capitalists when dealing with poverty. Idleness will slow capital gains. "Opulence" for the individual or the public is dependent upon "productive hands," wise consumerism, frugality of investing, and the "accumulation of valuable commodities" (p. 332). The system, when functioning properly according to capitalist tenets, should allow even the common worker to employ a menial servant, according to Smith. But perhaps more importantly for Smith is that this opulence can lead to greater public good and the wealth of a nation.

Public Good, the Political Economy, and Civil Justice

Before discussing public benefits in book 5, Smith addresses the political aspects of economy in book 4. He defines political economy as a "branch of the science of a statesmen or legislator, [which] proposes two distinct objects": first to provide for the people and second to provide for the state for the advancement of "public services" (Smith 1776/1937, p. 397).

During the height of the mercantilist era, European nations felt it was of the utmost importance to obtain gold and silver in order to maintain fleets and armies for protection, exploitation, and colonization (Smith 1776/1937, p. 399). Subsequently, governments controlled the exportation and importation of goods, gold, and silver. For example, monarchs supported the importation of silver and gold but not their exportation. Trade was restrained, which merchants opposed because it restricted their potential profit. Thus, merchants made appeals to the parliaments of several different countries.

Arguments surrounding the importation and exportation of goods, gold, and silver gave way to discussions of supply and demand. To loosen the trade restrictions meant that imports of necessities that ran short and had high demand could be replaced more quickly through foreign trade. The fear that exporting gold and silver would weaken the value of the exchange was explained away with the promise that bank notes could more easily replace the gold, which acted as currency, anyway. And as Adam Smith pointed out, just because a commodity is more durable (gold versus a paper note) does not make it more valuable. Adam Smith also argued that what had been most beneficial to the wealth of the European nations was not the gold or silver or other products or resources found by explorers, but rather it was the opening of the new markets in the Americas.

Smith (1776/1937) spends little time addressing the "savages and barbarians" or their possible "wealth" (specifically, he suggests that Spanish writers exaggerated the wealth and civilization of ancient Mexico and Peru; see pp. 416–17) and quickly proceeds to address the concept of trade with the East Indies. Free trade had been blocked in the East Indies but promoted in America (i.e., the colonies). As noted earlier, Smith recognized free trade as a means to create a wealthy nation and feared that statesmen would shy away from free trade because it would put their constituents out of work. But as Smith suggested, it makes no sense to make at home what can be bought more cheaply in another country (p. 424). He assured his readers that people out of work in one area would certainly find jobs in another area. Although exceptions do exist for the adoption of free trade (for example, free trade may be regulated if another country ceases free importation), as a rule it should continue unhampered, according to Smith.

The role that the government plays in the wealth of a nation is not limited to regulating or deregulating trade. The state is held accountable for the defense of the nation, and an expense is incurred whether it has an army or a standing militia. The state is also expected to protect "every member of society from the injustice or oppression of every other member of it" (Smith 1776/1937, p. 669). Smith suggests that there are two types of injustice: one that stems from envy, malice, or resentment, and that leads one person to harm another in reputation or in body; and a second one that stems from avarice in the rich and a passion for the easy life in the poor, which results in crimes against the rich. As Smith suggests, "Wherever there is great property, there is great inequality" (p. 670). But Smith views the problem as one-sided. Property must be protected. The rich, in order to sleep through the night, must be promised civil justice. Subordination must necessarily follow the advent of property. Smith argues that there will always be different levels of superiority among people (e.g., by birth, in skills, intelligence, financially) that will create distress, but it is private property that demands the institution of civil justice. In short, the wealthy must be protected for the good of the nation.

In addition to civil justice, the state must tax individuals to care for public projects like roads and water works. Education of the young should be supplied so that they can grow up to be productive, but whether that education should be maintained through tuition or taxes is debated. Smith felt that public education, paid for by the taxpayers, led to the teaching of worthless subjects. For example, Smith found philosophy to be a nearly useless endeavor to which, he claimed, most universities had failed to provide any new contributions. Smith expected those schools and universities that paid "attention to the current opinions of the world" (p.727) were the ones that would/should prosper. He suggested that if all schools were stripped of public funding, then only useful subjects would be taught because they would be in demand.

However, Smith also suggested that it is quite possible that with the division of labor as it is, workers would slip into "drowsy stupidity" (p. 735) from performing the same mundane job repetitively. Mentally, people would lack inventiveness; physically, men would not be ready for military duty. Thus, Smith encouraged the state to support a certain amount of mandatory education and encourage as well as foster continuing education. The arts and entertainment as well as philosophy are granted educational value in this way, but no teacher or professor or artist should be paid entirely by the state, or they would grow lazy, according to Smith.

Contemporary Scholarship

Almost any research that advocates efficiency and effectiveness for profit-making corporations is grounded in capitalist theory. For example, in an upcoming chapter on scientific management, the reader will see how work can be organized so that maximum efficiency and high output result. Efficiency and effectiveness are qualities that can be sought by nonprofit organizations, as well. Therefore, the inclusion of self-interest becomes an important criterion in determining which contemporary economic models are guided by capitalism. When studies are conducted to improve a system in order to make the organization more profitable, whether directly or indirectly, then capitalism is usually the theoretical framework, and Smith's concepts of self-interest and the invisible hand are hard at work. "The invisible hand is not a power that makes the good of one the good of all. . . . It is simply the inducement a merchant has to keep his capital at home, thereby increasing the domestic capital" (Grampp, 2000, p. 441). Whereas domestic production and the wealth of individual nations were the focus of Adam Smith's philosophy, contemporary versions of capitalism are expanding beyond national borders.

Today's push toward globalization is grounded in capitalism. *Globalization* is a term that refers to the disappearance of boundaries around the world, suggesting at the very least that cultures are beginning to overlap. But the term also refers to the expansion of businesses across countries, creating the "McWorld" (for an overview see Parker, 1996, p. 485) or the *McDonaldization of Society* (Ritzer, 2004). Use of the term *globalization* to describe one's research usually indicates a preference for capitalist expansion. Those opposed to capitalist expansion more often describe the phenomenon as capitalist imperialism or organizational colonization. Parker suggests that an earlier term, *international business*, was used to describe the phenomenon before concern for global issues, especially related to resources, entered the picture.

International business studies emerged in the wake of World War II and focused on economic trade across countries and foreign direct investment. By the 1960s, multinational mergers had called for new "streams of research" (Parker, 1996, p. 486). By the 1970s, international business (IB) studies had become established at universities and focused on a number of international business issues, such as banking, manufacturing, shipping, and advertising (see Nehrt, Truitt, & Wright, 1970). The increased complexity of operating in different countries, with different cultures, brought about cross- or intercultural studies of business.

Hofstede's (1983, 2001) studies are probably the most famous but also the most criticized (McSweeney, 2002a, 2002b; Triandis, 1994).[1] Hofstede's work is framed in a Western conceptualization of the world, suggesting that cultures can be easily categorized and subjected to statistical analyses according to values that the researcher determines are most salient. According to Parker (1996), "The disciplinary basis and the Western orientation that continue to characterize much of the research in IB hamper comprehensive international research and teaching" (p. 488).

Confusion also surrounds the contemporary terms *global* and *globalization*. Parker (1996) suggests that global enterprises were once thought of as large American companies that had satellite companies in other countries, but global enterprises today are large, medium, and small companies that come from any home country and move to any other country. They can be government- or business-oriented. They can be for-profit or nonprofit organizations. They cross all industries today. Global organizations cross national borders and cultural boundaries, consider alternative structural or organizational differences, and establish a "world-wide presence" (Parker, 1996, p. 490). Parker's definition is not merely that of global enterprises but that of "successful" global enterprises (p. 490). For Parker, the term *globalization* (as opposed to *global enterprise*) needs to include not only business and economy but "politics; culture; technology; [and] natural resources" (p. 491). Parker calls for an awareness of the new business power in politics (consider NAFTA, CAFTA, and WTO). She says that globalization has expanded beyond business as we know it; global prostitution rings now exist that exploit women and children; global policies diminish the power of governments; globalized cultures come with benefits and risks, especially with religious conflict, which is also true of global technologies; and global companies have the world to answer to when they use or abuse natural resources.

Globalization, defined as the advance of capitalism, raises serious concerns. Stohl (2001) suggests that globalization raises new communication questions for researchers and organizational members. Parker adds, "globalization, in permeating far beyond the confines of business, creates significant new challenges for all parts of society" (p. 497). Thus, Smith's theories and capitalists' practices raise issues not only for economists but for everyone.

Note

1. Triandis (1994) criticizes Hofstede for his deceptive use of bipolar categories; Hofstede and Bond (1988) later added Confucian dynamism. McSweeney (2002) criticizes Hofstede's work for its weak methodology. For example, as few as 37 Pakistan employees at IBM were used to determine the "national" culture of Pakistan. Hofstede confounded organizational culture with occupational culture and both of these with national culture by assuming that IBM employees were representative of the culture at large and used previously collected data. I would further criticize

Hofstede's work from a feminist perspective. After bifurcating cultures into either masculine or feminine, he names the dimension masculinity, privileging the masculine. He further privileges men, admitting that he used respondents who "were mainly men" (Hofstede, 2001, p. 285). Although this is not a problem if you are trying to say that one culture leans toward feminine/masculine values (whatever they might be), it is a problem to marginalize nearly half the culture when determining what the culture is like.

Chapter Six

Karl Marx

A Challenge to Capitalism

Introduction

Karl Marx, a philosopher of historical proportion, left a legacy that stretched well beyond the written word. His writings range from philosophical critiques to political treatises. His thoughts on economy spawned new socioeconomic arrangements in Russia, China, and numerous smaller countries. Most famous for his critique of capitalism and his development of a communist manifesto, Karl Marx's philosophy lives on and continues to spark debate.

Biography

Born in 1818 in the city of Trier, Karl Marx grew up in the second most powerful of the German States, Prussia (Randall, 1964). His parents were of Jewish descent but converted to Protestantism when he was only six. Converting to the state religion, Lutheranism, allowed Karl's father, Heinrich Marx, to practice law, a career that had been barred to Jews (Randall, 1964). The conversion to Lutheranism was not entered into lightly, nor was it done without an attempt to change the minds of the Prussian rulers. Heinrich Marx penned a letter asking Friedrich Wilhelm III, the new king of Prussia, to annul the laws that kept Jews from practicing jurisprudence; however, his efforts were in vain. In order to continue working as a lawyer, the elder Marx had himself and his entire family baptized.

Following in his father's footsteps, at seventeen Karl Marx went to the University of Bonn to study law. There the follies of a young man turned to drunkenness and bawdy behavior, which culminated in a duel that left Marx with a slight wound (McLellan, 1971; Singer, 1980). Without hesitation, his father had him transferred to the University of Berlin. A brief stay at home between his absence from Bonn and his transfer to Berlin allowed him time to secretly become engaged to Jenny von Westphalen, his neighbor and childhood sweetheart. Jenny's family was aristocratic and Lutheran. Baron von Westphalen, Jenny's father, eagerly engaged the young Marx as a friend of his son, Edgar, but his becoming a part of the Westphalen family through marriage seemed to be out of the question. The Marx family agreed, but Karl and Jenny persisted (Kamenka, 1983).

In his first year at the University of Berlin, Karl Marx experienced a flood of mixed emotions that he wrote of in his letters to his father. He desperately missed Jenny and turned to writing poetry and viewing art to take his mind off of her. These diversions were of little help, as this letter to his father indicates: "nor, finally, was any work of art as beautiful as Jenny" (Marx, 1837, as cited in McLellan, 1971, p. 2). Although at times it was difficult for Marx to concentrate on his studies, he also found them invigorating. He wrote, "But poetry was to be, and had to be, only a sideline; I had to study jurisprudence and felt above all impelled to struggle with philosophy" (p. 3; also see McLellan, 1977, p. 6).

Marx's passions were well-suited to the Romantic era. Although he personally criticized romantics who failed to include the rational with the idealistic, his own work has been labeled *ideological romanticism* (Randall, 1963). His earliest formal work considered the contemporary debates over philosophical differences in the writings of Democritus and Epicurus and drew from the writings of Georg Wilhelm Friedrich Hegel. Although this work is not considered one of Marx's more interesting contributions, it demonstrated his strong respect for Hegel, and it is where he "coined the term, so influential later, *praxis*," to refer to the synthesis of thought and action (McLellan, 1971, p. xiv).

As a Young Hegelian (i.e., enthusiastic young followers of Hegel who also moved Hegel's theory to the left), Marx found certain aspects of Hegel's philosophy pertinent to his own philosophical interests. First, Hegel challenged the philosophers of the Enlightenment, including Immanuel Kant. He did not believe that enduring eternal truths could be established; rather, he believed that reason was developed and challenged in a dynamic system. Hegel's *Philosophy of Right* suggests that ethics and morality are constrained by historical and political contexts. What seems right and just in one era may not seem so in another era or circumstance. Furthermore, no system of reason stands still; instead, Hegel argued that reason is progressive. For example, he argued, theories, like Kant's philosophy, will be critiqued, ameliorated, or challenged, adding to the growth of knowledge for humankind, which in turn explains the developing world spirit. According to Hegel, this progressive world spirit has been moving "toward an ever-increasing *self-knowledge* and *self-development*" (Gaarder, 1996, p. 364). Hegel argued that change occurs as a result of the dialectical process—a contradiction in opposites. For example, "as soon as one thought is proposed, it will be contradicted by another" (p. 365). This gives rise to two opposite ways of thinking, according to Hegel. A tension occurs between these two contradictory thoughts, and in order for the tension to be resolved, a third thought must synthesize the two prior thoughts. Thus, thesis, antithesis, and synthesis arise. Hegel applied his thoughts of the dialectical to religion, ethics, economics, and politics.

In addition, Hegel suggested that the self could only be created as a civil self, born into a certain time in history in a certain socioeconomic, religious, political situation. Individuals do not exist without these institutions, and it is their participation in them that leads to the world spirit. People begin with self-awareness (subjective spirit) and move toward a higher consciousness (objective spirit), which in turn leads to an expression of self-realization (absolute spirit). The absolute spirit finds its highest form in philosophy because it is a form of reflexivity that addresses the whole of human existence. Hegel's thoughts had an enormous impact on European philosophy (Dupré, 1966; Gaarder, 1996) and especially on Young Hegelians like Karl Marx.

Karl Marx's first article was a radical critique of the Prussian government's practice of censorship. Ironically, the Prussian government suppressed the article. This further infuriated Marx, who spoke with other Young Hegelians, including Bruno Bauer and Friedrich Engels, in order to garner support. As a result, a movement was born.

However, the group split into two factions, with Bauer leading the more traditional Hegelians, and Marx, Arnold Ruge, Moses Hess, Ludwig Feuerbach, and Engels leading the more action-oriented and political Hegelians. These Young Hegelians were influenced by the French Revolution of 1789, ideas about communism, and critiques of religion as a controlling force. They tried again to publish articles within their homeland, which resulted in Feuerbach's arrest and imprisonment. Marx then undertook a critique of Hegel's work that incorporated some of Feuerbach's ideas as well as his own notions of history, humanity, and the order of society (McLellan, 1971). He continued to write and search out other outlets for his articles.

Although his journalism jobs were scattered, Marx had saved enough money to marry Jenny, and in 1843 they moved to Paris, where Marx felt he might be able to express his radical ideas without suppression (Singer, 1980). In Paris, between 1843 and 1844, Marx immersed himself in the writings of British economists of the Romantic era—Thomas Malthus and David Ricardo. He rebelled against their negative portrayals of the working class and began to develop his ideas of the proletariat (Randall, 1964). Marx's ideas of the proletariat were, however, probably more influenced by his lifelong friend, Friedrich Engels.

Friedrich Engels's father was a conservative Calvinist from Prussia who owned cotton mills in both the Ruhr and England. He sent his son, Friedrich, to England to learn the family business, but when the young Engels witnessed the poverty and deplorable working conditions that the mill workers faced each day, his radical sentiments intensified. In addition, Engels fell in love with an Irish girl, Mary Burns, who worked in the factory. His out-of-wedlock relationship with her caused quite a social stir—Mary's being Irish, working-class, and living in sin during the Victorian age might have been more scandalous than Friedrich's espousal of communism (Randall, 1976).

Together over the next decade, Marx and Engels discussed and developed their ideas about economics, the working class, alienation, history, production, and communism. They continued to write critiques of the totalitarian regimes that plagued Europe. The Prussian government, tiring of the criticism, sought an expulsion order from the French. In short, the Prussian government pressured the French government to do something about these radicals. Marx and Engels traveled extensively during this time. Both activists attended a conference in Brussels, but Engels represented the pair in London while Marx traveled to Holland to visit relatives with the purpose of seeking a loan on his inheritance. Both Marx and Engels were expelled from France. Engels was expelled in February 1848, and Marx and his family were escorted to the French border in March 1848 (Kamenka, 1983).

Karl Marx, his wife, Jenny, and their first baby were forced to leave their home. Nevertheless, Marx continued his efforts toward reform. By 1848, Marx and Engels had completed and published the *Communist Manifesto* (Randall, 1964). However, it is more likely the French Revolution of 1848, which "triggered off revolutionary movements all over Europe" (Singer, 1980, p. 5), had more of an impact on change than did the little pamphlet, at least at first. Following the 1848 uprising, the Marx family returned to Paris, but after hearing that a revolution was stirring in Germany, they quickly moved to Berlin. In short order, the revolution failed, and Marx and his family were once again forced to move. After briefly returning to Paris and being expelled once more, the family fled to England.

Marx worked at odd jobs that barely fed the growing family. He welcomed financial gifts from Engels. Jenny's family sent a maid servant, Helen Demuth, to live with and work for the Marx family. In 1851, Helen Demuth bore an illegitimate son. The child was passed off as Engels's baby and sent to a foster home. However, in 1895, on his deathbed Engels "declared the child to be Marx's" (Kamenka, 1983, p. lxxiv).

Money woes continued to plague the Marx family; they relied heavily on the generosity of friends and relatives. Political troubles also plagued the family. Marx's work continued to be confiscated by the police in Europe. However, he did get his work published in America—the first article was published in 1853 for the *New York Daily Tribune*. In that same year, Marx's financial situation worsened, and when his wife became ill he was unable to pay for a doctor. Although Jenny survived, their son Edgar died. And in 1856 Jenny delivered a still-born baby.

Marx turned his attention to the injustices he saw occurring in Asia and America. Specifically, he addressed the horrors of slavery, which persisted in the United States. He wrote to President Lincoln, and after Lincoln's assassination, he wrote to President Johnson "calling on him to continue Lincoln's work" (Kamenka, 1983, lxxxvi).

Karl Marx also dedicated himself to intellectual projects. He studied the *Origin of the Species* by Charles Darwin and suggested to Engels that it "provides the foundation in natural history for their theory of class struggle" (Kamenka, 1983, p. lxxx). He buried himself in books about mathematics and calculus and worked laboriously on volumes of notes that were to become *Das Kapital*.

By 1866, the Marx family was so destitute that Jenny Marx pawned most of her own clothes and was still unable to pay the bills. For the next decade, Karl Marx continued to fight for the rights of workers and spoke at numerous rallies and conventions in order to promote the Counsel of International Workers. In addition, he began to support the Irish Independence movement, all the while falling deeper and deeper in debt. His health, as well as Jenny's, deteriorated.

In December of 1881, Jenny succumbed to cancer. Karl Marx died just one year and three months later, on March 14. He was buried in Highgate Cemetery outside of London on March 17, 1883. His grave draws large numbers of visitors to this day.

Philosophy and Rhetoric of Karl Marx

Although Karl Marx was a prolific writer, we have selected those articles and books that best reflect his developing and mature philosophy about alienation, labor, communism, and the critique of capitalism. Each of these issues contributed significant insights to Marx's philosophy and rhetoric of work.

On the Jewish Question and the Philosophy of Right

Many of the Young Hegelians opposed the Prussian government's "edict of 1816 [which] had excluded Jews from public office" (McLellan, 1971, p. xxv). Marx went even further.

First, Marx drew from Feuerbach's theory of religious alienation, which argued that "man estranges himself from himself by transposing his own greatness into an external object of worship" (Dupré, 1966, p. 98). He accepted the notion that religion does not alienate people but that alienated individuals create religion to overcome their feelings of isolation and frustration. Then Marx challenged both Kant's notion of faith and Hegel's notions of the absolute spirit and the philosophy of right. He argued that it was quite possible for a state to free itself of religious authoritarianism (as the United States had done), yet people might still practice religion. Specifically Marx wrote,

> The limits of political emancipation immediately become evident in the fact that the state can free itself of a limitation without men really being free of it, that a state can be a free state without men becoming free men. (Marx, 1844, "On the Jewish Question," as cited in Kamenka, 1983, p. 100)

Nor can the abolition of religion as a political matter do anything other than support it outside of the political sphere. That is to say, when a state annuls religion, it is presupposing religion's existence elsewhere and thus supporting its existence rather than controlling it. As in the United States, where the government allows people the freedom to choose any religion, the idea of practicing religion is supported by the granting of freedom to do so. Marx wrote that

> Political emancipation is indeed a great step forward. It is not, to be sure, the final form of human emancipation in general, but is the final form of human emancipation within the prevailing order. (Marx, 1844, as cited in Kamenka, 1983, p. 103)

By introducing the prevailing order as important, Marx could consider the right not only to religious freedom but also the right to private property as endorsed by the United States and France. Marx saw the right to private property as selfish:

> Man's right to private property is therefore the right to enjoy and to dispose over it arbitrarily à son gré [according to one's will], without considering other men, independently of society. It is the right of self-interest. (Marx, 1844, as cited in Kamenka, 1983, p. 108)

Marx argued that both the practice of religion and the practice of private property alienated humans from one another.

Not only did a parallel exist between religion and private property, but one actually supported the other, according to Marx. Marx described religion as "the *opium* of the people" (Marx, 1844, "Contribution to the Critique of Hegel's Philosophy of Right: Introduction," as cited in Kamenka, 1983, p. 115, emphasis in original). It created an illusion, offering a deferred happiness that was meant to substitute for "real happiness" (p. 115). "Thus the critique of heaven turns into the critique of earth" (p. 116). Religion, according to Marx, acts as a means of keeping people from critiquing their condition. Religion with the right to private property acted to maintain oppressive economic and social conditions.

The notion that religion actually supports the economic system exemplifies what Marx referred to as the infrastructure and the superstructure. The infrastructure is the economic practice (e.g., capitalism), and the superstructure is comprised of the cultural and political institutions that support the infrastructure (e.g., religion, education, democracy). The cultural practices are often institutionalized, making them more than difficult to change. These practices (e.g., religion) are so embedded in society that they seem natural and immutable; they are reified, and people cannot see how they would live without them. Marx argued that people would not be truly free until they became aware of the control that these practices had on their lives. Furthermore, to engage in any of them was certain to lead to alienation.

Alienation and the Meaning of Labor

Several manuscripts make up the *Economico-Philosophical* manuscripts of 1844. The first of those, *Alienated Labour*, criticizes private property and explains alienation. First, Marx argued that the political economy is a "war among the greedy" (Marx, 1844 as cited in Kamenka, 1983, p. 132) that exploits workers. Marx wrote that in order to "grasp" the power of the political economy a person must understand the interconnections between "private property, greed, the division of labor, capital and land ownership and the connection between exchange and competition, between value and devaluation of men, between monopoly and competition etc.—the connection between all of this alienation and the system of money" (p. 132).

At the heart of these connections is the notion that "the more commodities the worker produces the cheaper a commodity becomes" (p. 133). As commodities lose their value, so are the workers devalued. Furthermore, the more the workers produce, the more their value is reduced, the lower their wages become, and the less are their chances of being able to appropriate the very commodity that they help to make. This cycle of poverty contributes to alienation, but an even greater source of alienation comes through the capitalism under which the commodities are made. Specifically, "Political economy conceals the alienation inherent in the nature of labor by not considering the direct relationship between the worker (labor) and production" (p. 135). Not only do the workers produce commodities, but they become a commodity, much as a slave was considered a commodity.

Marx believed that labor, before it was co-opted by capitalism, held an inherently fulfilling and rewarding experience for people. Work, he felt, is an extension or expression of the self. For example, a seamstress might imagine a coat and mentally plan a design for it. Then the seamstress might lay out a pattern, cut the cloth, sew the seams, decorate the coat and give, sell, or barter it as she pleased. But in the capitalist system, the seamstress neither creates the coat nor sews the entire thing. She is separated from the process of creation—praxis. Furthermore, when the commodity is made under factory conditions, the worker does not even see the final outcome of her labor. Thus, people are alienated in terms of both the praxis and the product. The more the worker is alienated from the "producing activity," the more the activity seems to belong to someone else. When the activity of life belongs to another, the individual becomes alienated. For Marx, "the externalization of the worker into the product does not only mean that the work becomes an object, and external existence, but that it exists outside of the worker independently, as something alien to him" (Marx, 1844 as cited in Kamenka, 1983, p. 134). When people lose touch with what they make, they lose a part of their humanity, "for what is life but activity" (p. 137).

"Man knows how to produce according to the standard of every species and always knows how to apply the intrinsic standard to the object. Man, therefore, creates according to the laws of beauty" (Marx, 1844, as cited in Kamenka, 1983, p. 140). Labor is intended to be an expression of the person's creativity, an expression of self, an extension of self. When the creation is produced under capitalist guidelines, the labor that produces, according to Marx, is *appropriated*. But by whom? Marx asks rhetorically in his essay and answers with, "Neither the gods, nor nature, but only man himself can be this alien power over man" (p. 142). The capitalist owns the labor. Clearly, "the relation of the worker to the labor produces the relation of the capitalist. . . . Private property is therefore the product, the result, the necessary consequence of *externalized labor* . . . of alienated labor, of alienated life, and of alienated man" (p. 143).

For Marx, communism held the promise to rectify the abuses of capitalism. Communism, he held, would be achieved through revolution. He summarized his position in the *Communist Manifesto*.

The Communist Manifesto

The *Communist Manifesto* opens with the following sentence: "A specter is haunting Europe—the specter of communism" (Marx & Engels, 1848/1964, p. 55). Yet, communism was not a powerful force, and no countries had yet taken up the practice in 1848. Nevertheless, Marx and Engels believed that European governments felt the threat of communism breathing down their necks. Consequently, they decided it was time to write a manifesto that put forth their specific ideas concerning communism.

First, the manifesto argued that "the history of all hitherto existing society is the history of class struggles" (Marx & Engels, 1848/1964, p. 57). These class struggles had culminated in a struggle between the bourgeois and the proletariat, owners of capital versus exploited laborers of capital. Based on the argument that the more commodities are made the cheaper they become and so does the worker's labor, Marx and Engels criticized modern industry as well as capitalism. As machines are incorporated into production, the skill and value of the worker are lost, they argued. Not only is the work "repulsive and monotonous," but the "wage decreases" (p. 69). In addition to exploiting laborers, capitalism must expand in order to maintain its grip on society: "The need of a constantly expanding market for its products chases the bourgeoisie over the whole surface of the globe. It must nestle everywhere, establish connections everywhere" (p. 63). It seeks "free trade" (p. 84).

Capitalism, according to Marx and Engels, is the monster that will swallow up men, women, and children into its labor pools. It will put small "shopkeepers," "tradespeople" and "farmers" (p. 70) out of business, unless the proletariat band together in "a union of workers. This union is helped by the improved means of communication that are created by modern industry and that places the workers of different localities in contact" (p. 73) with one another. Marx and Engels predicted that even though these unions are disrupted by the competition of capitalism, they will continue to surface. As workers are alienated and exploited to the extreme, they will continue to join together, use the "developments of modern industry," (p. 78) and rise up as one voice, as one revolution to destroy the means of their oppression.

In part 2 of the *Communist Manifesto*, Marx and Engels summed up the basic philosophy of the movement as the "abolition of private property" (p. 82), not just bourgeois ownership but all private ownership. Marx and Engels explained that communists support the notion of capital as "a collective product" to be shared among all workers. In addition to challenging the bourgeois forms of production, the young revolutionaries challenged the bourgeois culture, law, and even family as institutions that promote the oppression of the working class. Women are exploited for their reproductive or sexual labor; they are treated as if they are no more than "mere instruments of production" (p. 89). Being married, for women, represents a form of private "prostitution," which Marx and Engels decried. Children are exploited by parents and educated in the ways of an unequal system that privileges one class over another, they argued. Each of these cultural and ideological aspects of oppression is met with an additional aspect of oppression through nationalism, they added. In its conclusion, the *Communist Manifesto* calls for an end to nationalism and proposes that all workers unite despite their nationality.

Marx and Engels argued that history has been nothing more than a series of class struggles, "antagonisms that assumed different forms at different epochs," and that each one has been based on the material means of production. "The communist revolution is the most radical rupture" of these past practices (p. 92) because it is meant to end all antagonisms by ending the existence of class itself. Exactly how this is to be done is spelled out in Marx's famous ten-point plan for communist reform at the end of part 2 of the *Communist Manifesto*.

In parts 3 and 4 of the *Communist Manifesto*, Marx and Engels solidify their arguments by specifically pointing to why their brand of socialism is superior to others of the day, and they call for action. Specifically, the proletariat must "openly declare that their ends can be attained only by the forcible overthrow of all existing social conditions" (p. 116). They expect the ruling classes to "tremble at a Communist revolution" (p. 116), and in their most famous quote, they assert that "The proletariat have nothing to lose but their chains" (p. 116). This is followed by their final call to action: "WORKINGMEN OF ALL COUNTRIES, UNITE!" (p. 116).

Das Kapital

Das Kapital, or *Capital*, is the most extensive of Marx's works and was edited by Engels. It took Marx several years to write this voluminous critique of political economy. Marx had already developed his ideas of alienation of praxis and product, the division of labor, the evils of private property, and the concept of historical materialism, as well as the roles of the proletariat, the bourgeoisie, and the petty bourgeoisie. *Das Kapital* further illuminates these issues as well as the objectification of humans and the development of the commodity as a dominating force. The commodity becomes a focal point when it begins to rule the desires of humanity and develops into what Marx called *commodity fetishism*.

Chapter 1 of volume 1 of *Das Kapital* defines the commodity. All commodities are objects "outside of us" that satisfy some "human wants" that "may be looked at from the two points of view of quality and quantity . . . and may therefore be of use in various ways" (Marx, 1867, p. 437, as cited in Kamenka, 1983). And each commodity, according to its role in history, has a use-value as determined by the standards of the society. Use-value "is independent of the labour required to appropriate its useful qualities" (p. 438). "Use-values become a reality only by use or consumption" (p. 438) and have a direct bearing on exchange value.

Exchange value represents what is generally accepted as equitable according to quantity and usefulness by an equation of the day. That is to say, in two different things, such as iron and corn, there exists something common, and both can be related to a third thing, such as silver or gold. Thus, exchange value tends to take precedence over use-value. What is truly common to all goods is the "human labour [that] is embodied in them" (p. 441).

Measuring human labor is not an easy task. Even if one attempted to measure labor by duration or exertion, these measures would be complicated by numerous other factors (e.g., skill, process of production, physical conditions, and environmental factors). Although labor might be an elusive phenomenon to define, the commodity, at first glance, seems far from mysterious: it is a thing with useful value. But with a deeper look one finds something quite enigmatic about the commodity, according to Marx.

The commodity is a transformed bit of nature, transformed by the mind and hands of humans, and as such these commodities are more than useful; they help to create the economy, and at the same time they symbolize the economy—they are produced, and they produce capitalism. When alienated labor produces commodities for another person, a social relation develops with respect to the commodity. Commodities then have a social relation embedded in them as the laborer works for another, who claims ownership of the commodity that has been produced by the laborer. The invisible labor is only apparent in the exchange, not in the item. As the product is exchanged, it enters into yet another social relation. Thus, the thing has no value without social relations—"So far no chemist has ever discovered exchange value either in a pearl or in a diamond" (Marx, pp. 460–461). Its value is socially constructed. Commodity fetishism—the mysterious value of the commodity—is grounded in social relations.

Chapter 1 of volume 1 sets the stage for discussions of the creation of artificial needs, exchange value, labor, capital, surplus value, accumulation, distribution, fictitious capital, and the antagonisms embedded in capitalism. This opening chapter gives a glimpse into the ponderous chapters that lie ahead. Volume 4, the final volume, is more than one thousand pages long, and its last chapter ends abruptly, unfinished, as it only begins to define what constitutes class. Only volume 1 was published in Marx's lifetime. The other volumes were organized later by Engels and published after Marx's death.

Contemporary Scholarship

Contemporary scholars find Marx's ideas surrounding the social relations of capital significant in their quest to understand the socioeconomic organization of societies and the meaning and practices of work. Paul Willis (1977), for example, used Marxist critique to explore the world of working-class boys in England. He followed their everyday lives as they moved through their last two years of school and on into the workforce. He discovered that the school was designed in such a way as to promote the status quo while offering an illusion that working class boys could step beyond the drudgeries of factory life.

Willis (1977) specifically followed twelve boys from a working-class neighborhood, which he calls Hammertown. Hammertown is filled with factories and pubs and working-class houses. These twelve boys were compared to five other groups of boys at similar schools in order to be sure the original group was indeed representative of working-class teenage boys. Slightly different academic regimens existed at the various schools, but overall the boys seemed typical of working-class youth.

Willis (1977) discovered that the boys defied authority through "dossing, blagging, and wagging" and having "a laff" at the expense of their superiors. By the time they were close to graduation they had learned various ways to beat the system (i.e., to get out of studies), including everything from sleeping in class to mixing up their day so that they never actually attended a single class and yet were never truant. They accept sexism and racism and allow the working-class machismo to define them; thus, they may only in part subvert the dominating ideology.

Schools used *education* rather than class to support the ideology of hierarchy, control, rules, regulations, compulsory attendance, coercive punishment, and control of resources. The boys, in a way, willingly accepted their lot in school and their projected lot in the workforce. Yet they put on a good front, for to do otherwise would position them as "ear'oles"—people who listen without thinking critically or acting on their own. The boys always reacted to the authority-laden environment, often with sarcasm, which represented not only an awareness of the imposed ideology but also a certain form of resistance. As Willis noted, "The working class does not have to believe the dominant ideology. It does not need the mask of democracy to cover the face of oppression" (p. 123). And so the boys thumb their noses at public education. They have, in part, penetrated the disguised contradictions of capitalism. However, yet another contradiction traps them in a working-class paradox.

Willis (1977) exposes the irony of the boys' condition in spite of their ability to see through the system. "The tragedy and the contradiction is that these forms of 'penetration' are limited, distorted and turned back on themselves, often unintentionally" (p. 3), often by class ideology and patriarchal domination. The boys almost eagerly join their fathers in the factories, as defiance against the imposed *education*. In doing so they join the exploited working class, and furthermore they engage in racist and sexist practices.

Critical theory, a contemporary version of Marxism that emphasizes the cultural institutions of oppression and the ways in which communication either perpetuates or challenges the dominant ideology, has been influential in helping scholars to understand how societies arrange work and maintain the status quo, especially in a capitalist system. Willis's (1977) work used Marxist concepts to unravel the discursive and materialist practices of working-class boys that support their own domination. Other scholars have drawn from Marxism to address how workers are pitted against each other and how they participate in their own oppression.

Chapter Seven

Booker T. Washington and W. E. B. Du Bois

Out of Slavery

Introduction

Two men—one a freed slave, the other a descendant of slaves—addressed the meaning of work and the organization of labor in society with such persuasion that their voices reached thousands during their life time and many more afterward. Booker T. Washington and W. E. B. Du Bois have been recognized for their oratorical skill, intellectual prowess, and contributions to improving race relations. However, each man promoted a unique and diverse philosophy. Specifically, these two great contributors disagreed vehemently on how African Americans should proceed from slavery to equality. Washington followed a conservative, practical path, whereas Du Bois espoused a radical philosophy. Washington's rather conservative approach was unsettling, to say the least, for Du Bois. Nevertheless, each man respected the other, and each man contributed new insights from his individual perspective.

Biographies

Booker T. Washington's name is a story in itself. Born on April 5, 1856, in Virginia, he was named Booker Taliaferro by his mother, a slave who worked on a small farm owned by James Burroughs. His father was an unknown or un-named white man. Booker's mother later married a fellow slave by the name of Washington Ferguson, and Booker, as a boy, took his stepfather's first name as his surname (see Booker, 2005). Until that time, Booker had been unaware that his mother had given him the last name of Taliaferro, but once aware of this fact, he kept it as a middle name and employed its initial, thus creating the full name Booker T. Washington.

Washington (1902) detailed his days as a slave in his autobiography, *Up from Slavery*. As a child he lived in destitute conditions, evidenced by the fact that he never had a meal but, rather, survived on pocketed sweet potatoes and morsels of pork and cornbread that were distributed to slaves. As did most slaves, he wore a flaxseed shirt, which he described as being made of rough material, stinging the skin like a thousand tiny burrs. His older brother James did him the greatest kindness by wearing his new flaxseed garment until it was "broken in" and less abrasive to the skin. As a child, one of his jobs was to take heavy sacks to the mill. The double sacks were loaded onto a horse, one bag hung over the left side and the other hung over the right, distributing the weight evenly; young Booker rode in the middle. However, time and again, the sacks would become uneven and slip from the horse causing Booker to fall as well. He tells of being too small to lift the sacks up again and of being very afraid of being discovered on the road alone because he had been told that stray black boys found in the woods by white men met a terrible fate—their ears were sliced off (Washington, 1902).

Washington described being cold in the winter, hot in the summer, and hungry year round. Despite the cruel conditions, he noted things that inspired him as well, stories of Lincoln, for one, and the possibility of learning to read, for another.

Following the Civil War, the family moved to West Virginia, where Washington's stepfather gained employment at Lewis Ruffner's salt mine and took his stepsons along. Together they worked the furnaces and packed salt. Later, young Washington worked in a coal mine that was also owned by Ruffner. While working there he heard that the Ruffner family had a vacancy for a house servant. His mother spoke with Mrs. Ruffner, who in turn hired young Washington to work as a houseboy. Considered difficult to please, Mrs. Ruffner had fired several boys; others had quit. But Washington was determined to prove to this "'Yankee' woman" (p. 43) that he could learn to sweep and clean to her satisfaction. Booker T. Washington's persistence paid off when she took him under her wing and encouraged him to continue his schooling.

Washington underwent a trying time in his attempt to gain an education. Having heard of a school that educated freed slaves, he set off to find it. With little money and no place to stay, Washington slept under a boardwalk in Richmond, Virginia, before landing a job as a pig-iron mover on the docks. He earned enough money to continue on his way but not enough to enter Hampton Normal and Agricultural Institute (currently Hampton University). Upon his arrival, he was given a test—to clean a room. Washington dusted and swept the room until it virtually gleamed, unaware that it was his dedication that was really being tested. Hampton administrators accepted the young man and gave him the job of janitor to help pay his tuition and living expenses (Washington, 1902).

At Hampton, Washington met General Samuel Armstrong, a Northerner and an advocate of practical education. Upon graduating, he taught school under Armstrong's direction for two years. Then he ventured to Washington, D.C., in order to undertake higher education. When Washington returned from Wayland Seminary in 1878, Samuel Armstrong employed him to teach in a program for Native Americans (Washington, 1902).

In 1880, Lewis Adams, an influential black leader, helped to promote the election of two democratic whites in Macon County. They returned the favor by supporting the building of an institute for higher learning for African Americans. Adams asked Armstrong, the education advocate and Washington's early mentor, to recommend a white teacher to put in charge of this new institute. Instead, Armstrong recommended that Washington be placed in charge. Subsequently, Tuskegee Negro Normal Institute opened in 1888 under the head administration of Booker T. Washington. Washington designed the Tuskegee Institute program by relying on a curriculum that placed importance not only on academic learning but also on industrial and agricultural training (Washington, 1902).

Students and faculty struggled during the early years at Tuskegee. They made do with a shanty building in order to stretch their funding to pay salaries. Later, Washington persuaded the treasurer of the Hampton Agricultural School to lend him enough money to buy an old plantation, where he and his students erected a sturdier building. Eventually, Tuskegee Institute purchased 540 acres of land that could be used for practical courses in agriculture. Male students learned carpentry, cabinetmaking, brickmaking, shoemaking, and printing. Female students learned skills in laundry, cooking, kitchen duties, dining services, sewing, and other practical arts (Washington, 1902). Washington spent long hours meeting with parents and speaking to community leaders.

By 1895, Washington had become a featured speaker, and on September 18 of that same year he presented what some call his compromise speech. Newspapers around the country reprinted the speech, which satisfied many whites who feared Negro empowerment. Its contents included comments that suggested that full social equality between Negroes and Caucasians was simply not realistic; Negroes would or should not seek such a dream, yet they should seek to improve their condition and contribute to society, according to Washington. Washington's speech, despite its conservative tone, resonated for many African Americans who agreed with his positions on work, race, and education. With the death of Frederick Douglass in 1895, numerous African Americans turned to Washington for leadership. He held a prestigious position within the African American community until his death.

In 1915, Washington became ill in New York City; doctors told him that he had very little time to live. He returned to his beloved Tuskegee, where he died of arteriosclerosis on November 14, 1915 (Booker, 2005). Although he was respected by many, some African Americans criticized Washington's conservative views. W. E. B. Du Bois, for one, challenged certain aspects of Washington's racial philosophy.

William Edward Burghardt Du Bois was born in the northern town of Great Barrington, Massachusetts, on February 23, 1868. New England at that time promoted an egalitarian philosophy grounded in a tradition of abolition (Murrel, 1984). However, among a population of around 5,000, Great Barrington only had between 25 and 50 African American residents (Hynes, n.d.).

Du Bois was enrolled in school by the age of five. His mother, Mary Burghardt Du Bois, who had been abandoned by her husband, encouraged young William in his studies. Murrel (1984) notes that "his intellectual superiority and dedication earned him the respect of his teachers and the admiration of his classmates, most of whom were white" (p. 233). Hynes (n.d.), on the other hand, suggests that Du Bois faced "a constant barrage of suggestive innuendoes and vindictive attitudes of its residents" (p. 1). The truth probably lies somewhere in the middle, for Du Bois (1903) explains in the book *The Souls of Black Folks* (also see Lester, 1971, for excerpts) that he had made many friends among the white population with the exception of the Irish. The Irish, who were poorer than the Negroes, hurled insults at him when he ventured into their section of town. But it was also the Irish situation that opened Du Bois's eyes to the realization that poverty was not necessarily dependent upon race. His mother reiterated this point suggesting that, had their kin attended school rather than quitting for more practical jobs, they could have achieved the status of whites. While Du Bois suggested that most whites treated him quite well, as he matured, he recognized the day-to-day reality of the race:

> I was beginning to feel lonesome in New England. Unconsciously, I realized that as I grew older, and especially now that I had finished public school, the close cordial intermingling with my white fellows would grow more restricted. There would be meetings, parties, clubs, to which I would not be invited. (Du Bois, as reprinted in Lester, 1971, p. 8)

A contradictory picture of Du Bois again emerges in different biographies when portraying his teenage years. Murrel (1984) portrays him as a boy struggling to support the family with "odd jobs—splitting wood, shoveling coal, and selling tea at the local A&P store" (p. 233). Hynes (n.d.) focuses on the fifteen-year-old Du Bois's accomplishments as a "local correspondent for the *New York Globe*" writing editorials about race relations. Once again the truth lies somewhere in the middle. It should be noted that while he was in high school Du Bois did write for the *New York Globe*, a paper with a primarily African American readership, where his race editorials were targeted for an African American audience and that Du Bois did work at odd jobs. But in *Dusk of Dawn*, Du Bois (1940) recounts that he also had time to play and went swimming in the summer and sledding in the winter. After high school he worked on a construction site as a timekeeper while he earned money to go college (Lester, 1971).

Although Du Bois longed to attend Harvard University, his financial situation would not allow it. Some of the local community residents felt that Fisk College in Nashville, Tennessee, might be the solution for Du Bois's future, while others longed to keep him in the North. One local woman promised to pay for his books, but of course that would not be enough. Fisk offered Du Bois a partial scholarship, and the local churches of Great Barrington provided further financial assistance. Subsequently, he accepted the offer from Fisk but never gave up his dream of attending Harvard.

Some neighbors suggested that a trip to the South would be *educational* for Du Bois, opening his eyes to a different world. After arriving in the South, Du Bois reported a range of novel experiences including a newfound appreciation of his race as well as intense discrimination. Du Bois (1940) wrote that he found an astonishing array of beautiful African Americans at Fisk: "I was thrilled to be for the first time among so many people of my own color. . . . Never before had I seen young men so self-assured and who gave themselves such airs, and colored men at that; and above all for the first time I saw beautiful girls" (p. 24). However, Du Bois discovered social and institutional racism in the South as well. The ugly side of his encounters with segregation, personal insult, and violence led him to new views on the world and in particular on race and labor. His graduation speech of 1888 laid the foundation for the philosophy upon which he built his career.

After graduating from Fisk, he taught school in the South, but continued to vie for entry into Harvard. Eventually, he achieved his dream of attending Harvard. Scholarships enabled him to enter Harvard as a junior, and after successfully completing his senior year, he continued on for a master's degree. Following graduation, he studied independently and traveled abroad for two years before returning to complete his Ph.D.

His work took several paths, including teaching, researching, and writing on race relations. He taught first in Ohio and later at Atlanta University, but before beginning his teaching, he conducted a study sponsored by the University of Pennsylvania on the state of the Philadelphia Negro. The work was highly praised and published in 1899. He continued to write, publishing *The Souls of Black Folks* in 1903 and *Dusk of Dawn* in 1940. He engaged in activism, founding the Niagara Movement in 1905 and cofounding the National Association for the Advancement of Colored People (NAACP) in 1910. In addition, he combined his political interests with his writing skills and founded the publication *The Crisis*. *The Crisis* began as a tool of the NAACP; within a short time, it was self-supporting, growing from a circulation of 1,000 people in 1909 to 10,000 in 1919 (Hynes, n.d.), which allowed Du Bois to speak out even if and when he disagreed with the views of the NAACP. The rhetorical arguments found in *The Crisis* extol the philosophy to which Du Bois dedicated his life.

Du Bois provided the original scholarly arguments that led to an understanding of racial oppression as an international phenomenon, one grounded in imperialism. He challenged capitalism for its oppressive aspects and was met with derision by many Americans for these ideas. His struggle for a socialist-communist America died an early death. Discouraged with the United States and its promotion of capitalism, at the age of ninety-three Du Bois joined the Communist party and moved to Ghana. After becoming ill in 1962, he underwent three surgeries—in Ghana, Bucharest, and London. He traveled to China to convalesce and watched the thirteenth anniversary of the People's Republic in Tienanmen Square with Chairman Mao. Months later, he fell ill again. He died on August 27, 1963, one day before the largest civil rights demonstration in the history of the United States was held in front of the Lincoln Memorial. Tributes were made in his honor at that meeting in Washington, D.C., as well as in Ghana, where torches were held high.

Philosophy and Rhetoric of Booker T. Washington and W. E. B. Du Bois

Booker T. Washington

Booker T. Washington (1902) believed that slavery had done not only an injustice to the African race but also an injustice to the concept and practice of work. Slavery led both Whites and Blacks to consider work demeaning and disgusting. Work was considered something to be avoided at all costs. Physical labor was considered especially deplorable, and Washington realized that many of his students came to Tuskegee with the hope of learning academic skills that would allow them to escape drudgery. Instead of satisfying their dreams, Washington set out to change their minds with respect to the social construction of work. He advocated both practical as well as academic learning.

Simple hygiene, taken for granted by many, such as bathing, brushing one's teeth, sleeping between sheets, and having regular meals was new to Washington when he arrived at Hampton Normal (Washington, 1902). He found each of these practices well worth the time and energy to learn and practice. He began education for his own students at Tuskegee with these basics. He also included lessons on how to use silverware, lay a table, and take care of one's clothing. These practical endeavors gave way to other practical needs' being taught. How to grow one's food, erect housing, and build furniture became the foundation courses at Tuskegee. Although Washington did not neglect the academic side of education, he approached it with caution. His concern lay in the fact that too many of his students thought that if they learned to read the classics and studied Latin they would enter into a world of professional work, freeing them from manual labor (Washington, 1902).

Washington (1902) attempted to instill a new image of labor in his students. He claimed that labor could provide a sense of satisfaction in a job well done and would provide a solid foundation for the students' learning. He felt that it was wrong to simply apply a previous educational mold to every situation. In the case of recently freed Southern slaves, a standard model of education could not be used as a template. Instead, Washington found General Armstrong's approach of combining the industrial with the academic as most useful. Washington added the practice of having his students participate in building their school. This, he said, would create a sense of pride and ownership, as well as a new way of thinking about work (Washington, 1902). Specifically, Washington wrote:

> From the very beginning, at Tuskegee, . . . My plan was to have them, while performing this service, taught the latest and best methods of labour, so that the school would not only get the benefit of their efforts, but the students themselves would be taught to see not only utility in labour, but beauty and dignity; would be taught, in fact, how to lift labour up from mere drudgery and toil, and would learn to love work for its own sake. (Washington, 1902, p. 148)

Changing students' minds about work was no easy task. Washington encountered resistance not only from students but also from their parents. He thus undertook a speaking tour of the South to explain his educational philosophy.

Once the students and parents understood Washington's mission, they engaged it with enthusiasm. Tuskegee thrived under the devoted efforts of Washington and his students: they built the buildings and beds; they made the mattresses and the sheets, grew the food and cooked and served it in an orderly manner. Eventually, Washington sought suggestions from the students through open forums and letters of criticism. The students began to realize that indeed the school was of their making (Washington, 1902).

When people mentioned the good luck that Washington had with Tuskegee, he quickly pointed out that luck had little to do with it. Success comes from hard work, he told them. Indeed, both he and his students worked very hard. Night school students, for example, worked ten hours a day at trades and two hours a night on their academic lessons. He permitted no one to attend Tuskegee who did not do manual labor (Washington, 1902). Washington also believed that hard work and dedication could overcome racial prejudice. Specifically, he felt that if people perfected a trade they would be justly rewarded; however, he added a pragmatic point. He felt that people must be economically savvy. That is, his students needed not only to do their best but also to supply what the community needed. Washington (1902) wrote:

> I think the whole future of my race hinges on the question as to whether or not it can make itself of such indispensable value that the people in the town and the state where we reside will feel that our presence is necessary to the happiness and well-being of the community. No man who continues to add something to the material, intellectual, and moral well-being of the place in which he lives is long left without proper reward. This is a great human law which cannot be permanently nullified. (p. 282)

The last chapter of his autobiography repeats this sentiment: "labour is beautiful and dignified—to make each one love labour instead of trying to escape it" is a worthy goal (p. 312).

While Washington (1902) asserts that the same holds true for Whites as for Blacks, he does make distinctions between the races. Keenly aware of the "colour line" (p. 102), Washington believed that the Negro of the 1800s was expected to fail and that this was a great disadvantage. Furthermore, most freed slaves did not have knowledge of their heritage, did not have a family name that would be shamed by misbehavior. He felt knowledge of one's ancestry helped Whites to engage in conduct that would bring respect to the family name. Furthermore, Blacks were burdened with the role of representing their race.

Serious controversy surrounded Washington (1902), especially following the speech he delivered at the Atlanta Cotton States and International Exposition in Atlanta, Georgia, on September 18, 1895. An African American had never spoken in the South with such a prestigious panel of speakers nor to such a large crowd. Approximately two thousand people attended, including Whites and Blacks, Northerners and Southerners. Filled with anxiety, Washington envisioned himself giving this speech as one who faces the "gallows" (Washington, 1902, p. 210). He wanted to maintain the decorum that promised a continuation of "the good feeling prevailing between the two races" (p. 210), while exhorting the progress that his race had made. "I was determined to say nothing that I did not feel from the bottom of my heart to be true and right" (p. 213), Washington asserted. Furthermore, Washington claimed that:

> Our greatest danger is that in the great leap from slavery to freedom we may overlook the fact that the masses of us are to live by the production of our hands, and fail to keep in mind that we shall prosper in proportion as we learn to dignify and glorify common labour and put brains and skill into the common occupations of life; we shall prosper in proportion as we learn to draw the line between the superficial and the substantial. . . . No race can prosper till it learns that there is as much dignity in tilling a field as in writing a poem. It is at the bottom of life we must begin, and not at the top. Nor should we permit our grievances to overshadow our opportunities . . . (p. 220)

Addressing the White Southern portion of his audience, he said:

> Cast down your bucket . . . among the eight million of Negroes whose habits you know . . . cast it down in making friends . . . cast it down in agriculture, mechanics, in commerce, in domestic and in profession. . . . Casting down your bucket among my people, helping and encouraging them as you are doing on these grounds . . . you will find they will buy your surplus land, make blossom the waste places in your fields and run your factories. (pp. 220–221)

But to the dismay of some, Washington did not encourage his listeners to cast down their bucket in hopes of finding political, social equality. Instead he switched metaphors: "In all things that are purely social we can be as separate as the fingers, yet one as the hand in all things essential to mutual progress" (pp. 221–222).

Washington (1902) promised that the Negroes of the South would help pull the South out of its antebellum economic depression, but he did not encourage agitation for social equality, at least not until his race had proven itself in regard to industry. He did not feel the vast majority of African Americans were prepared to take on political issues and suggested that a test of property or skill or both be administered for the right to vote. This he believed should also apply to Whites who were not skilled or academically prepared to understand politics. "The opportunity to earn a dollar in a factory just now is worth infinitely more than the opportunity to spend a dollar in an opera-house" (p. 224).

Yet, he held out hope that from:

the product of field, of forest, of mine, of factory, letters, and art, much good will come, yet far above and beyond material benefits will be that higher good, that, let us pray God, will come, in blotting out of sectional differences and racial animosities and suspicions, in a determination to administer absolute justice, in willing obedience among all classes to mandates of law. This, this coupled with our material prosperity, will bring into our beloved South a new heaven and a new earth. (pp. 224–225)

W. E. B. Du Bois

William Edward Burghardt Du Bois held both respect and disdain for Booker T. Washington's philosophy on race, economics, and labor. Early on Du Bois wrote of his "great admiration" for Washington, who appeared larger than life. As for Du Bois, he saw himself as "a scientist, and neither a leader nor an agitator" (Du Bois, 1940, p. 69), but that changed following his education in the South. Du Bois began with a puritanical work ethic and a firm belief in education. Although he argued that oppressed people should protest, it was also their responsibility to pull themselves up from the degradation they suffered. The more Du Bois encountered new and different situations, the more he recognized the powerful forces of imperialism, capitalism, and cultural constructions of the revered, privileged whiteness of the world.

In *The Souls of Black Folks*, Du Bois (1903) wrote a mixed message with a complimentary tone but one that mentioned Washington's "silence" with regard to politics:

Easily the most striking thing in the history of the American Negro since 1876 is the ascendancy of Mr. Booker T. Washington. . . . His program of industrial education, conciliation for the South, and submission and silence as to civil and political rights, was not wholly original. . . . But Mr. Washington first indissolubly linked these things; he put enthusiasm, unlimited energy, and perfect faith into his program, and changed it from a bypath into a veritable Way of Life. (from *The Souls of Black Folks*, 1903, as cited in Booker, 2005, n.p.)

In a more straightforward statement on Washington, Du Bois charged that

Mr. Washington, or any other person, is giving the impression abroad that the Negro problem in America is in process of satisfactory solution, he is giving an impression which is not true. We say this without personal bitterness against Mr. Washington. He is a distinguished American and has a perfect right to his opinions. But we are compelled to point out that Mr. Washington's large financial responsibilities have made him dependent on the rich, charitable public and that, for this reason, he has for years been compelled to tell, not the whole truth, but that part of it which certain powerful interests in America wish to appear as the whole truth.—A statement on Booker T. Washington signed by William Du Bois and twenty-two other African Americans 26 October, 1910. (Booker, 2005, n.p.)

Whether Du Bois is correct in his explanation of Washington's silent politics' being due to his financial indebtedness to Whites cannot be known for sure. Clearly, Washington disagreed, claiming that he spoke what was in his heart; Du Bois did likewise, blaming powerful interest groups for influencing Booker T. Washington. Those powerful interests included the president of the United States as well as wealthy capitalists, all of whom had decided to support the ascendancy of Booker T. Washington. Eventually, Du Bois came to see Tuskegee as a machine of capitalism that promoted racial oppression.

Du Bois tackled the problem of racial oppression from a wider perspective, both historically and globally. For Du Bois, slavery had been a historical institution, but racial oppression had been a more recent invention. He considered the elevation of whiteness as an invented thing. "'But what on earth is whiteness that one should so desire it?' Then always, somehow, some way, silently but clearly, I am given to understand that whiteness is the ownership of the earth forever and ever, Amen" (see *The Souls of White Folks*, as cited in Lester, 1971, p. 487). Du Bois speaks of the greatness of Europe, which came about on the backs of the African slaves and at the exploitation of African resources, and all of this in pursuit of wealth.

Small wonder, then, that in the practical world of things-that-be there is jealousy and strife for the possession of the labor of dark millions, for the right to bleed and exploit the colonies of the world where this golden stream may be had, not always for the asking, but surely for the whipping and the shooting. (Du Bois, as cited in Lester, p. 496)

From an international and historic perspective Du Bois drew conclusions about racial oppression as born of imperialism. Although imperialism preceded World War I, it was through that "Great War" that Du Bois recognized the dangers of imperialism for the darker people of the world. He wrote:

> The present war in Europe is one of great disasters due to race and color prejudice and it but foreshadows greater disasters in the future.... It is not merely national jealousy, or the so called "race" rivalry.... It is rather a wild quest for the imperial expansion ... between Germany, England, and France primarily and Belgium, Italy, Russia, and Austria-Hungary to a lesser degree.... A theory of the inferiority of the darker peoples and a contempt for their rights and aspirations has become all but universal in the greatest centers of modern culture ... civilized nations are fighting like mad dogs over the right to own and exploit these darker peoples. (Du Bois, as cited in Lester, 1971, p. 68)

Du Bois's awakening began at Atlanta University, where he attempted to undertake a massive project on the state of the American Negro. His interviews and questionnaires demonstrated that "in a long series of lynchings less than one-fourth of the victims had been accused of rape" (Lester, 1971, p. 35) and that education for Southern Blacks was far from equal to that for Whites. In addition, he presented the history of Africa as a place of culture and education. He faced continual insults related to segregation, resulting in emotions that Du Bois had not felt with any great intensity when he lived in the North. In 1899, he witnessed the state of Georgia's passing laws to disenfranchise African Americans. He also saw a drop in funding for his scholarly pursuits.

Eventually, Du Bois began studying both Freud and Marx in order to understand "the economic foundations of human history" (Du Bois, *The Autobiography of W. E. B. Du Bois*, 1968, p. 228, as cited in Lester, 1971, p. 51). In 1905, he joined the Niagara Movement, an ideological group that eventually spawned the National Association for the Advancement of Colored People (NAACP), and became editor of *The Crisis*. Du Bois challenged the right of White liberals to lead African Americans, the Jim Crow laws, and the colonization of Africans worldwide, and although he supported World War I in order to protect and advance African Americans, he later wrote that perhaps his race should have passively resisted.

The Russian Revolution of 1917 intrigued Du Bois, who felt that Russians were actually attempting to answer the questions and concerns about the poverty of the masses in a time of great industrial wealth (Du Bois, 1940). He maintained, however, that "I could never regard violence as an effective, much less necessary, step to reform the American state" (Du Bois, 1940, p. 286). Du Bois visited Russia in 1928 and later wrote:

> Marx was one of the greatest men of modern times ... he put his finger squarely upon our difficulties when he said that economic foundations, ...

> are the determining factors in the development of civilization, in literature,
> religion, and the basic pattern of culture. (Du Bois, 1940, p. 303)

Du Bois then recognized that the argument as to whether African Americans should be trained in industrial skills or higher learning was moot if capitalism reigned supreme. The more that African Americans became educated in either skills or higher education, the more they became a part of a new capitalist scheme with both blue collar and "white collar proletariat" (Du Bois, as cited in Lester, 1971, p. 563). Furthermore, he argued, the system had been using Blacks as scabs against working class Whites and working class Whites had retaliated. Neither the liberal arts colleges nor the industrial schools of the South taught African Americans about the politics of work. Labor continued to be viewed as a deplorable endeavor divided between the haves and the have-nots, carried out by the laborers and the professionals to the profit of the capitalist, Du Bois argued. "Thus the world market most widely and desperately sought today is the market where labor is cheapest and most helpless and profit is most abundant" (Du Bois, from *The Souls of White Folks* as cited in Lester, 1971, p. 498).

Du Bois (1940) developed another plan; he advocated "consumers' co-operation for American Negroes" (p. 280). As a result, several store cooperatives were founded. For example, in a public school in West Virginia plans to teach cooperation through a hands on cooperative store were put into place and heralded as a "splendid piece of work" by Harvard University Graduate School of Education director W. C. Matney (p. 280). However, the state of West Virginia declared cooperatives illegal and closed down the project. Du Bois concluded that a democratic government gave people no say in how they "work and earn a living and [in] distributing goods and services; that here we did not have democracy; we had oligarchy" (p. 285). Du Bois wrote:

> I was early convinced that Socialism was an excellent way of life, but that
> it might be reached by various methods. For Russia I was convinced that
> she had chosen the only way open to her at the time. I saw Scandinavia
> choosing a different method, . . . After the depression and the Second
> World War, I was disillusioned. The progressive movement in the United
> States failed. (Du Bois, as cited in Lester, 1971, p. 144)

From this Du Bois concluded, "Capitalism cannot reform itself; it is doomed to self-destruction. No universal selfishness can bring social good to all. Communism . . . is the only way of human life. . . . I want to help bring that day (Du Bois, *Letter of Application to the Communist Party*, as cited in Lester, 1971, p. 144).

In a speech to the youth of his day, Du Bois asked them to consider certain ideals, including the ideal of poverty, the exact opposite of the ideal of wealth, which is promoted in the United States. Let them seek a simple life, he argued. The second ideal is the ideal of work, which he explained as putting every effort into what is worth doing. The third is the ideal of knowledge. He instructed students to question the taken-for-granted even if it is religious dogma. He encouraged critical systematic and creative thinking. Finally, he discussed the ideal of sacrifice, not the religious kind that has been embellished with religious overtones of heavenly reward but rather the kind of sacrifice where one surrenders personal ease and gratification for the betterment of humanity.

In his *Credo*, Du Bois proclaimed that he believed in God, "who made of one blood all nations that dwell on earth," that he believed in service, and that "Work is heaven." The devil made hate; the Prince of Peace exists; and "War is Murder." He believed that liberty is meant for all and that children, "black even as white," should be educated so that life is lit with "a vision of beauty and goodness and truth" (Du Bois, as cited in Lester, 1971, p. 485). Finally, he promoted patience in the long journey to end prejudice.

Contemporary Scholarship

Nkomo and Cox (1996) provide an excellent overview of contemporary research interests in organizational diversity. They begin by saying "that diversity is perceived to be such a new issue, an implicit assumption appears to be that there is little available knowledge relevant to its development as a topic," especially a topic related to "identity" (p. 339), but that is not the case. The authors explain that there are multiple definitions of diversity, which can be confusing, but the idea of diverse identities, be they ethnic, racial, gender, nationality, or organizational, exists and has been discussed in scholarly literature. The vast majority of this literature focuses on "managing diversity," a concept and practice that for the most part is intended to study what effect diversity has on production outcomes and how those outcomes can be controlled to the benefit of the organization.

Nkomo and Cox (1996) divide the literature into five main bodies of scholarship. The first is conducted under the framework of *Social Identity Theory* (SIT), which suggests that individuals tend to classify themselves and others into categories. Individuals can define themselves in multiple ways, including according to age, race, gender, or occupation. The focus of the SIT research is on how one defines oneself and others. Most research in this area addresses "the effects of diversity [a heterogeneous group of people who define themselves in varying ways] on work groups and organizational processes and outcomes" (p. 341).

The second approach to the study of diversity is called *Embedded Intergroup Relations Theory* (EIRT). This theory divides groups into two kinds: identity groups and organizational groups. An identity group is based on a biological trait (e.g., sex, age, race), while organizational groups are based on common organizational positions. The two groups can be related. For example, white males tend to dominate positions in upper management in the United States. Thus the theory notes that suprasystem identification can wield power that effects one's place in the organizational world.

Organizational Demography, a third approach, tends to focus on traditional demographic variables as indicators of identity and places the greatest attention on age, tenure, education, and occupation. This theory has promoted studies of diversity's effect on organizational and work-group outcomes, suggesting that "heterogeneity (compared to homogeneity) reduces . . . cohesiveness, lowers . . . satisfaction . . . and increases turnover" (p. 343). However, heterogeneity can have positive effects as well by increasing creativity, improving decision making, and stimulating innovation. Managing diversity is meant to find ways to decrease the negative outcomes and increase the positive ones.

A fourth approach focuses mainly on *Racioethnicity and Gender.* The major issue for these theorists "was assumed to be assimilating white women, racial minorities and those who were 'different' into organizations" (p. 344), but basically the research in this area has restricted itself even further to "blacks and women" (p. 344). For the most part, these studies characterize gender and race as innate properties and generalize to entire groups. For example, studies of women and leadership make dichotomous claims and generalizations.

Ethnology, or comparative cultural analysis, exemplifies a fifth current in the literature. This category seems a bit confusing because Nkomo and Cox (1996) include in it Hofstede's work even though his main focus has been on a quantitative assessment of nationality, which he generalizes to mean culture and then ascribes to it what he considers to be cultural traits. This does not fit the traditional definition of ethnology. We would not point this out except that Nkomo and Cox continue in this vein by providing yet another example that stresses how U.S. workers' expectations of management differ from those of French, Indonesian, and Japanese workers. In short, they are comparing nationalities, not cultures, and when they generalize to the U.S. they miss all the subtle distinctions between the various cultures embedded in the U.S.

All of these theories work under the assumption of capitalist tenets. They are focused on making the current system more efficient and effective. They do not challenge the economic lay of the land. However, diversity of identification has been studied from critical and postmodern perspectives. Nkomo and Cox give attention to this area without ever turning back the pages of history to see the contribution of W. E. B. Du Bois. Nevertheless, it is good to see organizational scholars at least pointing out the rich body of literature on the topic, even if they think it is a fairly recent development. To the contrary, critical thinking about identity dates back to Marx and has been promoted and developed through the ages via such people as Du Bois.

Rhetoricians like Kenneth Burke (1966) gave impetus to critical studies of organization, language, and identity decades ago. Some of those studies have highlighted organizational identity itself as a social construction that causes workers to behave in certain ways (see Cheney, 1991). Critical scholarship that turned to a cultural emphasis explored the construction of identity in terms of race and nationality through the work of Barthes (1972). Barthes in turn, influenced people like Stuart Hall (1992), whom Nkomo and Cox do mention. Hall was also influenced by postmodernists like Foucault, who addressed the discursive construction of the subject (or identity), the existence of multiple identities, and the shifting nature of identity, as well as hegemony.

Hall (1985) specifically addresses the shifting discourses around the identification of Black males. Born in the islands, he tells the story of his own family's bringing him home from the hospital as a baby and having his sibling describe him as a "coolie baby," that is, one who is darker-skinned than the rest of the family. In short, there is a hierarchy of privilege (Clair, 1998). Hall continues to explain that his blackness is perceived differently, and he is interpellated differently when he, as a young man, lives in England. He suggests that identification of a Black male shifts according to the cultural and political situation. Hall, as well as Laclau and Mouffe (1985), discusses representation and the nonfixity of identities.

Clair (1994, 1998) explored the discourses of identity between different groups and within shared groups and found that hierarchies do indeed exist within groups as well as between groups. There are certainly examples of wealthy women privileging themselves above and abandoning poor women and of white women privileging themselves above and abandoning minority men, women, and children (of course the opposite is true as well in that the already privileged group sometimes protects the oppressed group). With respect to privileging between different groups, Clair (1998) noted that under certain circumstances Black males have privileged themselves above females without regard to race. With respect to privileging self over others within the same group, Clair found that, in a group of female experts who came together to discuss publicly the topic of sexual harassment, an African American female privileged herself above "feminists" and did not want to be associated with them (p. 65). Clair suggests that this form of privileging may be related to the act of abandonment and that, in this case, the African American woman is abandoning other women who are feminists. These are complex issues of identity, issues that Nkomo and Cox (1996) call for researchers to explore.

Contemporary scholars do need to explore these issues further in the future, but they also need to look to the past to see the whole picture. For example, Booker T. Washington broke through racial barriers to become the first African American to head a university, as well as the first African American to receive an honorary degree from Harvard University. Washington's focus on practical education may have given further impetus to an industrial age with a "rags-to-riches" focus and may have contributed, albeit unwittingly, to the social organization of labor with respect to race in a unique and paradoxical way. While he prepared students for jobs, he also laid out a future for African Americans within certain trades, partially or potentially limiting them to blue-collar work; for those who reached professional, white-collar positions, capitalism became the guiding light. African American women especially became "stuck" in jobs that included domestic work, laundry, and restaurant drudgery, a way of life that would not change, for the most part, until World War II. Nonetheless, Washington's ideas about work and education spread across the South, helping thousands of freed slaves to achieve skills and education previously denied them.

W. E. B. Du Bois's contributions were also widespread and far-reaching. His graduation from Harvard cum laude in 1890 and his experiences in life and education prepared him to advance an educational agenda that led to the development of Black studies in universities today. W. E. B. Du Bois attempted to highlight the culture of Africa, but also noted that many "American Negroes" were not ready to be associated with anything African, which they met with "fierce repugnance, . . . the natural result of the older colonization schemes" (Du Bois, 1940, p. 275). Cognizant of the irony in the term *black Frenchman*, Du Bois consistently exposed the subtle and overt oppression of colonization via imperialism, and for this he should be granted the title of father of postcolonialism; yet, he is rarely cited today among the scholars of this growing trend. Nor is his deconstruction of language heralded as the beginning of postmodern discursive critique. Nevertheless, Du Bois's theoretical arguments on imperialism, labor, and race gave birth to new organizations, including the NAACP, which has promoted the intellectual, emotional, cultural, political, and economic advancement of African Americans. He elevated the identity of the oppressed and exposed the exploitive aspects of work in ways that deserve further scholarly attention.

Chapter Eight

Mother Jones and Emma Goldman

Labor Activists

Introduction

The American story of labor has been a long and tumultuous one, particularly in the late nineteenth and early twentieth centuries. The strong push toward capitalism and tremendous growth in industry led to the exploitation of thousands of workers (Chandler, 1991). From the mines to the factories, workers faced cruel conditions. Various activists ranging from liberal union organizers to radical anarchists offered avenues of hope. The voices of reformists, socialists, communists, and anarchists could be heard across Europe, Russia, and America. Unions like the Industrial Workers of the World (IWW), which used activist tactics such as strikes, boycotts, and propaganda and only later promoted collective bargaining, grew in strength. Revolts erupted in various European countries and culminated in Russia's October Revolution in 1917. Unions made a strong stand in America. Leading figures of the day ranged from liberal workers' advocates to anarchists. "Mother Jones" and "Red Emma" Goldman, two of the most compelling and colorful activists of the time, captivated audiences across America.

Biographies

The early life of Mary Harris, later known as Mother Jones, is difficult to describe with any precision because Jones may have altered her personal history to fit her activist persona. For instance, consider the example of her birth date. When Mother Jones first entered the public sphere in the early twentieth century, newspapers reported that she had been born in the late 1830s or early 1840s.

However, once she became more famous, she began insisting that her birth date was May 1, 1830; journalists later affirmed this claim but offered no supporting evidence. This date may have been promoted for symbolic and political reasons because the earlier year served to exaggerate her age and May 1 was the international workers' holiday, May Day (Gorn, 2001a). Indeed, the first sentence of her autobiography insists on this date (Jones, 1925/1969), yet according to Gorn (2001a), Mary Harris was in fact born in Cork, Ireland, on August 1, 1837.

When Harris was ten years old, her family left Ireland in the midst of the potato famine and immigrated to Toronto, where she learned the art of dressmaking and trained to be a teacher. In her early adulthood, she traveled the midwestern United States teaching and eventually married George Jones, a member of the International Iron Molders Union. In 1867, a yellow fever epidemic swept Memphis, Tennessee, where Mary Harris Jones, her husband, and their four children resided. Its victims were primarily poor workers because the wealthy fled the city to avoid the disease. Mother Jones described the horrific experience of losing her family to the fever:

> One by one, my four little children sickened and died. I washed their little bodies and got them ready for burial. My husband caught the fever and died. I sat alone through nights of grief. No one came to me. No one could. Other homes were as stricken as mine. (Jones, 1925/1969, p. 12)

Following the tragic loss of her family, Harris moved to Chicago. There she operated a dressmaking shop. She made an adequate living until the Chicago fire destroyed her home and possessions as well as her shop in 1871 (Gorn, 2001a). Homeless, Jones camped with thousands of other refugees. During this time, she witnessed the suffering souls of humanity, and perhaps this experience combined with the loss of her family is what sparked the nurturing anger that drove her activism.

Mary Harris Jones traveled between mining towns, where she found miners like her late husband working long hours in dangerous conditions. She took their cause to heart and began encouraging workers to unite and strike if necessary. Jones became deeply involved in the labor movement, particularly in organizing miners, and adopted the persona of Mother Jones. However, the exact date that Mother Jones appeared remains a mystery.

Although arrested on numerous occasions for her organizing efforts, she remained resolute in her responsibility to help the miners, whom she called "her boys." Jones recognized that the battle for humane working conditions and fair wages was difficult and dangerous at times but necessary. As she often told the miners, "Pray for the dead and fight like hell for the living!" (Jones, 1925/1969, p. 41).

In the later years of her life, Mother Jones began to suffer from rheumatism and other illnesses that progressively weakened her. The woman who had once told a congressional committee, "My address is like my shoes. It travels with me wherever I go" (Gorn, 2001b, p. 60), was forced to slow down. In 1923, Jones wrote her autobiography with the help of Mary Field Parton, a journalist who already had written several pieces about her. *The Autobiography of Mother Jones* proved to be a commercial failure, and the name Mother Jones began to disappear except in the militant circles of the labor movement. But her efforts were not in vain, and in following years her contributions became memorialized. On November 30, 1930, Mother Jones succumbed to her age and passed away. As her physician said, "She just wore out" (Gorn, 2001a, p. 292).

Mother Jones's legacy survives today in the magazine *Mother Jones* and the Web site motherjones.com, which are committed to "social justice through investigative reporting" (About Mother Jones, 2002, p. 1). Furthermore, her work is present in America's laws that regulate working conditions and strive to prevent the exploitation of workers.

Emma Goldman, born roughly thirty years after Mother Jones and an equally intense and passionate activist, also became known as a fiery speaker and social advocate for workers. Emma Goldman was born in Kovno, a Lithuanian section of Russia, in 1869. Her childhood had few moments of happiness as her family's income dwindled and her father became more abusive toward her. "Once father lashed me with a strap so that my little brother Herman, awakened by my cries, came running up and bit father on the calf," Goldman wrote (1931, p. 59). On another occasion, no one came to Emma's rescue, and her father beat her until "he grew tired and fainted" (p. 59). On a more hopeful note, her father allowed her to live with her aunt and uncle some distance away in order to attend school. As a strict disciplinarian, he expected excellent grades. However, Emma's uncle took her out of school, pocketed the father's tuition money, and forced the girl to work like a servant. Although her aunt protested, nothing was done until neighbors discovered the bruised and wan child and sent for her father. However, it should also be noted that Emma Goldman was an "impulsive, rebellious girl" who refused to be married off according to custom (Ganguli, 1979, p. 9). Furthermore, she spoke her mind and at the age of fifteen threatened to commit suicide if her father refused to let her join her half-sister in the United States (Goldman, 1931).

Emma Goldman's immigration with her sister Helena in 1885 to the United States could not have come soon enough for her. She and Helena moved in with their married half-sister Lena, who lived in Rochester, New York. Emma Goldman earned her keep by working in a garment factory, "sewing ulsters [corsets] ten and a half hours a day, for two dollars and fifty cents a week," not even enough to pay her rent (Goldman, 1931, p. 14). Goldman had worked in a glove factory prior to her immigration, but she found the American factory more intolerable because the work was harder, one had to ask permission to use the toilet, and every movement was under supervision. After asking for a raise and being denied, Goldman left that factory and a found a job in another factory where the pay was four dollars a week and the conditions slightly better. There she met Jacob

Kershner, whom she married after a short engagement. The marriage, however, was a dismal failure, and they eventually divorced, setting Goldman against marriage but not against "free love" as advocated by Marxist philosophy.

During those years, Emma Goldman and her sisters followed the news stories about the strikes in Chicago by workers at the McCormick Harvester plant. Workers had been joining unions to increase their wages, reduce their working hours, and gain respectable treatment. The Knights of Labor had been the most successful union to date; however, with the ascent of Terrance Powderly to the head of the organization, matters changed (Stewart, 1991). Powderly did not support the practice of strikes; instead, he advocated an educational plan, which many workers, such as Albert Parsons and August Spies, considered naïve. When Spies and others went on strike, Powderly betrayed their efforts by first promising to support them and then secretly telling workers not to attend the strike. In 1886, Spies and others headed the strike for the eight-hour day. The gathering was peaceful until police used brutality to break up the crowd, beating men and women and killing several people.

"To protest against the outrage a mass meeting was called in Haymarket Square on May 4. It was addressed by Parsons, Spies, and others, and was quiet and orderly. This was attested to by Carter Harrison, Mayor of Chicago, who had attended the meeting to see what was going on," according to Goldman (1931, p. 8). After the mayor left, the police ordered the protestors to leave. Some of the crowd began to disperse under a light rain; others argued for their right to peacefully protest, "whereupon the police fell upon the people, clubbing them unmercifully. Then something flashed through the air and exploded, killing a number of police officers and wounding a score of others" (p. 8).

Following the event, police rounded up anarchists, some of whom had not even been at the meeting, and held a rushed trial where "the jury was picked for conviction" (Goldman, 1931, p. 8). Workers charged that the men were innocent, whereas the press described the anarchists as violent terrorists. In the end, eight "innocent" men were convicted, five sentenced to hang and the others to life imprisonment, with one given a fifteen-year sentence. Goldman wrote, "The last words of August Spies rang in my ears: *Our silence will speak louder than the voices you strangle today*" (p. 51). From that day forward Emma Goldman dedicated herself to the activism of anarchism.

After moving to New York City and being encouraged by leading anarchists, she became a speaker for the movement. Her first speaking tour included Rochester, Buffalo, and Cleveland. She parroted the party line, not relying on her own thoughts (Goldman, 1931). The audience response from the first two cities left her disappointed. Attendees asked questions that seemed mundane, lacking in concern for the workers and the overthrow of capitalism. When Goldman faced the same response in Cleveland, she shot back with a sarcastic assessment of her audience from the stage. To her surprise, "The audience seemed to enjoy being handled in such an outspoken manner," (p. 52) but more importantly they engaged her with important questions. One elderly man asked why he should set aside the goal of the eight-hour day in favor of the overthrow of capitalism when he probably wouldn't live long enough to see the latter but might have a chance at the former. This question and others led Goldman to rethink her philosophy. She realized that she had been mimicking her teachers rather than critically thinking through the ideas for herself and she began to reflect more earnestly on her philosophy of work.

Following her first tour, she began to write her own speeches and develop a fiery style that was often followed by witty repartee. Her passionate dedication to the workers' cause brought more attention to the problems of the day. However, her "wizardry on the stump, fusing fervid rhetoric with spectacular delivery marked by a theatrical presentation," placed her in constant jeopardy of being arrested as a threat to the state (Oz, 1996, p. 908).

Early on Goldman met Alexander Berkman, with whom she fell in love and to whom she referred as her Sasha. Although the couple tried to lead a quiet life by opening an ice cream parlor to support themselves, the young Berkman became horrified by events that took place in Pittsburgh in 1892. Worker exploitation reached a breaking point at Carnegie Steel Homestead Mills, where workers went on strike. During the night, a group of men led by the chairman of Carnegie Steel, Henry Clay Frick, rode down the river and under the cover of darkness opened fire on the strikers, killing several workers, including a little boy, and wounding many more (Goldman, 1931).

Both Emma Goldman and Alexander Berkman felt compelled to leave their quiet life and return to activism. Berkman, in particular, became so distressed over the events that had taken place at Carnegie Steel Mills that he planned to kill Frick, and Emma helped him gain the resources to travel to Pittsburgh to do so. His assassination plot failed and Berkman was arrested, tried, and sentenced to twenty-two years in prison. Distraught over Berkman's arrest, but dedicated to anarchism, Emma Goldman continued to give anti-capitalist speeches across the country as she evaded the law. Eventually, she was arrestedt and tried for inciting a riot. After being found guilty, Goldman refused to appeal and was sent to prison. While in prison, she overcame her own suffering by helping the other women, many of whom had been arrested for prostitution or stealing as means to counter poverty and hunger. In prison, she became the doctor's assistant and learned nursing skills that would prove beneficial in the future. Her prison sentence ended just shy of one year, at which time Goldman reentered society and worked as a certified nurse and midwife, ministering to poor women. She continued to speak in public, especially on behalf of women and their needs (e.g., with regard to birth control). These public appearances led to Goldman's arrest on numerous additional occasions (Goldman, 1931).

During one of her speaking tours, more specifically, following the Cleveland lecture in 1901, Emma Goldman met a quiet young man named Leon Czolgosz. He asked for information to read so that he might better understand the anarchist philosophy. Later that year, Czolgosz, was arrested for shooting President McKinley, and Goldman was arrested for contributing to the young man's assassination plot. Police detained her in Chicago in the same Cook County jail where the Haymarket strikers had been hanged. Goldman felt that she had come full circle (Goldman, 1931).

Eventually the judge dropped the charges. Goldman was released and returned to her life on the lecture circuit arguing for freedom of speech, women's rights, birth control, and anarchism. She and several other advocates decided to publish their own magazine. Goldman thought of the title *Mother Earth*, "The nourisher of man, man freed and unhindered in his access to a free earth" (Goldman, 1931, p. 378), and the first edition, sixty-four pages long, was released on March 1, 1906. The magazine included essays on birth control, indoctrination in schools, and anarchism. It became illegal under the Comstock Act to distribute literature on birth control, and Goldman once again in 1915 found herself behind bars.

With a world war looming, Goldman's lectures diverged in emphasis, especially building the theme of antipatriotism. By this time, she had developed a nonviolent anarchistic philosophy. She argued that war is the equivalent of murder, which solved nothing, and she, therefore, spoke against U.S. involvement in the Great War. World War I brought new laws that jeopardized Goldman's freedom to speak. They included the selective service act (the draft); laws against espionage, which made it illegal to interfere with the draft or encourage disloyalty; and the Sedition Act, which prohibited antigovernment speech and anticonscription activities. Goldman spoke out against these laws and published essays on them in *Mother Earth*. She was arrested again in June 1917 for conspiracy to violate the draft act. In December 1919 she and her longtime activist friend and lover, Alexander Berkman, were deported to Russia (Goldman, 1931).

Upon arriving in Russia following the Red Revolution, Goldman discovered that Russian communism was a disappointment at best (Goldman, 1923). She reported that the Russian people were exploited, living in poverty, coerced under tyrannical forces, subjected to censorship, and worked as hard as capitalist workers. Upon learning that revolutionists had executed counterrevolutionists, Goldman spoke out fiercely. "I must be crazy, Jack," Goldman (1931) reported saying to her friend and fellow anarchist John Reed, "or else I never understood the meaning of revolution. I certainly never believed that it would signify callous indifference to human life and suffering, or that it would have no other method of solving its problems than by wholesale slaughter. Five hundred lives snuffed out on the eve of a decree abolishing the death penalty!" (p. 740). Under the excuse of a speaking engagement in Germany, Goldman and several other fellow anarchists who originally had been deported to Russia, left that country forever.

Goldman spent the next two decades writing her memoirs, *Living My Life* and *My Disillusionment in Russia*, and speaking out against worker exploitation in the world. She traveled to England, Spain, Italy, Germany, and other European countries. She suffered from "diabetes," "bouts of tuberculosis," painful "varicose veins," and the effects of a "strenuous life" (Ganguli, 1979, p. 9), but despite her poor health she traveled to Spain when she heard that anarchists were fighting against a despotic regime. "Sixty-seven year old Emma pottered about the trenches in the Aragon front where she met soldiers whom she described as courageous and dedicated. Vowing to assist them, she prepared documents of record and took photographs. . . . to rouse public opinion and organize relief. . . . It was to be a story of anti-fascist struggle" (Ganguli, 1979, pp. 74–75). Goldman took the story to England, where she hoped the people would support the workers who were fighting against the growing fascist movement. But the British remained unconvinced, and Spain fell into the hands of the fascists.

At the age of seventy, Emma Goldman left Europe but did not give up her dream (Ganguli, 1979). A following of supporters invited her to Canada, where she celebrated her seventieth birthday in 1939. In 1940, she suffered a stroke that left her paralyzed on one side of her body and unable to speak. On May 14, 1941, Goldman died. Perhaps inappropriately and most certainly ironically, a priest spoke at the atheist-anarchist's funeral. More appropriately, authorities returned her body to the United States for burial. "She was buried next to the *Haymarket Five*, whose death had transformed her life" (Ganguli, 1979, p. 77). Like Mother Jones, her spirit remains alive through numerous magazine and academic articles and books.

Philosophy and Rhetoric of Work of Mother Jones and Emma Goldman

Mother Jones

Upon embracing the labor movement, Mary Harris Jones adopted the maternal role of Mother Jones.

> Her symbolic May 1 birthday . . . and her accelerated aging were engineered to fit her self-cast leading roles of labor's prophet and matriarch. . . . Costumed always in matronly black silk and white lace, Mary Harris Jones answered only to "Mother." She called miners her "children," her "boys." (Tonn, 1996, p. 2)

Tonn (1996) believes that this motherly identity was effective for female agitators such as Mother Jones because agitating and mothering both involve nurturing as well as militancy. Furthermore, by taking on the role of the workers' "mother," Jones both usurped and overcame the traditional domestic role of women and could help the miners (Tonn, 1996).

Miners worked long hours for low pay in unsafe conditions. These men and their families lived in typically dilapidated and unsanitary communities built by the mining companies. Furthermore, mining families had no choice but to purchase food and clothing from company stores using scrip. "Scrip was a medium of exchange that coal companies issued to their employees instead of cash; outside of the company store it was worthless" (Samosky, 2001, p. 1). Mining companies could inflate the prices at the company store, and workers would have no choice but to pay the unfair amounts.

These conditions led miners to strike, which at times took a militant turn and at other times was met with violence from owners, as in the previously mentioned case of Carnegie Steel Mills, where several workers were shot in 1892 and one young boy killed.

Although the militant aspects of agitation are often more striking than the nurturing aspects, it is important to recognize the necessity of the latter. Mother Jones worked for the "fostering of emotional and intellectual growth, and development of group identity and social responsibility" for the coal miners (Tonn, 1996, p. 2). Most of the miners were poorly educated and were unaccustomed to making decisions for themselves. As one of her primary goals, Mother Jones attempted to instill independence. She typically accomplished this by telling stories with embedded dialogue that demonstrated independent thinking to the workers (Tonn, 1996, p. 12). She hoped to diminish their fears and encourage independence.

In addition to fostering courage, Mother Jones also worked to promote a group identity, knowing that change would only come about through working collectively. Evidence suggests that she was astoundingly successful. When she began working for the United Mine Workers in the 1890s, the organization had only 10,000 members. Within a few years of her activism, more than 300,000 men had joined the union (Gorn, 2001b).

Nurturing independence and collective identity were prominent concerns for Mother Jones, but a third concern, maternal protection, also surfaced in her rhetoric. Tonn (1996) argues that "mother in myth, cave mother, and even animal mothers remind us [that] maternal love entails the fierce protection of children, often at any cost" (p. 3). Not surprisingly, Mother Jones often stood up to the miners' oppressors, typically through verbal attacks (Tonn, 1996). In addition to speaking for the miners, her "children," Mother Jones taught them how to represent themselves. For example, she ridiculed the miners so they would learn how to defend themselves and she told stories that showed opponents of labor to be weak and conquerable (Tonn, 1996).

Tonn (1996) demonstrates that the maternal persona of "Mother Jones" allowed Mary Harris Jones to drastically influence mine workers and the entire labor movement. Tonn (1996) also shows that confrontation, which typically is seen as a masculine trait, is consistent with maternal instincts. By nurturing and challenging her children, Mother Jones succeeded in helping them achieve better working conditions and better lifestyles.

In addition to working to secure rights for miners, Mother Jones also addressed the issue of child labor with her Crusade of the Mill Children. In July 1903, Mother Jones, union leaders, and a group of children, some crippled by the machinery of textile mills, began a march from Philadelphia to New York City. Throughout the journey, the group stopped in numerous towns, where the children performed skits demonstrating the luxurious lives of the mill owners and Mother Jones delivered speeches denouncing child labor (Gorn, 2001a). Mother Jones described the first demonstration in Philadelphia:

> A great crowd gathered in a public square in front of the city hall. I put the little boys with their fingers off and hands crushed and maimed on a platform. I held up their mutilated hands and showed them to the crowd and made the statement that Philadelphia's mansions were built on the broken bones, the quivering hearts and dropping heads of these children. That their little lives went out to make wealth for others. (Jones, 1925/1969, p. 72)

Although the march had numerous problems, including dissent among the followers and summer weather that was unbearable at times, it is viewed historically as a success. As Mother Jones (1925/1969) explained,

> We had drawn the attention of the nation to the crime of child labor. . . . Not long afterward, the Pennsylvania legislature passed a child labor law that sent thousands of children home from the mills, and kept thousands of others from entering the factory until they were fourteen years of age. (p. 83)

In communities where the exploitation of children was commonplace, thousands of citizens turned out to listen to the words of Mother Jones (Gorn, 2001a). In a time when children were viewed as a necessary part of the workforce, she dared to condemn the practice of child labor and greatly influenced social change to eliminate it. The Crusade of the Mill Children demonstrates the concept of theory in action. Mother Jones's rhetoric was not limited to oratory but also included creative acts and performances used to draw attention to the plight of workers.

Although Mother Jones fought for the rights of workers in the early twentieth century, it should be noted that she did not embrace other movements for social change. As Gorn (2001b) notes, "Mother Jones opposed giving the vote to women—or, to be more precise, she believed that suffrage was a false issue, a bourgeois diversion from the real problem of worker exploitation" (p. 60). Although she frequently worked to organize the wives of union members into "'mop and broom' brigades, [groups of] militant women who fought alongside their husbands" (Gorn, 2001b, p. 60), she did not want these women to end up as part of the workforce. She believed that women were better off in the home.

In short, Mary Harris Jones was an activist who clearly understood the power of rhetoric to change the world. She created a persona to capture the hearts of miners, and she created dramatic moments and persuasive speeches to spread her emancipatory philosophy. She worked tirelessly for the exploited mine workers of America, and she devoted her efforts to ending child labor.

Emma Goldman

Anarchism, of course, was the most influential philosophy in Goldman's arsenal and served as the foundation for her other philosophical tenets. However, as Ganguli (1979) points out, there are several different schools of thought with respect to anarchism. They range from the mutualism of Proudhon to the communism of Marx and Engels, from the atheist anarchism of Nietzsche to the Christian anarchism of Tolstoy, from the violent anarchism of Lenin to the passive-resistance anarchism of Ghandi and Thoreau. Emma Goldman was well read on the topic of anarchism and developed her own distinct version of anarchism.

In hopes of dispelling some of the fears associated with anarchism, Goldman wrote an essay for *Mother Earth* entitled "Anarchism" in which she defined the philosophy. She began by telling the reader that anarchy, like any other new idea, was being met with resistance before people had the opportunity to fully understand it. She blamed ignorance, especially the ignorance of the masses, for the initial resistance to anarchy and suggested that once ignorance was replaced with knowledge few objections would exist. She then addressed the objections of those who were knowledgeable on the topic: "First, Anarchism is impractical, though a beautiful ideal. Second, Anarchism stands for violence and destruction, hence it must be repudiated as vile and dangerous" (Goldman, 1910, p. 55). But even these criticisms may be grounded in ignorance, Goldman explained: "Anarchism is indeed practical. More than any other idea, it is helping to do away with the wrong and foolish; more than any other idea, it is building and sustaining new life" (p. 55). Stories of the violence and horror of anarchism are fed to people by those who oppose anarchism. Ignorance, not anarchy, then becomes the violent and destructive force that controls the minds of the people, she argued. "Anarchism urges man to think, to investigate, to analyze every proposition" (p. 56). Anarchism is "the philosophy of a new social order based on liberty unrestricted by man made law; the theory that all forms of government rest on violence, and are therefore wrong and harmful, as well as unnecessary" (Goldman, 1910, p. 56).

Although governments are based on controlling people, Goldman, felt that economic arrangements are more responsible for maintaining the evil brought upon people. In addition to government and economics as modes of control, Goldman argued that religion and education maintained the status quo. Thus, according to Goldman, the government, the economic arrangement, and the religious and educational institutions all play a role in perpetuating the current conditions that keep individuals from knowing their own potential. "Anarchism is the only philosophy which brings to man the consciousness of himself; which maintains that God, the State and society are non-existent, their promises null and void" (Goldman, 1910, p. 58).

Governments continue to impose laws that are meant for all without "regard to individual and social variations" (Goldman, 1910, p. 67). Anarchism means to end authority. "Only in freedom will man grow to his full stature" (p. 67). That freedom is not restricted to freedom from government authority but also includes freedom from religious and social authority.

Goldman (1910) argued that "Religion speaks of God"; yet, "God has created a kingdom so despotic, so tyrannical, so cruel . . . [that] tears and blood have ruled the world since gods began" (p. 59). Anarchism (with the exception of Tolstoy's Christian version) suggests that religion presents a "great obstacle to progress" (p. 59), as does private property.

The theory against capitalism, most fully developed by Marx and Engels, asserted that private property is a great evil. Proudhon referred to it as "robbery." Goldman (1910) concluded that capitalism is saturated with greed. "The A B C student of economics knows that the productivity of labor within the last few decades far exceeds normal demand a hundredfold. . . . The only demand that property recognizes is its own gluttonous appetite" (p.60). As a result, "the power to subdue, to crush, to exploit, the power to enslave, to outrage, to degrade" has become the order of the day. "America is particularly boastful of her great power, her enormous national wealth," but all of this is achieved on the backs of the "wretchedly poor" who live "in squalor, in filth, in crime, with hope and joy gone, a homeless, soilless army of human prey," Goldman argued (p. 60). It is the goal of anarchy to end exploitation.

Goldman (1910) believed that "real wealth consists in things of utility and beauty" and that if we are "to continue in machine subserviency, our slavery is more complete than was our bondage to the King" (p. 61). She called for a "society where man is free to choose the mode of work, the conditions of work, and the freedom to work" (p. 61). She called for "voluntary productive and distributive associations, gradually developing into free communism" where individuals' rights would be protected, freedom would be encouraged, and choice would be recognized: "Anarchism aims to strip labor of its deadening, dulling aspect, of its gloom and compulsion. It aims to make work an instrument of joy, of strength, of color of real harmony, so that the poorest sort of man should find in work both recreation and hope" (Goldman, 1910, p. 67).

Subordination is in direct conflict with the tenets of anarchism. Government has worked hand in hand with capitalists to reduce "mankind to clockwork" (Goldman, 1910, p. 63) while protecting the property of capitalists. Those who believe that government maintains order and reduces crime are naïve. It is government that protects the criminal activities of exploitation, "stealing in the form of taxes, killing in the form of war and capital punishment" (p. 66), and does little to protect people from hunger and despair, the reasons that the people commit crimes.

Goldman (1910) asserted that anarchism stands for "the spirit of revolt, in whatever form, against everything that hinders human growth" (p. 69). Anarchism is about liberty of mind, liberty from religion and authority, and liberty from exploitation. Democracy cannot, or has not, given people liberty. Goldman explains in her essay that the states with the most rigid laws against child labor continued to have the highest levels of exploitation and the states with the strictest protections for miners continued to have the greatest number of mine disasters. Only revolt brings about radical reform; from the American Revolution to John Brown this fact is made clear, she asserted. Goldman calls for "direct action" to end the oppression of the current order, which actually represented disorder. She concludes her essay with a vision of the future grounded in her definition of anarchism: "It is the theory of social harmony. It is the great, surging, living truth that is reconstructing the world, and that will usher in the Dawn" (p. 73).

On Violence

Emma Goldman's essay on anarchism minimized the role of violence and ironically blamed violence on the government and the capitalist owners. She became aware early on of the plot to assassinate Frick, although in the end she had not directly participated. Arrested on more than one occasion for inciting to riot and influencing two young men who turned to violence to solve political problems, she certainly contributed to aggression in her youth. Some of her speeches were more than fiery. For example, in a speech that she gave to a crowd in New York City in 1893, she said, "They will go on robbing you, your children and your children's children, unless you wake up, unless you become daring enough to demand your rights. Well then, demonstrate before the palaces of the rich. Demand work. If they do not give you work, demand bread. If they deny you both, take bread. It is your sacred right!" (Goldman, 1931, p. 123).

However, time and maturity changed her position on violence, which confused many including one reporter who asked about her feelings toward President McKinley after he had been shot. Goldman denounced McKinley as an imperialist but swore that should he need her she would nurse him back to health; at the same time, she announced that she sympathized with Leon Czolgosz, McKinley's assassin, and that he probably needed her more than did McKinley. Following the assassination she spent much time meditating on the state of affairs, concluding that life is precious, McKinley's and Czolgosz's included.

Goldman was influenced by anarchist Peter Kropotkin who had explained "that an anarchist society had to be non-violent" (Ganguli, 1979, p. 78) if it was to be grounded on freedom. Yet, "Force had to be used in the present society because society itself was responsible for anti-social deeds" (as cited in Ganguli, p. 79). The ensuing moral dilemma, then, was that the only way out of tyrannical and imperialist regimes, including the capitalist system, was through revolutionary acts. Most forms of "anarchism did not preach submission to injustice, tyranny or exploitation" (p. 83). Most anarchists "rejected Tolstoy's principle of non-resistance to evil" (p. 83). Goldman understood the violence of the Russian revolution, but as mentioned earlier, she was incensed over the execution of anti-revolutionaries. Near the end of her life, Goldman made statements opposing World War I on the grounds that war is murder and unnecessary violence, but she dove into the trenches with anarchist soldiers in Spain who fought against fascism, and she rallied for their support.

On Sexuality

Freedom for women, like freedom for workers, was inextricably linked to the major institutions of society. Furthermore, workers, working women, and women who stayed at home existed in a tangled web. Goldman (1910) wrote on the history of prostitution as being supported by the institution of religion, capitalism, and government, beginning with accounts from Herodotus about women in Babylonia, Greece, Cypress, North Africa, Western Asia, and the Mediterranean, where prostitution was required. In Babylonia the law stipulated that all women must at least once in their life provide sex to a stranger in return for money for the temple. According to Goldman, this ancient practice was neither heathen nor dead. She continued to explain that Pope Clement II had said that "prostitutes would be tolerated if they pay a certain amount of their earnings to the Church" (p. 189). Pope Sixtus IV required payment from the brothel instead of the individual; "he received an income of 20,000 ducats" (p. 189). Contemporary religious leaders simply turned a blind eye to the practice, and except for a few activists, no one attempted to uncover the primary reasons for prostitution—commodification of women and poverty, two issues that Goldman had faced in her own life. Her father had tried unsuccessfully to marry her off as a girl, which was when she first felt the commodification of her sex in a personal way. Later, as a young woman working in a factory, she did not earn enough money for her rent. When she and Berkman wished to put their anarchist ideals to the test by assassinating Frick, Goldman considered and came close to prostituting herself to get the money to accompany Berkman on his trip. Thus, capitalism's low wages, the police and politicians' corrupt participation, and the religious leaders' apathy of the day encouraged prostitution.

While in prison, Goldman met many women who had succumbed to prostitution as a means of economic survival. Upon her release she became closely acquainted with women whose economic situations were made nearly intolerable by pregnancy, another mouth to feed. She protested the fact that birth control and even birth control information were illegal. Furthermore, she opposed abortion on the grounds that too many women died from the procedure. Women of wealth faired little better because they were subject to subordination and control by their husbands and were also subject to constrained birth-control laws, according to Goldman.

At every anarchistic turn, Emma Goldman met sexism, even from her colleagues and mentors. Radical thinkers like Karl Marx had called for "free love," that is, love that was not subjected to the laws or constraints of economics, government, or religion. Yet Marx had a wife by law and a servant/mistress whom he impregnated. Ownership and control of the female ran deep within the male psyche. For example, Nietzsche has been quoted as saying, "When you go to woman, take the whip along." Johann Most treated Goldman as inferior intellectually, but sought her sexually. Nevertheless, Goldman quoted these philosophers and others (Goldman, 1910).

Patriarchy loomed large; it reared its ugly head not only in personal relationships and the home but also in religion and politics. Women hegemonically became the church workers and missionaries of a philosophy that undermined their very stature as equal human beings, according to Goldman. She drew this idea from Nietzsche, who suggested, "Christian morality was the morality of the slave," and from Emerson, who called for the "active soul" (Ganguli, 1979, p. 63). With regard to politics, women demanded equal suffrage, much to Goldman's dismay. For in her estimation, women who called for the vote were calling for participation in more of the same—capitalism, corrupt government, and authoritarian rule. And sadly, Goldman asserted, in states where women did have the right to vote, women's working conditions had not improved at all, and women of privilege turned against prostitutes, not allowing them the vote. Women's emancipation has been the story of tragedy, grounded in such concepts as democracy, liberty, patriarchy, religion, and marriage, Goldman argued. She wanted women to denounce suffrage, religion, and marriage and hoped that women would recognize how contemporary institutions exploited and controlled them.

Goldman's work on birth control rights was met with much criticism. "Her blend of sexual and political radicalism, the aura of violence surrounding her, seemed to mobilize the deepest anxieties among conservatives" (Wexler, 1984, p. 177). Her rhetoric of violence, connection to political assassins, her anarchist literature, and her antipatriotic rhetoric combined to make her voice too radical for the average American (Solomon, 1988; Fox, 2005).

On Art

Emma Goldman confessed that a man she names only as Fedya, an artist whom she and Berkman helped to support and who in turn became her other lover, had influenced her thoughts on beauty. He suggested that beauty was a necessary part of life and on occasion brought flowers to Goldman. Berkman criticized this act as bourgeois indulgence. Goldman considered both sides of the issue and concluded that flowers were a joy to have in the house, even though they were a luxury. Rarely extravagant, Goldman did feel that beauty brought joy to life and should be included within the anarchist dream. Once criticized for dancing because frivolity could only hurt the cause, Goldman (1931) responded: "I did not believe that a cause that stood for a beautiful ideal, for anarchism, for release and freedom from conventions and prejudice, should demand the denial of life and joy . . . If it meant that, I did not want it" (p. 56).

Art came into Goldman's philosophy in other ways, as well. For example, although she disagreed with Marx on the nature and development of communism (too centralized and controlling), she agreed with his notion that the ontological nature of work is self-expression. Work as an extension of the individual is corrupted by capitalism. Goldman, who longed at one point in her life to be a designer and dressmaker, not a seamstress in a girdle factory, clearly understood this Marxist maxim.

Further, a friend whom Goldman names only as P. Yelineck, asserted that, "All creative people must be anarchists" (Goldman, 1931, p. 194) because creative people could not exist under the constraint of authority. The role of the artist is to self-express, to create, to break the rules. She agreed with her friend and asserted that Nietzsche was a good example.

Ganguli (1979) believed that Goldman had a streak of the romantic. She admired much of Nietzsche's work and from her writings seems to have been unaware of his misogynistic side or had transcended his sexist attitudes (see Mahowald, 1983, for a discussion of Nietzsche's views on women). Nietzsche's statement that "Art and nothing but art! is the great possibilizer of life" (Nietzsche, *Will to Power*, 653, I and IV, an unused draft for a preface for a new edition of *The Birth of Tragedy*, as cited in Hollingdale, 1973, p.155) addressed the ways in which reality is created as well as the means to express philosophy. Goldman took to heart much of what the poet-philosopher wrote.

Recognizing the power of art to portray and teach philosophical concepts, Goldman spent the later years of her life using dramatic literature as the central theme of her speeches. This approach allowed her to speak with less interference from authorities, who saw her not as promoting anarchy but as interpreting great works of literature.

Contemporary Scholarship

Today, debates rage over the free-trade agreements and their implications for workers worldwide. American workers may fear the loss of their jobs as businesses move production offshore, and activists may continue to worry about the treatment of workers in underindustrialized countries. With the development of NAFTA, the recent passage of CAFTA, and the upcoming changes in the textile import/export regulation laws, business arrangements are expected to take a more dramatic turn toward the exploitation of workers, and activists are not sitting still as this happens. Workers in underindustrialized countries and American students have united to bring attention and protection to workers.

In 1996, Charlie Kernaghan, director of the National Labor Committee, exposed Kathie Lee, TV host with her own clothing line sold at Wal-Mart, for supporting sweatshop activities. Lee denied the charges at first but later discovered that indeed her line of clothing was being made by child labor under gruesome conditions. Sweatshops at the time were believed to exist elsewhere, not in the United States. Pressure to end sweatshop abuses both in the U.S. and around the world led President Clinton to form the Apparel Industry Partnership (AIP) through the U.S. Department of Labor to create an enforceable code of conduct for apparel manufacturers (Galestock, 1999, p. 1). Eventually, this partnership developed into the Fair Labor Association (FLA), an organization whose purpose is to monitor the apparel manufacturing business in order to reduce and ultimately end abuses. However, the design of the FLA board left activists unhappy because they saw businesses gain too much control and workers and unions have too little voice. Activists were disappointed to see Nike on the FLA Board and to find out that the FLA did not support open disclosure, the living wage, or union activism at apparel factories (Esbenshade & Bonacich, 1999). Workers in underindustrialized nations along with university students and union leaders spearheaded their own movement—United Students Against Sweatshops (USAS) to start the Workers' Rights Consortium (WRC).

According to Featherstone (2002), who has written a history of the USAS movement:

> With a *joie de vivre* that the American economic left has lacked since the days of Emma Goldman and John Reed, college students are harnessing their creativity, irony, and media savvy to launch a well-organized, thoughtful, and morally outraged resistance to corporate power. (p. 29)

Students learned more about the situation as they accepted internships with unions in New York City. When they returned to their universities they began campaigns to end university participation in buying goods (i.e., university logo apparel) from factories that abused workers. From Tico Almeida at Duke University (1998) to the students of Purdue University who went on an eleven-day hunger strike in the spring of 2000, college activists gained the ear of administrators (Featherstone, 2002).[1]

These student activists are outraged not only by the worker abuse but also by the corporatizing of U.S. universities. Capitalism, they suggest, is turning universities into businesses that care more about money than ethics and education. When Brown University joined the WRC, Nike canceled its contract with them and denounced the WRC (Featherstone, 2002). USAS members used this action to launch a campaign against Nike.

It is important to note that advances being made are due not only to university students' activism or to universities' jumping on board, but also to the workers in these underindustrialized countries. Yesenia Bonilla of Lima, Honduras, at the age of sixteen joined union activists at the maquiladora where she worked. They fought for pure water, an improved transportation system, and lighted pathways for those who had to walk home in the dark. She was fired for her activities, along with forty-eight other workers (Featherstone, 2002). "In January 2001, over 850 workers at Kudong International Mexico, a Korean-owned garment factory in Atlixco de Pueblo, went on strike when five of their co-workers were illegally fired for trying to organize an independent union" (Featherstone, 2002, p. 80). Kudong contracts with Nike and Reebok to supply logo apparel to U.S. universities. Subsequently, the USAS members became involved, and the workers and students worked together to bring in an independent monitoring board who confirmed the complaints (worm-infested food served at high prices with no alternative to leave for lunch, low pay, and other inhospitable conditions; Featherstone, 2002). Making this known to Nike and Reebok through the media eventually moved the shoe companies to act. But constant vigilance and pressure are required to keep corporate giants from slipping back into apathy about worker conditions.

USAS members are challenging globalization with their own "internationalization of resistance" and the resurgence of the motto, "Workers of the World Unite!" and Mexican workers are uniting under the motto, "Sí, se puede!" (Yes, it can be done!; Featherstone, 2002, p. 85) It is an eye-opening experience for both workers and affluent students. "People are drawn in by the horror stories, . . . but then they start seeing how the whole system works," Maria Roeper of the WRC explained (Featherstone, 2002, p. 95). Living in capitalism's midst does not always automatically provide understanding and awareness of its impact locally or globally; capitalism surrounds people like a fog that too often obscures from view the exploitation of people and the world.

Activists from the past to the present devote their efforts to securing safe, sufficient, and dignified working conditions. Both Mother Jones and Emma Goldman devoted their lives to the emancipation of the workers.

Note

1. Purdue University student members affiliated with USAS staged a second hunger strike in 2006, which lasted nearly a month and brought renewed visibility of the plight of workers to the public (see Clair, R. P. November 2007, *Organizations as arguments: A case of monitoring sweatshops.* Paper presented at the Annual Meeting of the National Communication Association, Chicago, Ill. and under review with *Management Communication Quarterly.*)

Chapter Nine

Emile Durkheim

The Division of Labor

Introduction

Emile Durkheim is by far one of the most notable scholars of sociology. His work on the division of labor and suicide has had a significant influence on both the humanities and the social sciences. He is credited with bringing scientific methods to sociology by incorporating unique demographic analyses in his studies. In addition, he supported the introduction of anthropological studies into sociology. Furthermore, he relied on both methodological approaches to develop his theoretical positions. Durkheim's work examined the organization of society, especially in terms of the division of labor and its effect on workers. He proposed that all aspects of human society are interrelated, suggesting that different types of societal structures (e.g., mechanical or organic) lead to different outcomes. Both his theoretical and his methodological contributions have added to the understanding of work.

Biography

David Emile Durkheim was born on April 15, 1858, in Epinal, in the eastern French province of Lorraine. His mother, Melanie, was the daughter of a merchant. His father had been a rabbi in Epinal since the 1830s and was also chief rabbi of the Vosges and Haute-Marne. Durkheim's grandfather and great-grandfather also had been rabbis. Following the family tradition, Durkheim spent the earliest part of his education in a rabbinical school (Jones, 1986). However, after his traditional Jewish confirmation—bar mitzvah—at the age of thirteen, Durkheim broke away from Judaism altogether (Coser, 1977). Nevertheless, as Jones (1986) points out, he lived with the daily anti-Semitism that permeated Europe. Furthermore, Jones notes, "Later, Durkheim would argue that the hostility of Christianity toward Judaism had created an unusual sense of solidarity among Jews" (p. 12).

Durkheim skipped two years at the College d'Epinal, graduating with baccalaureates in letters and sciences in 1874 and 1875, respectively. He then left Epinal for Paris to seek admission to the prestigious École Normale Supérieure. After failing the entrance examination on his first two attempts in 1877 and 1878, Durkheim was finally admitted near the end of 1879. Ironically, following these efforts for admission, he found himself dissatisfied with the style of education at the École Normale Supérieure, seeing it as too literary and unscientific. Nevertheless, he stayed, continued his studies, and graduated in 1882. Upon successfully passing the examination required for admission to the teaching staff of state secondary schools, he began teaching law and philosophy. Eventually, Durkheim taught sociology at the University of Bordeaux and later at the University of Paris. Durkheim devoted his career to the development of sociology as a respectable science (Edwards, 1967). His accomplishments include being named as "Chargé d'un Cours de Science Sociale et de Pédagogie" at Bordeaux in 1887, founding the first social science journal in France (*Annee Sociologique*) in 1898, and being named professor of science of education and sociology in 1913 (Jones, 1986).

Durkheim started a school of sociological ethnography. His son and his nephew, as well as other students, trained with him. However, these promising young students were taken away by the demands of World War I, which resulted in the tragic death of Durkheim's son, leaving only his nephew Marcel Mauss to continue the ethnographic tradition (Moore, 1997).

The death of his son in 1916 left Durkheim devastated, leading him to withdraw from his academic endeavors. Several months later he collapsed from a stroke; Durkheim died on November 15, 1917, at the age of 59 (Jones, 1986).

Philosophy and Rhetoric of Work

One of Durkheim's earliest works focused on how societies function. Specifically, book 1 of *The Division of Labor in Society* opens with an explanation of the term *function*, which can be thought of in two different ways. First, function refers to a system of vital movements without reference to the consequences of these movements (e.g., digestion, respiration). Yet *function* also refers to the relationship between these movements and the corresponding needs of the organism (e.g., digestion replenishes nutritional resources; respiration cools the biological system; Durkheim, 1893, 1933/1984). Durkheim observed that the latter use of the term *function* was the more appropriate when referring to the function of the division of labor. "Thus to ask what is the function of the division of labour is to investigate the need to which it corresponds" (p. 11).

The division of labor is the separation and specialization of work among people. Furthermore, "it is the necessary condition for the intellectual and material development of societies; it is the source of civilization" (Durkheim, 1893, 1933/1984, p. 12). According to Durkheim, as technology and industry continue to advance and populations grow, people must recognize the need to specialize in order to ensure survival, both for society at large and for the individual. Specialization of labor makes each worker more or less irreplaceable as people continue to learn the intricacies of different types of work. For society, this means that there will be more efficient production of goods. Civilization is thus protected. However, Durkheim also questioned whether civilization defined in this way was really good for people. He proposed that there is nothing morally inherent in civilization. Furthermore, he suggested that the division of labor does less to satisfy needs and more to create needs that perpetuate the system. But if this were all that the division of labor achieved, that is, to bind "up the wounds that it inflicts" (p. 15), then individuals might "submit to it, but there would be no reason to desire it" (p. 16). This notion impelled Durkheim to investigate what other functions the division of labor served.

Before detailing Durkheim's (1893, 1933/1984) arguments, it should be noted that Durkheim based the rationale for his theory on suspect data, leading him to draw racist and sexist conclusions. For instance, Durkheim initiated his arguments on the division of labor with comparisons between "primitive" and contemporary societies. Specifically, he focused on the skull size of women as compared to men and argued that in primitive societies the differences were less than in contemporary societies, suggesting that men became smarter because they handled the intellectual jobs in society and women actually suffered a "regression" (p. 21) because they handled the affective aspects of the home. Marriage, he suggested, demonstrates the first division of labor. Dependence, as seen in marriage, develops as the result of the division of labor. This dependence, in turn, facilitates solidarity. Durkheim suggested that this modulating relationship between dependence and solidarity could be applied to society at large.

With increased specialization in society, Durkheim argued, people naturally become separated from each other. Their values, interests, and social norms vary, in both work-related and social-related settings. Because people are performing different tasks from one another, they come to value different things. These differences do not hinder a society but, rather, give rise to a unique type of society. Durkheim proposed that although people like and are drawn to those who resemble themselves, the opposite is also true. As humans, people are also drawn to those who are different, simply because they are different (Durkheim, 1893, 1933/1984). Differences between people, then, become a factor in what attracts people to one another. The differences between people can act in a complementary fashion. Durkheim refers to this as *positive attraction,* in which people seek in others what they themselves lack and vice versa. Associations are then formed between people, and there is an exchange of services that arises from this division of labor. According to Durkheim(1893, 1933/1984),

> if the division of labor produces solidarity, it is not only because it makes each individual an exchangist, as the economists say; it is because it creates among men an entire system of rights and duties which link them together in a durable way. (p. 406)

Durkheim (1893, 1933/1984) pointed out that the division of labor gives rise to solidarity, which can be classified in two different ways in this regard. First, Durkheim proposed that societies that evolve from a simple, nonspecialized form engage in mechanical solidarity. In this type of society people behave and think alike. The work that people perform and the tasks that they do are more or less similar in nature, thus proposing the same group-oriented goals. Mechanical solidarity is possible only insofar as individual differences are minimized and group devotion is emphasized. Durkheim contends that this type of social structure prevails to the extent that the ideas and tendencies that pertain to individuals are not as intense or numerous as those that pertain to all people in society. This type of solidarity grows inversely to personality. In short, Durkheim considered mechanical societies simple, primitive, and comprised of people who were similar and lacked individual definition as well as independence. Once again Durkheim's position rested on prejudicial data that assumed "that he who has seen one native of America has seen them all," whereas, "By contrast, among civilized peoples two individuals can be distinguished from one another at a first glance" (p. 89).

Whereas mechanical solidarity emphasizes the similarities between individuals, organic solidarity focuses on the differences and is built upon the interdependence of people in society. Organic solidarity exhibits a more extensive division of labor. In this type of society, work becomes more and more complex (organic), and people perform more specialized tasks. Because people are performing distinct tasks of a specialized nature, they come to rely on each other for survival. Durkheim (1893, 1933/1984) recognized the social structure in an organic society as a sort of system made up of different organs, each of which has a special role. Each person in society has a specific, differentiated part that is coordinated and subordinated to those around them. Durkheim wrote:

> As the progress of the division of labor demands a very great concentration of the social mass, there is between the different parts of the same tissue, of the same organ, or the same system, a more intimate contact which makes happenings much more contagious. A movement in one part rapidly communicates itself to others. (p. 224)

Hoping to "deduce what is the contribution of that organic society to the general cohesiveness of society" (p. 102), Durkheim once again pointed to "lower societies" to make his point. Durkheim argued that tribal and clan-based societies had weaker ties between people, and although his assumption may be based on faulty data, it led him to explore the ties that bind people together and a means to measure solidarity. Without religion, custom, or clan relationships, people do not have a means to link themselves socially. People living in a society that is continually differentiating itself need more than exchange to tie them together. Durkheim suggested that contracts and the law acted to give order and connection to people in an organic society.

Book 2 of *The Division of Labor in Society* focuses on the causes of differentiation. Durkheim (1893, 1933/1984) suggested that to assume that dividing work would provide more happiness was a psychological answer to the question of why we work the way we do; he further suggested that to say that work was divided in order to produce more abundant products was an economic answer. He sought a social answer. He suggested that both of these aspects, happiness and abundance, play a role and need to be given special attention because "the suicide of sadness, is an endemic state among civilized people" (p. 191), but neither happiness nor exchange alone explains what gave rise to the division of labor.

Durkheim (1893, 1933/1984) suggested that a vicious cycle exists between the division of labor and the increase in population as well as its concentration in certain areas. Yet this concentration will not necessarily lead to conflict. Using the example of a blacksmith, Durkheim argued that a town can support several blacksmiths, and even if the town reaches the point that the blacksmiths would enter into serious competition, they avoid conflict by specializing. Specializing reduces antagonism. However, the specialization must correspond to some need of the townspeople. Durkheim suggested that new needs would be created as people grew more intellectual, which is the natural outcome of civilization and the division of labor. Some of these new products would support music, arts, and science; other products would have an apparent (as opposed to a real) need. Not all of these products would make workers happy, yet their manufacture would be necessary to survival. And as people further specialized they could establish a sense of uniqueness as long as that uniqueness stayed within the bounds of the collective. Briefly put, people can assert their individuality while they resemble every one else, living the collective life. Limited variation allows the organism (organic society) to survive. In short, "Durkheim advanced an essentially Darwinian argument" (Coser, 1984, p. xvi) that addressed the criticisms of capitalism.

The system of collective representations in society is that which constitutes its *collective conscience*, the sharing of common values. Durkheim rejected the idea that biological or psychological factors were determinants of human collective representations of social phenomena (Edwards, 1967). He argued that these collective representations are more collective than universal and that they operate coercively, independent of free will. In other words, collective representations exist outside of one's own individual conscience. They seem to be accepted norms. For instance, that it is wrong to kill may appear to be universal, but it is not. The proscription against killing may vary from culture to culture, from situation to situation, and across time. In order to determine these collective representations, one must analyze the social facts within forms of the law or customs as well as the punishments. These constraints come into play whenever social demands are being violated (Durkheim, 1933) and can tell a great deal about the mechanical or organic society. Law became the index by which Durkheim measured the organic society and its solidarity.

In book 3 of *The Division of Labor in Society*, Durkheim tackled the notion of limited variation in the sense that many people seem to be relegated to certain positions in society. Although heredity plays a role and past societies with caste systems have had an influence, Durkheim wrote that the division of labor cannot be pushed to the point of isolating individuals or it will become the "source of disintegration" (p. 294). If work is so diverse that there is no longer a standard, a norm, then anxiety will ensue. Furthermore, if a worker feels like a cog in a machine with no recourse from a monotonous job, then the worker will suffer a sense of separation. The worker must have meaning as well as the promise to overcome social inequities. The division of labor cannot be forced; it must be spontaneous but not to the degree of laissez-faire government. Thus, Durkheim offered a theory that negotiated a place between pure capitalism and radical communism.

Furthermore, he explained that rules are needed to dispel feelings of anomie, and justice is needed to dispel feelings of inequity. To feel lost or worthless would inevitably lead to alienation. *Normlessness* is what makes individuals unable to find their places in society without the help of rules to guide them. Without these rules, habits, and beliefs, sudden change occurs, which may lead to conflict and deviant behavior (Durkheim, 1883, 1933/1984). Durkheim further developed his idea of anomie in his study on suicide but noted in *The Division of Labor* that suicide is the direct result of anomie, especially when

> The new life that all of a sudden has arisen has not been able to organize itself thoroughly. Above all it has not been organized so as to satisfy the need for justice. . . . We need to put a stop to this anomie . . . and. . . . We need to introduce . . . a greater justice by diminishing those external inequalities that are the source of our ills. (pp. 339–340)

Thus, Durkheim paved the way for a more regulated form of capitalism with an emphasis on law, morality, and justice.

Contemporary Scholarship

Durkheim's concepts have acquired a new relevance for the contemporary sociology of business ethics (Hendry, 2001). As a sociologist, Durkheim focused much of his attention on the idea that moral rules are socially constructed and that they change as society changes. Durkheim was convinced that these moral rules that guide behavior would be required in the professional world. To him, society could not survive and be effective without such moral discipline. However, he feared that businesses at the time did not possess the sociology of morals necessary for the health of a society. In the past, Durkheim noticed the tendency for the business world to focus on economic life and self-interest rather than social, moral rules. Morality, in Durkheim's opinion, was not an individual but a social phenomenon. Without morality, a social structure could not survive. According to Durkheim:

> It is not possible for a social function to exist without moral discipline. Otherwise, nothing remains but individual appetites, and since they are by nature boundless and insatiable, if there is nothing to control them they will not be able to control themselves. (Durkheim, 1957, pp. 10–11, as cited in Hendry, 2001)

In other words, without an existing social morality in business, the appetites of the individual would reach such levels of greed that society would not be able to function. Writing in 1893, it is not surprising that Durkheim worried about economic greed. That period, the era of "robber barons and rebels," as Zinn (1995) put it, saw a great deal of greed, violence, and mayhem. Oil, railroads, agriculture, and other industries were controlled by wealthy magnates who were creating monopolies in the United States. Workers banded together, struggling to develop unions. Violence was commonplace. Durkheim was convinced that the economic function of society was completely unstable without the presence of moral codes and that the economy could not be left to laissez-faire economics.

Durkheim feared the idea that organizations might operate without social morals and with purely economic self-interest. He saw this as a potential social problem that could lead to the collapse of society. As the evolution of businesses progressed, so did the rise of the bureaucracy, which Durkheim also feared. In the early part of the twentieth century, business organizations evolved from the "individual pursuit of economic self-interest to a bureaucratic model based on large organizations in which traditional moral values held sway" (Hendry, 2001, pp. 209–210; the rise of bureaucracies, their characteristics, and their sway on society will be discussed in further detail in the next chapter).

Hendry (2001) notes that even in the last twenty years, however, it seems that the trend toward bureaucracy has lessened, whereas the trend toward the market has increased. Traditional moral values have taken a backseat to corporate issues. Individuals are more likely to take on an entrepreneurial way of thinking—the pursuit of individual self-interest. The moral discipline and concern for ethical behavior that is motivated within an individual seems to have faded into the background (Hendry, 2001).

However, as Hendry points out, the modern bureaucratic corporation has little to do with ethics, as well (Chandler, 1962, 1977; Chandler and Daems, 1980; Lazonick, 1991, as cited in Hendry, 2001). Although Durkheim feared that the members of a business organization would live according to self-interest, people in organizations in the twentieth century were governed by personal obligation and moral constraint. That is to say, cultural institutions, such as religion, guided the moral behavior of individuals. The members of an organization were expected to maintain loyalty to that organization and to act in its interest rather than their own. What Durkheim feared most, the loss of morals and the increase in suicide has surprisingly not yet surfaced, according to Hendry (2001).

With respect to organizational structure, the trend among business organizations has continued to change dramatically in the last two decades. Although the strictest forms of hierarchy and bureaucracy have become the exception rather than the rule, the elements that sustain this type of function continue to exist. According to Hendry (2001):

> The balance of organizations has shifted, the problems of bureaucracy have receded, and those of the market have returned to the foreground. In the flexible economy of the late twentieth and early twenty-first centuries, the relationships between firms and their employees, and the relationships between employees, are increasingly governed, quite openly, by the rules of the market rather than by those of traditional moral obligation. (p. 213)

Hendry (2001) provides interesting insights but may fall short of discussing the full implications of the new market trend. As Pomery (2006) notes, it is important to raise a variety of questions concerning the role of the worker

> (a) as an interchangeable commodity; (b) as part of hierarchy; (c) as an individual subject to control but also with discretion, intrinsic motivation, sense of self, and more; (d) as a potential stakeholder; (e) as having the capacity for acquiring and embodying human capital, at the individual, social, and firm-specific levels; (f) as a political being with interests in his or her real wage and also in the *general will* for society; (g) as an individual with survival needs and life goals; and (h) as a human with rights.

This roller coaster of trends among business organizations continues to evolve. Today, numerous organizational members have shown characteristics of self-interest, as have many business owners, some moving toward the extreme. And these self-interests have taken precedence over the moral values that Durkheim argued are necessary to maintain a healthy society. Durkheim's argument that extreme market self-interest is destructive to moral values and threatens the stability of society is certainly salient amid the social problems that are related to business today.

When considering corporate greed, Achbar, Abbott, and Bakan (2004) suggest that the corporation has grown so morally decrepit that it has reached the extreme. They provide the example of Bechtel Corp.'s claim over the water rights in Bolivia. Bechtel charged Bolivians extravagant amounts of money for water use after working in concert with the Bolivian government to make it illegal for citizens to draw water from the rivers or even to catch rain water in containers. The people staged protests where clashes with the police resulted in two deaths and scores of injuries before the Bolivian citizens reclaimed the rights to the water. Others quickly mention Pacific, Gas, & Electric; the tobacco industry; or Enron as examples of corporate self-interest gone mad with greed.

As traditional morals continue to weaken and self-interest continues to dominate, Hendry (2001) argues that the marketization of business life will also penetrate many other aspects of society, including the public and political arenas. Consumers have begun to see economic growth as an end in itself rather than as a means to a morally sound life, he argues. That the pursuit of economic contentment is the route to getting ahead in society has been demonstrated and encouraged. People are inspired to be effective in their own entrepreneurial endeavors and to make it on their own in the world. To do otherwise would be considered naive (Hendry, 2001). Hendry's (2001) somewhat pessimistic perspective may be balanced by those who see organizations as moving toward sustainability, as well (Achbar, Abbott, & Bacon, 2004), and by those who see the workers as Pomery (2006) does—as human beings who have multiple goals and multiple roles and have the abilities to participate in the system as active agents of change.

As Emile Durkheim's theories continue to be revisited, the powerful and substantial influence that this very prolific sociologist has had on the philosophy and rhetoric of work will become even more apparent. His life and writings can and will, no doubt, continue to be the source of considerable insight as well as debate, especially concerning the organization of labor and the moral fiber of society.

Chapter Ten

Max Weber

The Father of Sociology and Theorist of Bureaucracy

Introduction

Max Weber is considered one of the most deliberate thinkers of the nineteenth century, and his influence stretched well into the twentieth century. His most famous contribution—an explanation of the relationship of the Protestant work ethic and the development of capitalism—addressed the role of religion and other factors as motivators of work behavior. Although intriguing, the theory faced criticism then and continues to face it now (Giddens, 1992). Weber's writings on organization and leadership promoted bureaucracy as a means to reducing nepotism and subsequently alienation. The concluding premise of these writings is facing contemporary challenges, as well (Barker, 1993; Barker & Cheney, 1994; Ferguson, 1984). However, Weber may have been his own best critic because he, too, questioned the outcome of a bureaucratic world.

Biography

Max Weber, born April 21, 1864, in Erfurt, Germany, spent his early years under the protection of his parents, Max and Helene Weber (Coser, 1971). In 1869, the family moved to Berlin because Max Sr. accepted a position with the Berlin city government and also served as deputy of the National Liberal Party in the Prussian and Imperial Diet (Kaelber, 2003). While Max Sr. excelled in politics, he remained indifferent to religious and philanthropic concerns. This contrasted sharply with the altruistic viewpoint of his wife, Helene. Helene descended from a wealthy family, yet she avoided any great displays of affluence.

She had been raised a Calvinist and, unlike her husband, was strongly devoted to social causes.

This difference of opinion grew into larger rifts throughout their lives. Early in their marriage, one of their children, Anna, died as an infant. "Helene was taken aback by what she perceived as Max Sr.'s lack of concern for her by not sharing her grief over the loss" (Kaelber, 2003, p. 1). Max Sr. also insisted on being the sole decision maker in the family, including all monetary decisions, even though Helene's inheritance had comprised the majority of the family's wealth.

Throughout Max Weber Jr.'s adolescence, Helene attempted to attract him to her side of the marital dispute and to cultivate Calvinist values in the boy; however, Max Jr. tended to identify more with his controlling father. At eighteen years of age, Max began attending the University of Heidelberg and chose to major in law, as his father had done (Coser, 1971). Influenced by his parents' differing ideologies, "Max could not make up his mind whether to lead the life of a scholar or that of a gentleman" (Specher, 1962, p. 7). While away at school he shrugged off his ascetic side and joined a rather rowdy fraternity. His crude behavior followed him home, and his mother was so displeased with his conduct that she slapped him. According to Specher, "the effect was lasting" (p. 7).

After three terms at Heidelberg, Max Weber Jr. left for a term of military service in Strasbourg. During this period, he came under the influence of his mother's sister, Ida, and her husband, Hermann Baumgarten, whom he came to view as second parents. Whereas Weber's father had always treated him as an inferior, his uncle regarded him as an intellectual equal. Also, his aunt succeeded in instilling the sense of social responsibility that his mother never could. His time with his aunt and uncle led him to sympathize with his mother and increasingly dislike his father (Coser, 1977).

In 1884, Weber returned to his parents' home to study at the University of Berlin. He remained financially dependent on his father until he was thirty years old. In 1892, Weber began teaching law in Berlin and became engaged to Marianne Schnitger. A year later, they were married (Weber, 1978). During these years, Weber wrote his second major work, "a penetrating analysis of the social, political and economic developments of Roman society. It was published in 1891" (Specher, 1962, p. 9). Not wanting to be isolated in his scholarly pursuits, Weber joined a group of socialists, mostly students and faculty, who wished to make a difference in world conditions, especially for the working class. The members of this group eventually became known as "academic socialists" (Specher, p. 9).

In 1897, possibly encouraged by his newfound financial and personal independence, Weber confronted his father about his role as a controlling husband and father. Unfortunately, the strained relationship continued, and the two had not reconciled when Max Sr. died later that year. Unable to cope with this traumatic event, Max Weber Jr. suffered a nervous breakdown (Kaelber, 2003). His attempts to resume teaching in 1899 were in vain and only made his mental condition worse (Weber, 1978). He did not fully recover for nearly five years. His wife later wrote, "For hours . . . he would sit at the window and stare into space; . . . during which time he never opened a book or wrote a line" (Specher, 1962, p. 10).

Eventually, Weber's emotional health returned and he accepted an appointment—an honorary professorship at Heidelberg in 1903. He spent the next seventeen years of his life lecturing throughout the world and writing on topics ranging from religion to political-economics. He developed basic concepts in theory and methodology of sociology and became known as the "father of sociology."

In 1920, Weber's sister Lili committed suicide, leaving behind children that Max and Marianne Weber planned to adopt (Kaelber, 2003). However, before the adoption was finalized, Max Weber fell ill and died of pneumonia in Munich on June 14, 1920 (Coser, 1977). His last words were, "The Truth is the Truth" (Coser, 1977).

Philosophy and Rhetoric of Work

As Runciman points out, "Max Weber has been described as not merely the greatest of sociologists but *the sociologist*" (see Weber, 1978, p. 3); however, during his life, Weber did not consider himself a sociologist. He disagreed with sociology's tendency to apply holistic concepts to people. Instead, he argued that sociological explanations should result from the conscious behaviors of individuals (Weber, 1978). Nevertheless, many of his contributions in both theory and method moved the field of sociology forward.

Weber defined "sociology as the science which aims at the interpretive understanding of social behavior in order to gain an explanation of its causes, its course, and its effects" (Specher, 1962, p. 13). *Verstehen,* or understanding, as Weber meant it could be gained in one of two ways: intellectually or empathically. Intellectually, one relies on rational thought and the unfolding of patterns as witnessed through observation and empirical analysis in order to make sense of the world. Empathically, one relies on understanding and being able to take the place of the other. Thus, if a behavior seems irrational, one needs to step into the other person's proverbial shoes in order to understand and explain what is motivating the person to behave a certain way.

In relation to behavior, Weber (1962) proposed that four types of motivators affect behavior: goal-oriented, value-related, affect-related, and traditional. The first of these is "*rational* in the sense of employing *appropriate means to a given end*" (Weber, 1978, p. 28). In this type of action, a person uses his or her expectations of others' behaviors to determine how to act in order to achieve his or her own rationally determined purpose. The second type of action, Weber (1978) described as "*rational* in the sense that it is an *attempt to realise some absolute value*" (p. 28). That is, a person acts rationally to achieve something ethical, religious, or having some other form of intrinsic but immeasurable value. A third type of social action is "*affectively* (and in particular *emotionally*) determined" (Weber, 1978,

p. 28). In this instance, a person is not considering the consequences of his or her actions but, instead, is acting out based upon his or her current state. The final motivator of social action that Weber (1978) identified is "*traditional* behaviour, [or] the expression of a settled custom" (p. 28). This is the most common form of action and consists of people's acting a particular way simply because they have always acted in that way. The level of intentionality varies from motivator to motivator, and more than one motivator may be working at the same time.

Weber suggested that behavior could be analyzed in comparison to "typical ideal behavior patterns" (Specher, 1962, p. 14). Thus, he developed what he called the *ideal type*. The ideal was not an image of perfection but, rather, an existing representation of the type, to which all other types could be related in order to assess, explain, or understand them. "Thus, the construction of an ideal type can also be regarded as a working hypothesis" (p. 14). Furthermore, the ideal type is descriptive, not prescriptive; it is a means of classification.

Weber's interest in the workers' plight and the organization of labor in general led him to explore how people organize themselves. Specifically, he investigated the ideal type of bureaucracy. However, before exploring his insights and concerns about bureaucracy, a few comments should be made about his most famous hypothesis related to work, which is that the Protestant work ethic was the driving force behind the development of modern capitalism.

The Protestant Work Ethic

Weber believed that in order to understand socioeconomic behavior a scholar needed to explore the historical and cultural context as a whole. For example, in order to understand the development of modern capitalism, one needed to look at historical implications, religious changes, technological developments, and much more. However, in his book *The Protestant Ethic and the Spirit of Capitalism*, Weber minimally addressed all but religion as a motivator. He minimized social, political, economic, and psychological motivators and maximized his discussion of religion. The book is based on lengthy articles that were first published in 1904–5 and later posthumously published in a collection in 1930 and republished in 1992. Weber's thesis is that although forms of capitalism have existed for many generations in many different societies, Protestantism alone, as developed from New England Puritanism, advanced capitalism in the direction of the modern form that exists today.

Unlike Durkheim, Weber argued that reliable theories could not be based on racial neurology and psychology. These fields of study were only in their infancy, and although they might be "promising," he held that that they were as yet unreliable (Weber, 1992/1904–5, p. 31). He also suggested that other explanations held validity and might even have had a hand in the development of capitalism but not with the same rigor that Protestantism has had. Protestants who drew their philosophy from Puritanism developed an ideology distinct from the Catholic Church and from eastern religions. Specifically, Protestants did not believe that they could use accumulated grace to achieve salvation. Nor could they atone for sins committed. They believed that salvation was predetermined through divine providence and the best that they could do to stave off the loneliness of this ideology (because no priest or person could help them into heaven) was to act as if they were part of the chosen few. Those who wished to appear chosen could exhibit the persona of a good person by being a hard worker. Treating work as a *calling* performed to glorify God would speak of the goodness of the individual as well as the goodness of God (Weber, 1992/1904–5).

If people work with religious fervor, then they are bound to make a profit. Making a profit actually creates a paradox for Protestants who derive their ideology from Puritanism because the Puritans believed in the ascetic life, devoid of worldly pleasures. Thus, Protestants were encouraged to work, make a profit, and then save their money. As Weber noted, *A penny saved is a penny earned.* Weber's pointing out this proverb is double edged. He meant that this practice would keep Protestants from indulging in frivolous behavior, and he also meant to highlight the fact that this adage came from Benjamin Franklin, the son of a Calvinist, who even though he did not share his father's religious ideals promoted them through tradition (both a traditional and value-related motivator) (Weber, 1992/1904–5).

Protestants, unlike eastern worshippers, could not consider meditation as a means to enlightenment; only work would suffice. And unlike Catholics, they could not atone for their sins, but work might keep them from sinning in the first place because *idle hands are the devil's workshop*, or so they believed. In addition to idleness, wealth could create temptation; thus, the Protestant needed to work, earn, save, and invest. Investing is crucial to capitalism, and hard work is necessary to the development of a middle class.

The unequal distribution of wealth in society was attributed to divine providence that humans could not be expected to understand. As such, Protestantism supplied workers with the means to salvation; they worked as if their very soul depended upon it, saved, and invested in order to reach salvation, and they did not question their circumstances (Weber, 1992/1904–5).

Finally, Weber wrote that Protestants were taught that their "care for external goods should lie on the shoulders like a cloak" so that it might be easily tossed off; instead, "fate decreed that the cloak should become an iron cage" (Weber, 1992/1904–5, p. 181). In short, whether we are moved by religion or tradition matters not; what matters is that the ideas are so embedded in the mind that we cannot act otherwise; we are trapped in the iron cage. As Weber notes, "the idea of duty in one's calling prowls about in our lives like the ghost of dead religious beliefs" (p. 182) so that one day these activities might be driven as if one were engaging in a "sport" (p. 182). Weber feared that sport-like capitalism might lead to unhealthy ways of behaving, but he preferred not to pass judgment; instead, he moved onto discussions of what kinds of organizations would best regulate modern capitalism.

Bureaucracy

Weber considered bureaucracy a superior form of organization. He concluded that

> The decisive reason for the advance of bureaucratic organization has always been its purely technical superiority over every other form. A fully developed bureaucratic apparatus stands to these other forms in much the same relation as a machine does to non-mechanical means of production. (Weber, 1978, p. 350)

It is important to note that Weber did not invent the bureaucratic system, nor did he address actual bureaucracies; instead, he "defined the ideal type of bureaucracy . . . on a *pure* or abstract level" (Dalby & Werthman, 1971, p. 1) but a level that nonetheless had to have the probability or possibility of existence.

Weber outlined six basic criteria that characterize modern bureaucracy. Weber's discussion of these characteristics begins with the concept of (1) rules followed by discussions of (2) hierarchy, (3) separation of public and private resources, and issues, (4) separation of jobs according to specialization, (5) unbiased selection and promotion of workers, and (6) written descriptions and rules concerning job duties.

The first of these characteristics is "the principle of official *jurisdictional areas*, which are generally ordered by rules" (Weber, 1968, p. 956). This includes the idea that all activities required for the function of the organization be assigned to individuals as official duties. The authority to command others to perform these duties is strictly limited by rules. Furthermore, written rules provide for the regular and continuous fulfillment of the duties, and only people who qualify under general guidelines are employed to perform the duties (Weber, 1968).

The second characteristic of modern bureaucracy is the concept of "*office hierarchy*" (Weber, 1968, p. 957). According to Weber, the effective bureaucracy has clearly established superordinates and subordinates. Lower offices are supervised by higher offices, and decisions of lower offices can be appealed to higher ones through a clearly established process. However, the idea of hierarchical subordination does not mean that higher offices can simply take over the work of a lower office. Once an office has been established, it must be filled with a qualified individual to manage its affairs (Weber, 1968).

The third characteristic that Weber identified in the ideal modern bureaucracy is the separation between official and private lives. "In principle, the . . . office is separated from the household, business from private correspondence, and business assets from private wealth" (Weber, 1968, p. 957). This practice is common in today's business world, but Weber noted that its beginnings could be found as early as the Middle Ages (Weber, 1968). It is meant to reduce corruption and greed, as well as the abuse of workers.

The fourth characteristic of bureaucracy is that office management "usually presupposes thorough training in a field of specialization" (Weber, 1968, p. 958). Thus, all employees, including managers, are trained in a particular field and then specialize in that field. The fifth is that personnel should be selected and promoted according to their competence and performance. This characteristic of bureaucracy is intended to reduce nepotism. Finally, the sixth characteristic mandates that the selection and promotion decisions should be based on a pre-determined written job description, which clearly describes the procedures for work performance to be evaluated.

In summary of the characteristics, Weber (1968) noted that "the management of the office follows *general rules*, which are more or less stable, more or less exhaustive, and which can be learned" (p. 958). By reducing management to explicit rules, an organization works to eliminate affective and traditional social action and instead encourages rationality in decision making. These rules would help to establish and reinforce hierarchy. Furthermore, the system was intended to separate the public from the private, position workers in specialized jobs, and promote fair hiring and promotion practices. Finally, the above practices needed to be written. Keeping a written record was meant to act as documentation that would protect workers and allow the bureaucracy to continue operating in spite of individual personnel losses.

In addition to describing the characteristics of an organization, Weber worked to identify the role of the individual within a bureaucracy. First, Weber (1968) observed that positions in modern offices are "vocations" (p. 958). That is, they entail specific courses of training and examinations as prerequisites of employment. Also, employees usually work in the same capacity for a long period of time. Weber argued that when a person enters an office, he or she is agreeing to work for the purpose of the office in return for the promise of a secure existence. The agreement is based on functional rather than personal purposes (Weber, 1968).

The individual in the bureaucracy relies on "fixed career lines and status rigidity" (Weber, 1968, p. 963). That is, he or she expects to move up through the established hierarchy to positions of higher seniority and prestige. The bureaucratic employee is compensated by salary rather than by wage. Thus, pay is not determined by work completed but instead according to status. Therefore, the longer an employee remains within a bureaucratic organization, the more prestige he or she is accorded, and the more pay he or she expects to receive.

While Weber observed that bureaucracies are the most effective means for managing an organization, he did not necessarily see them as entirely positive. Weber recognized that bureaucracies succeeded by depersonalizing, if not dehumanizing, the people within them. "Bureaucracy develops the more perfectly . . . the more completely it succeeds in eliminating from official business love, hatred, and all purely personal, irrational, and emotional elements which escape calculation" (Weber, 1968, p. 975). Although these restrictions and others were meant to reduce the capriciousness of supervisors, the practice of nepotism, and thus the alienation of the workers, Weber realized that they might lead to extreme control. While bureaucracies ensure management of the organization, they do so at the expense of the individual.

Weber feared that in time bureaucracies would continue to spread, and the individual would continue to be destroyed.

> It is horrible to think that the world could one day be filled with nothing but those little cogs, little men clinging to little jobs and striving toward bigger ones. . . . It is as if in politics . . . we were deliberately to become men who need "order" and nothing but order, become nervous and cowardly if for one moment this order wavers, and helpless if they are torn away from their total incorporation in it. That the world should know no men but these; it is in such an evolution that we are already caught up. (Weber, as cited in Elwell, 1996, p. 1)

Clearly, Weber feared the path to which bureaucracies could lead in the future.

Authority

Weber discussed authority as a complex aspect of organization. He clarified three types of authority. The first is rationalized authority that is constituted through legal means. Weber believed that the bureaucratic system tends to regulate authority through its system of rules and fixed promotions. Weber identified this type of authority in his writings as "rational-legal authority" (Weber, 1978, p. 217). This concept of authority is most prevalent in the modern world. The second type of authority, traditional authority, is prevalent in premodern societies. Under this system, authority is not codified but, instead, is passed from one individual to another, usually along hereditary lines (Weber, 1978).

The final type of authority Weber described is charismatic authority. According to Weber, "the bearer of charisma holds his authority in virtue of a mission held to be incarnate in his person" (Weber, 1978, p. 232). That is, the charismatic leader gains authority due to his personal characteristics rather than from his or her position. This idea of authority differs greatly with that established by bureaucracies.

> In contrast with all forms of bureaucratic administrative systems, the charismatic structure recognises no forms or orderly procedures for appointment or dismissal, no "career," no "advancement," no "salary;" there is no organised training either for the bearer of charisma or his aides, no arrangements for supervision or appeal, no allocation of local areas of control or exclusive spheres of competence, and finally no standing institutions comparable to bureaucratic "governing bodies" independent of persons and of their purely personal charisma. (Weber, 1978, p. 227).

Charismatic leadership differs significantly from the other two forms of authority; however, Weber pointed out an interesting paradox. In order for charismatic authority to continue, it must "routinize itself." This can occur in one of two ways. In the first, the charisma is passed down from the leader to someone s/he designates as his or her successor (Weber, 1968). This typically occurs along hereditary lines and is therefore similar to traditional authority.

The second means of institutionalizing charisma occurs when the charisma becomes attached to the office rather than to the individual. When this occurs, incumbents to the office are afforded the same authority that had been given to the charismatic leader. Eventually, a bureaucratic order develops, and authority depends on a legal-rational basis (Weber, 1968). In theory this legal-rational basis should eliminate the practices of nepotism and favoritism by superiors in terms of hiring and promotion; Weber thought this might reduce alienation.

Although Weber described each of these types of authority as distinct from one another, he recognized that in reality this is not the case. Actual examples of authority are almost always combinations of the different types of authority. It is for this reason that Wrong (1970) proposes that Weber's three types "are better put to use in examining societies in terms of their transitions from one form to another rather than their relative conformity to one or another of these types" (as cited in Hilbert, 1987, p. 83).

Contemporary Scholarship

Contemporary feminist Kathy E. Ferguson (1984) challenged the ideal aspects of bureaucracy as not only dehumanizing but specifically as "a primary source of the oppression of women and men" (p. ix). Ferguson challenges the very core of bureaucracy through its assigned characteristics. For example, the ideal bureaucracy is based on stringent rules; those rules can be reified to the point that they seem like immutable laws rather than rules generated by and for the organization and its members. Law-like rules alienate individuals who feel like they have no power to alter the circumstances. Second, Ferguson argues that the hierarchal arrangement of the bureaucracy *reproduces subtle forms of domination.* For example, welfare clients are far too often painted as incompetent, subordinate individuals, and case workers may suffer the same fate when viewed from their supervisor's position. Third, bureaucracies have a tendency to *normalize* people. Foucault (1979, 1978/1990) addressed this in several of his works, and Ferguson draws from his discussions about the subject. For example, clients in government programs become *cases*, and students in public schools and universities become *numbers,* all of whom should fit a certain expected profile. Clients and students are expected to behave in certain ways, ways that fit within the normal. Deviance from the norm, even if it is creative, is usually seen as disruptive. Fourth, Ferguson points out that although bureaucracies were intended to be efficient, they have become bogged down with *red tape* and spend an inordinate amount of time *perpetuating themselves.* Finally, because bureaucracies are so large, people get lost in them; they become isolated and alienated within the crowd of bureaucratic members, the flood of rules, and the avalanche of paperwork. In short, what the ideal bureaucracy was meant to alleviate has actually intensified.

In addition to these general problems, Ferguson (1984) sees bureaucracies as *feminizing.* Here Ferguson, is suggesting that in bureaucracies "the political consequences of male dominance are such that women learn the role of the subordinate" (p. 94). Sadly, too many women take on this subordinate role (as do many men who have lower organizational status). They internalize an image of themselves and act accordingly. Bureaucracies feed this subordinate, inferior, construction of women, and to a certain extent men, and perpetuate control over these organizational participants.

One final area that scholars are exploring related to bureaucracy is the promotion of an impersonal approach to hiring, firing, organizing, and treating employees. Weber encouraged impersonalization in order to end nepotism and other forms of favoritism. However, scholars today argue that bureaucracies have gone too far in their quest for impersonalization. Ferguson (1984) provided an example of flight attendants who depersonalized "themselves from their work as a defense against being swallowed by it, only to suffer from a sense of being false, mechanical, no longer a whole integrated self" (p. 54). Hochschild (1983) discussed how employees' emotions are kept under control through coercive work rules; Ritzer (2004) pointed to a similar phenomenon's happening through workplace technology, as in the drive-through window's controlling the behavior of workers. They become mechanical robots, he argued. Whether it is emotions (also see Mumby & Putnam, 1992) or behaviors, the discursive and technological practices of the workplace today continue to alienate employees.

Ferguson (1994) points out that this type of subordination through non-democratic organizational practices silenced not only women but also minorities. She called for more studies of "language, politics, and subjectivity," "diversities and inequalities," and "democratic practices" (p. 81). Promoting a possible solution to the vagaries of bureaucracy, Ferguson (1984) notes that "political theory can be transformative . . . to rethink our lives, reshape our possibilities, and resist the official definition of reality" (Ferguson, 1984, p. x).

Ferguson (1984, 1994) is not alone in her criticism of bureaucracy. Barker (1993) and Barker and Cheney (1994) provide a postmodern critique of the iron cage. They argue that Weber's fear that workers would internalize the controlling order of the bureaucracy has come true and is best explained through a Foucauldian analysis. After observing workers who were *empowered* to supervise themselves, Barker discovered that the employees enacted stricter discipline on themselves than supervisors had in the past. They disciplined one another in a Foucauldian sense of the term, behaving as if they were still under the watchful eye of a supervisor and made few to no allowances for workers with special circumstances. Foucault (1975/1979) described this behavior according to Bentham's panopticon where prisoners placed in cells could be viewed by guards from a central tower, but the prisoners could not see whether a guard was in the station or not. Eventually the prisoners would behave as if a guard were always present.

In hope of developing a less alienating form of organization, Weber argued on behalf of the ideal bureaucracy. Ending capriciousness and nepotism of past tyrannical behavior in dictatorial organizations encouraged Weber to detail the ideal bureaucracy. However, these same practices intended to reduce alienation have ironically perpetuated it. His observations of bureaucracy and authority allowed contemporary scholars to interpret modern organizations in ways that speak to the sacrifice of humanity for efficiency. Nevertheless, he clearly identified characteristics of bureaucracies that have held true for nearly a century and some that have indeed promoted certain types of organizational success.

Chapter Eleven

Frederick Winslow Taylor

The Father of Scientific Management

Introduction

Antagonism between workers and management escalated in the late 1800s and early 1900s, which begged action. At the same time, the scientific method increased in popularity, both in the United States and England. Seeing the possibilities, Frederick Winslow Taylor applied science to work management, resulting in a method commonly known today as scientific management. Scientific management proved to be an effective method that brought workplace efficiency to heights never before known. It also changed the workplace to an even grimmer place for workers who lost what little independence and freedom they had in the past if, indeed, they were able to keep their jobs at all. While production increased and costs went down, unemployment rose. The methods that Taylor ushered into the workplace are considered nothing short of genius by some and more than disturbing to others.

Biography

On March 20, 1856, Frederick Winslow Taylor was born into a wealthy upper-class family. His father, Frederick Taylor, a lawyer, and his mother, Emily Winslow, an abolitionist and feminist, were members of Quaker merchant families. Despite their independent wealth, the Taylor family lived a fairly simple life in Germantown (now a section of Philadelphia), Pennsylvania. The parents valued a moderate life-style in terms of materialism and promoted education and intellectual pursuits for their children (Wrege & Greenwood, 1991). Although this brief description of Taylor's early life is undisputed, Wrege and Greenwood (1991) explain that much of the later biographical material about Taylor is exaggerated or "erroneous" (p. 1) because "Mrs. Taylor [his wife], along with the Frederick W. Taylor Cooperatives [controllers of the estate] . . . desired a book that would glorify Taylor's life" (p. 1). One early biographer Frank B. Copley attempted to provide a balanced portrait, according to Wrege and Greenwood, but his efforts were derailed, and the location of the original manuscript is unknown.

It is believed that in school, Taylor excelled at math and sports. At least one source suggests that he combined these two talents in 1881 when he won the U.S. Lawn Tennis Association doubles championship using a patented spoon-shaped racket that he personally designed (Papesh, n.d.,); however, Wrege and Greenwood (1991) found newspaper reports that suggest he and his partner did well but did not necessarily win the tournament and although he did have a patent for a "scoop-handle tennis racket" (p. 125) it is not clear whether he used it at the match. The *New York Times* credits him with winning the tennis match in its obituary of Taylor (F.W. Taylor, 1915), but it is not clear on what source the *Times* relied. In short, some "facts" about his life have been questioned. Nevertheless, the multiple sources combine to give a general impression Taylor's life.

Although Taylor came from a wealthy family and was expected to uphold the Taylor family name by attending Harvard, after a year at Phillips Exeter Academy, a leading prep school he chose not to go to Harvard. At least one biographer attributes this choice to "poor health and eye problems. . . . The family feared that he might actually go blind if he were to try the rigorous studies of a Harvard education" (Wrege & Greenwood, 1991, p. 6). In his own words, Taylor claims to have "graduated at Phillips Exeter in 1874 and entered Harvard College in the same year. I started to serve my apprenticeship as a pattern maker in 1874, and during the years between 1874 and 1878 completed my apprenticeship" (as cited in Wrege & Greenwood, p. 7). Taylor undertook a four-year apprenticeship as a pattern maker and a machinist at Enterprise Hydraulic Works in Philadelphia where he cultivated quite a talent for swearing that would continue throughout his life. He liked to use swear words at the most unexpected of times; for example, rather than "swear on the golf course" he would "swear when lecturing at Harvard" (Wrege & Greenwood, p. 222). In 1878 he accepted employment at the Midvale Steel Company. Over the next four years Taylor worked as "a laborer, machinist, gang boss, assistant foreman, and foreman of the machine shop" (Wrege & Greenwood, p. 7). In addition, during this time he took "a home study course in mathematics and physics" (p. 34) offered by a Harvard professor. This course sparked further interest in education and Taylor devoted his spare hours to studying for and receiving his "Mechanical Engineering degree from Stevens Institute of Technology in Hoboken, New Jersey" (p. 34).

Although Taylor's early career choices may have seemed mysterious to his parents, who hoped he would become a lawyer, the young engineer, whether he realized it or not, gathered the knowledge for what would be the foundation of his famous theory during those early years. While at Midvale Steel Company, Taylor observed the factory's inefficiency. He also noticed the carelessness and sloppiness of skilled workers on the job. By studying how long it took each worker to complete a step, as well as the quantity of work produced by that worker, Taylor hoped he could find the potential productivity of workers under optimal conditions. Dissatisfied with the status quo, he began to find ways to motivate the workers around him to be more productive (Jersey & Schwarz, 1994). At a time when most workers were paid very little, Taylor's objective was to find the most efficient way to perform tasks without aggravating tensions between the owners and the workers, although any goal of good labor relations has been disputed based primarily on the methods he employed (Kanigel, 1997).

Taylor's methods included the use of time and motion studies to set daily production quotas with his stopwatch in hand. Timing workers down to the fraction of a second, Taylor aimed to find efficient methods that he claimed would benefit both workers and the company owner. Workers would get paid by reaching their daily goal. Those who did not reach their daily goal received a significantly lower amount of money for that day's work. As a result of his time and motion studies, Taylor doubled productivity and created a new wage scheme, but he also contributed to massive layoffs by company owners. By 1890, when Taylor was age thirty-four, his innovations and productivity improvements were gaining widespread attention in the manufacturing community (Greco, 1999); they were also gaining widespread criticism (Kanigel, 1997).

At age thirty-seven, Taylor became a consulting engineer. As a consultant, he worked with such companies as the Simonds Roller Bearing Company and Bethlehem Steel Company. Taylor's contributions at Bethlehem Steel included the development of the functional foreman system, the institution of time-and-motion studies that dramatically increased productivity, and the development of a high-speed metal cutting process that was dependent on heating steel to the "breaking-down point" and also increased production. Taylor's obituary reports that he received the "Gold Medal from the Paris Exposition of 1900 for the Taylor-White process for treating high-speed steel tools" (F.W. Taylor, 1915, n.p.). What this obituary doesn't mention is that the patent came under attack and after a lengthy court trial Taylor and White lost the patent because the process had been in practice elsewhere for some time (Wrege & Greenwood, 1991). Taylor's new management techniques also created controversy at Bethlehem Steel and beyond. Many employees voiced concerns over the reduction of the yard force population. In addition, Taylor's firing of 85 of the 120 workers at Simonds caused many of his critics to believe his methods too harsh, causing people to either lose their jobs or become automatons. In spite of his achievements, and perhaps due to the surrounding controversies, Taylor's contract with Bethlehem Steel was terminated in May of 1901 (Wrege & Greenwood, 1991).

Shortly thereafter, Taylor decided to formally introduce his ideas on scientific management. He wrote a paper titled *A Piece-Rate System, Being a Step toward Partial Solution of the Labor Problem*. In 1903, Taylor presented this paper at the biannual meeting of the American Society of Mechanical Engineers in Detroit. Also around this time, Taylor (1911) wrote and published his famous book *The Principles of Scientific Management* on the subject of efficiency through time and motion studies and his new form of organization. The best seller was immediately translated into ten different languages (Greco, 1999). Although management praised the book, workers took the system to task. A strike in 1911 forced the government to investigate the use of time-motion studies in factories. The American Federation of Labor condemned the practice and Congress held hearings. Although private owners of factories were left unscathed, "Congress banned time and motion study methods from government factories in 1915," according to Taylor's obituary in the *New York Times* (F.W. Taylor, 1915, n.p.).

By 1910, Taylor's health had began to deteriorate. Several factors contributed to his declining condition. First, his wife's health deteriorated as she suffered serious bouts of depression. Second, social responsibility surfaced and became a matter of concern in the engineering societies, most of which saw Taylor's methods as questionable in this regard. His appearances before Congress were likely quite stressful. "By 1914, Taylor was emotionally and physically exhausted" (Wrege & Greenwood, 1991, p. 231). He managed to complete one last speaking tour through Ohio before succumbing to a cough that turned into a bronchial condition. In 1915, at the age of fifty-nine, he died of pneumonia. His gravestone includes the title, "Father of Scientific Management" (Wrege & Greenwood).

The Philosophy and Rhetoric of Work

Frederick Taylor and his theories are so widely known throughout business communities that his theory of scientific management is sometimes referred to simply as Taylorism. By the early 1920s, Taylor's theories had gained worldwide notoriety, reaching not only across the United States but also such places as Germany, Italy, and France. Lenin urged the Soviets to introduce Taylorism in Russia after he read one of Taylor's books, *Shop Management*, and Mussolini personally welcomed Taylor's ideas into Italy's congress in Rome (Beissinger, 1988). From this widespread attention, then, it is no wonder that Frederick W. Taylor became known as the Father of Scientific Management (Kanigel, 1996). However, his name also became synonymous with the word *strike*. Although Taylor (1911) claimed that no strike ever occurred where he instituted scientific management, violent protests and strikes did indeed revolve around the use of his method in the United States, France, and Russia (Beissinger, 1988). The method was without a doubt unique and controversial.

Taylor discovered a need for a more scientific method of work while employed at Midvale Company. He realized the vast inefficiency of the workers on the job could be defined through observation and eliminated through a scientific approach. There are two sources of this inefficiency, according to Taylor. The first is the worker's natural tendency to do as little work as possible, and the second is the propensity for the group of workers to control the output, slowing work to an easy pace. Deliberately working slowly to avoid doing a full day's work is referred to as "soldiering" in this country and "hanging out" in England (Taylor, 1911, p. 13). Taylor found these types of under-utilization of the workers unacceptable. There is natural and systematic soldiering, which according to Taylor, "powerfully affects the wages, the prosperity, and the life of almost every working-man, and also quite as much the prosperity of every industrial establishment in the nation" (Taylor, 1911, p. 14). Eliminating soldiering would provide a twofold benefit. First, for the organization, a more productive worker would mean lowering the cost of production and doubling its output. Second, for the employee, a more productive working environment would mean higher wages, better working conditions, and possibly a shorter work day. In sum, Taylor saw the potential for maximum prosperity for the company and maximum prosperity for the worker. Taylor proposed that to end soldiering and motivate workers to maximum efficiency, the organization had to be run scientifically. In the introduction to *The Principles of Scientific Management*, Taylor states, "In the past the man has been first, in the future the system must be first" (Taylor, 1911, p. 7).

Taylor's (1911) scientific management theory can be summarized in four basic principles, the first of which is that there is one best way to do a job. The one best way is determined through scientific analysis and requires workers to perform a task in the most efficient way possible. In Taylor's opinion, each element of a worker's work could be crafted down to a science to replace the old rule-of-thumb methods. The goal was efficiency, and any sort of wasted time and effort hindered an efficient process. Taylor's method prescribed clockwork, timing tasks down to the second.

Second, Taylor called for the scientific selection of personnel. Taylor believed that employers should choose and assign people their tasks according to their skills. Instead of allowing workers to choose and train themselves on their own tasks, Taylor believed that this process also should be perfected based on scientific principles. Adding to the notion of worker efficiency and productivity, Taylor believed it was essential literally to find the right person for the job. Finding the right challenge for each person would increase output due to the workers' being assigned to tasks for which they were best suited. Management should assume this responsibility. According to Taylor (1911), it is management's duty to study the workers individually in order to fully understand their capabilities and, thus, their potential. Then managers should set about to systematically teach and train the workers in the best way to approach their jobs. All of this according to management's design as assessed through scientific means.

With respect to selecting the appropriate person, it should also be noted that Taylor described the common laborer as "so stupid and so phlegmatic that he more nearly resembles in his mental make-up the ox" (p. 59). He described female workers as girls, when they might well have been women, who like "children" need "an actual reward . . . as often as once an hour" (p. 94). Although Taylor considered most of the workers "stupid" (pp. 59, 62, 63), he assured his reader that scientific management would work equally well for educated mechanics.

The third of Taylor's (1911) principles declares that workers should be paid directly for the work that they produce. Taylor thought an incentive plan would be more appropriate than an hourly wage because he thought workers would produce more if they were paid accordingly. Instead of paying workers futile bonuses, the incentives should be based on efficiency. Those who completed the work would be paid more, and those who fell short would not get as much of an incentive, he explained. In this regard, Taylor thought that workers would be motivated by the amount of monetary reward they would receive. Again, there is a matter to note; Taylor wrote, "Doubtless some of those who are especially interested in working men will complain because under scientific management the workman, when he is shown how to do twice as much work . . . is not paid twice his former wages" (p. 135). Taylor, without providing even anecdotal evidence, assures his readers that if workers are paid too much they will become lazy again and engage in unhealthy pursuits. Besides, if the worker were paid too much, then costs would go up and the economy would be threatened, which would be unfair to "the whole people—the consumers" (p. 136).

Last, Taylor (1911) believed cooperation between workers and management could be achieved if managers planned the work and workers followed the plan. Intimate and friendly relationships between management and workers could be brought about through scientific management and would lead to prosperity for all. Specifically, Taylor notes that "close, intimate, personal cooperation between the management and the men is of the essence of modern scientific or task management" (p. 26). In Taylor's principles, the establishment's actual work should be divided almost equally between workers and management (Taylor, 1911). Instead of the workers' being primarily responsible for most of the work, it should be divided in almost equal shares. Each group (workers and management) should take over the work for which it is best fitted. More accurately dividing and sharing the work reduces the likelihood of unfriendly relations between workers and management. However, it should be noted that Taylor's idea of shared work meant that managers (sometimes called *teachers* or *bosses*) would plan the work, time the worker, and create a work schedule; that is, managers should take care of "preparatory acts" (p. 26). Taylor was rapidly promoted by management, but faced threats from workers (Wrege & Greenwood, 1991).

This idea of division and cooperation between workers and management is further developed in Taylor's "task management" idea. Just as a teacher would give a class of students a clear-cut lesson plan stating what each child would be required to learn or accomplish, so must the manager treat workers. According to Taylor (1911), workers are all "grown-up children" (p. 120) and so will perform to the greatest satisfaction of everyone involved when given a definite task to be completed in a definite amount of time. The work of every worker is planned at least one day in advance by the management in the planning department. Each worker is then given detailed written instructions describing the task to be completed and how to accomplish that task. These instructions are the result of the combined work of a team of planning department members, each of whom is a specialist. Together, these planners have analyzed the best way for each job to be done and so have created a format for the workers to follow. "One of these teachers (called the inspector)" assures that the worker understands the job; "The second teacher (the gang boss)" trains the worker on the machine; "The third (the speed boss)" times the worker (p. 124). If agitation arises from some workers' saying, "I am not allowed to think or move without someone interfering or doing it for me" (p. 125), then "enforced cooperation" should rule the day (p. 83).

Some texts note that Taylor's methods resulted in massive layoffs (Spiker & Daniels, 1987). This may be a gross understatement, for massive layoffs not only resulted due to scientific management but were actually a planned part of scientific management. Scientific management was and is much more than the reorganization of job processes; it is a "philosophy in industrial management" (Taylor, 1911, p. 114). For example, a less often shared story from Taylor's book recounts how he introduced scientific management at the bicycle ball-bearing factory. Originally, 120 women and girls worked at the ball-bearing factory, inspecting the little balls of steel by placing them on the backs of their hands and rolling them in the knuckle valleys between the tendons. They did this work ten and a half-hours a day, at least five and a half days a week. Taylor offered the most talented workers a chance to help persuade the others to change their work hours to only ten hours a day. Oddly enough, the girls said they preferred not to change. It would seem that Taylor's reputation preceded him. Thus, he had to campaign for them to shorten the day, and then he let the workers vote on whether they wanted a shorter workday. He considered this the most tactful approach under the circumstances. The vote came back a resounding *no*. Thus, the situation called for *enforced cooperation*. Taylor shortened their workday against their wishes, first to ten hours and eventually to eight and a half hours. He then selected the most coordinated workers and dismissed 85 of the 120 as not suited to this kind of work. With the remaining 35 workers Taylor instituted the shortened day, increased pay, added systematic rest periods, and separated the workers so that they could not speak to each other during the workday. Output increased, quality improved, and pay was better, at least for those who had a job.

Taylor was famous for threatening to fire and for actually firing those workers who did not cooperate or who did not work fast enough or meet the criteria for selection. He considered this necessary for scientific management to succeed and, in turn, for the betterment of society as a whole. Taylor (1911) notes, "each man has been systematically trained to his highest state of efficiency, . . . he has acquired a friendly mental attitude toward his employers. [He no longer spends his time] in criticism, suspicious watchfulness and sometimes in open warfare" with his employer (p. 144). Is this not the solution that both America and England have been seeking, Taylor asked in the conclusion of the book.

Although Taylor's scientific management clearly had a positive impact on production, its impact on workers has received mixed reviews. Concerning their employability, the majority of workers lose their jobs when Taylorism is introduced. With respect to work conditions, having shorter days and higher pay is hard to complain about, but being turned into an automaton is worth objection. Taylor's insight, mathematical abilities, and powers of keen observation can be appreciated, and his creative solution to each individual task certainly has merit. Yet the outcome for many workers was the loss of their jobs.

Contemporary Scholarship

Although Taylorism was first introduced more than a century ago, its basic underlying principles have proven to be timeless. The elements of scientific management continue in many of today's factories and are applied to nonphysical tasks as well. Employee selection, high work standards, management research, and special employee bonuses are just some of the enduring concepts of Taylor's scientific management principles.

In fact, companies such as Pic 'n Pay Stores and Toyota presently apply some of Taylor's employee selection procedures. Many human resource publications contain articles about standardized employee selection methods based today on computerized programs. "In an effort to combat high employee turnover, Pic 'n Pay Stores has centralized its employee selection process with the help of a computer-hosted interview" (Robins, 1994, p. 34–35). The desire to hire dependable and productive employees remains an important element at any company.

Toyota is another well-known company that values having the best employees and uses many of Taylor's principles in its hiring process. At Toyota's Kentucky facilities, only one applicant in about thirty even makes it to an interview. The interview is then conducted by a panel representing a variety of Toyota departments. Personnel manager Dewey Crawford says that by then, "we're going to know more about these people than perhaps any company has ever known about people" (Butler, 1991, p. 23).

Toyota uses extensive testing to reduce the likelihood of hiring an incompetent person. A person applying for the lowest paying job on the shop floor goes through approximately 14 hours of testing. The tests are administered by state employment offices and Kentucky State University on behalf of the Toyota Company. The tests usually cover basics such as math skills, reading, and manual dexterity. Some tests include workplace simulations, with the intent of being a final check as to whether the company and those who are being trained are really right for each other (Butler, 1991).

The General Motors Company also has implemented some of Taylor's principles of employee selection and team performance. Of course, GM obviously uses scientific management to coordinate its assembly line work, but now it utilizes scientific management in other personnel related areas. GM recently implemented a program in which it ranked its employees against each other, grading on a curve. Management was asked to pick the top 10 percent, the next 25 percent, the next 55 percent, and the bottom 10 percent of their group. They then had to enforce pay differences between the categories, with specifications left up to individual managers. In the same way, GM set up a "recognition award" fund to be given to the company's highest performers regardless of their salaries. This plan was implemented in order to encourage better cooperation between coworkers, with the rewards stemming from overall team performance (Butler, 1991).

Taylor's ideas on basing higher wages and incentives on piecework also continue to be practiced in organizations today. At the Lincoln Electric Company in Cleveland, Ohio, piecework, combined with high wages, has been an overwhelming success since 1934: "About 90 percent of Lincoln's production workers are paid on a piece-work basis. Lincoln Electric's piece-work system, however, is rare—it works. It works for several reasons, not the least of which is a strong trust between shop-floor employees and management" (Chilton, 1993, pp. 23–30). And although Lincoln is listed with companies that have benefited from Taylorism, they also ushered in the Scanlon plan. The Scanlon plan, developed by union leader Joe Scanlon, promotes participation of workers in management and production. The workers in turn are rewarded handsomely for their contributions to the workplace (see Rogers & Agarwala-Rogers, 1976).

At the other end of the controversy, Ritzer (2004) points to the downside of Taylor's scientific management. Specifically, Ritzer argues that

> Like all rational systems, scientific management had its irrationalities. Above all, it was a dehumanizing system in which people were considered expendable and treated as such. Furthermore, because workers did only one or a few tasks, most of their skills and abilities remained unused. This had drastic consequences, and by the 1980s, American industry found itself outstripped by Japanese industry. (p. 32)

Ritzer considers scientific management the precursor of today's McDonaldization of the world and the global spread of the philosophy that there is one way to be, one way to act, and one way to flip a hamburger. Taylor's philosophy placed emphasis on efficiency, effectiveness, and predictability, all of which are found at McDonald's but not without some dehumanization.

It is no surprise that the management principles Frederick Taylor set in motion so many years ago still seem surprisingly current. Despite the controversy, scientific management continues to have an impact on management practices and worker job design. Over 100 years old, scientific management remains viable and controversial today.

Chapter Twelve

Mary Parker Follett

Ahead of Her Time

Introduction

During the age of scientific management, a new method of organizing business emerged from the writings of Mary Parker Follett. Follett's background in
economics, philosophy, and rhetorical politics influenced her perspective. She
advocated a more holistic approach to management than her contemporaries
(Parker, 1984). Specifically, Follett favored a democratic style of organization
grounded in communication.

Parker (1984) argues that Follett is commonly overlooked as one of the
early management writers, although she contributed significantly to the development of general system theory and the human relations movement. This
neglect may be due to the novelty of her writings, which could not be classified
within a particular school of thought at the time they were written. Even now,
textbooks commonly list her contributions under the rubric of eclectic theories
(e.g., see Daniels & Spiker, 1987, p. 52). "Chronologically, Follett belonged to the
scientific management era; philosophically and intellectually, she was a member
of the social man era" (Parker, 1984, p. 325). It seems Follett was years ahead of
her time because many of her views did not become commonly accepted until
the 1960s (Parker, 1984).

Biography

Mary Parker Follett was born to a Quaker family in 1868 in Quincy, Massachusetts. Her father died when she was in her teens, and because her mother was

an invalid, she took over responsibility for the family (Horne, 1997). In 1892, she began attending Radcliffe College, the women's branch of Harvard (Shapiro, 1996). She graduated summa cum laude six years later with a degree in economics, government, law, and philosophy (Horne, 1997). While still in college, Follett published her first book, *The Speaker of the House of Representatives*, in which she examined the traits and characteristics of successful office holders. Studying the elements of the persuasive speeches of politicians led her to develop a theory of communication and management that she hoped would be superior to the persuasive forms of rhetoric emphasized at the time.

Fox and Urwick (1973) suggest that Follett's study of the House of Representatives may have contributed to her later theories:

> It also presents an interesting contrast to her later work, in which she doggedly rejected the techniques of persuasion, compromise and pressure which normally figure so large in the legislative process, and shows that her later position did not stem from a naïve lack of appreciation for the way these techniques operate. (p. xi)

To the point, Mary Parker Follett was well informed as she proposed a communication theory grounded in participation through dialogue and democracy.

Following her graduation from Radcliffe Follett entered graduate studies in Paris, where she remained until 1900 (Parker, 1984). Upon returning to the United States, Follett dedicated her time to social work in the Roxbury neighborhood of Boston. During this time, she assisted in the formation of numerous social centers in and around Boston. She served on the Massachusetts Minimum Wage Board and became the vice president of the National Community Center Association.

In 1924, Follett wrote a book entitled *Creative Experience* in which she used the experiences she had gained through her social and administrative work to address management theory (Horne, 1997). Following this publication, she became recognized as an authority on business administration in addition to political science (Parker, 1984).

In January 1926, Follett suffered the loss of her dear friend and lifelong companion, Isobel Briggs. From 1929 to 1933, she lived in England and focused her attention on English industrial conditions. Upon returning to the United States to attend to personal business, she fell ill. Mary Parker Follett died on December 18, 1933, at the age of 65. "Her ashes were taken to a daisy field in Putney, Vermont, where she and Miss Briggs had had a summer home and which had, through the years, been for her a favorite place to relax with friends for the kind of pleasant, inquiring and stimulating conversation that was so much a part of her life" (Fox & Urwick, 1973, p. xxii).

As suggested earlier, it should be noted that in many respects, Mary Parker Follett was ahead of her time. She wrote during the age of scientific management, and her works precede both the human relations movement and systems theory. While Frederick Winslow Taylor and Henri Fayol were gaining popularity for their emphasis on using science to ensure effectiveness and on viewing employees as *cogs in the machine*, Follett emphasized the human nature of employees. "She was a pioneer in her emphasis on the 'human factor' in management" (Sethi, 1962, p. 215). Follett viewed an organization as more of an organism than a machine, and she believed that the whole is greater than the sum of its parts (Sethi, 1962). Although Sethi highlights Follett as the forerunner of a system approach, a human relations approach, and a human resources approach, others see her contributions as related more to a theory of organizational democracy.

Philosophy and Rhetoric of Work

Mary Parker Follett addressed the issue of conflict in several of her essays and speeches. Although many people view conflict as negative and something to be avoided at all costs, Follett argued that conflict is neither positive nor negative but rather the "appearance of differences" (Follett, 1940/1973, p. 1). When there are differences of opinion or of interests, conflict often ensues.

Follett identified three methods of dealing with conflict: domination, compromise, and integration (Follett, 1940/1973). In domination, one side "wins" and obtains its wants while the other "loses." According to Follett, the ultimate example of this is war (Follett, 1940/1973). The second means of dealing with conflict, compromise, is commonly recognized to be the best way to deal with differences. However, Follett disagreed with this generally accepted belief. She wrote, "If we get only compromise, the conflict will come up again and again in some other form, for in compromise we give up part of our desire, and because we shall not be content to rest there, sometime we shall try to get the whole of our desire" (Follett, 1940/1973, p. 6). Furthermore, Follett argued that compromise is inefficient and detrimental to open communication. For example, consider a dispute over the wages of factory workers. Those people representing the factory workers will initially ask for more of a raise than they want, expecting to lower their request as part of the compromise. The representatives of the company will offer less money than they are in fact willing to give, knowing that they will have to raise the amount as part of the compromise. Under this system, neither group ever knows for certain exactly what the other truly wants.

For these reasons, Follett advocated the use of a third method of dealing with conflict: integration. Under integration, a creative solution is found in which neither side has to sacrifice its wants and both desires have a place (Follett, 1940/1973). "Integration involves invention, and the clever thing is to recognize this, and not to let one's thinking stay within the boundaries of two alternatives which are mutually exclusive" (Follett, 1940/1973, p. 4). It is important to recognize that many disputes are not merely "either-or" situations and that another possibility may satisfy both parties' desires.

To achieve integration, Follett emphasized the need to reconceptualize business's ideas of power. Integration of competing interests requires shared power rather than one person's controlling another. "Whereas power usually means power-over, the power of some person or group over some other person or group, it is possible to develop the conception of power-with, a jointly developed power, a co-active, not a coercive power" (Follett, 1940/1973, p. 72).

Follett believed that the key to achieving "power-with" is participation. She makes a clear distinction between consent and participation. Voting is an example of showing consent and does not allow for genuine participation. It only allows for a group to give approval to the decisions of others. According to Follett,

> We cannot obtain genuine consent by a vote any more than you can *declare* peace. . . . Peace is a process and an attainment. In the same way, genuine agreement is part of a slow process of the interweaving of many activities and this is not consent but participation. (Follett, 1940/1973, p. 176)

Participation is ongoing and much more effective than mere consent because it allows for actual agreement. With participation, related thinking occurs, whereas voting merely registers people's previously formed opinions (Follett, 1940/1973, p. 187).

Follett argued that participation depends on understanding and coordination. She uses the example of a foreman's consulting with employees before implementing any new procedures to demonstrate the necessity of these two principles. In doing this, the foreman receives feedback and suggestions from the workers and can also work to prevent resistance. Furthermore, the workers have the opportunity to see the foreman's challenges and the difficulties connected with managing the plant (Follett, 1940/1973). In this instance, both sides gain understanding of the other's opinions and desires. Furthermore, coordination is attained as both sides work together to find a solution.

In contrast to scientific management, Follett argued that "you may bring together all the parts of a machine, but you do not have the *machine* until they are properly related. The chief task of organization is how to relate the parts so that you have a working unit" (Follett, 1940/1973, p. 177). The key to uniting the different parts of the organization is the active participation of all employees through coordination.

Follett believed that this coordination needs to begin at the lowest levels of the organization, as in the example of the foreman and workers, and work its way to the top of the company. When department heads meet, each one brings a separate view of the organization as a whole. However, because they are all actively participating in the decisions of the company, Follett concluded that they will see what is best for the company rather than what is best for them individually. As problems arise, by working together to do what is in the best interest of the company the different department heads will reach not only the best solution but also a solution that leaves each of them satisfied (Follett, 1940/1973).

Follett told the story of a workman who explained how successful coordination improved communication in his company: "You don't go into a conference committee with a gun under your coat, and that does away with suspicion, for when a man has a gun under his coat, he always thinks the other fellow has two under his" (Follett, 1940/1973, p. 47). When people are focused on the good of the company, which is the result of successful participation, there is less distrust between different sides, and significantly more can be accomplished.

Follett referred to this idea as collective responsibility. Unlike scientific management, which divides work so each person is responsible for the part of the work that he or she is best at, collective responsibility argues that everyone is responsible for all aspects of the organization.

A key to achieving collective responsibility is to recognize that every employee has authority, not simply those in management positions. Follett believes that authority does not rest with individuals but rather within a particular job. Therefore, the president does not have authority over everyone; he or she merely has the authority that lies within his or her position. "The dispatch clerk has more authority in dispatching work than the president" (Follett, 1940/1973, p. 118). Because each employee's ultimate goal is to accomplish the job, the job rules overall. Follett refers to this concept as the "law of the situation." The unique circumstances of a given situation dictate what needs to be done rather than the organization's hierarchy (Parker, 1984).

Although individuals cannot possess authority, they can hold leadership positions. Follett described three aspects of leadership: leadership of position, leadership of personality, and leadership of function (Sethi, 1962). The first of these, leadership of position, is perhaps what many people first think of when considering leadership within an organization; that is, the chief executive of the company as the leader. Follett believed that the chief executive's main job is the coordination of the organization and that this can only be achieved by clearly defining the business's overall purpose. "The chief executive should be able to define the purpose of the plant at any one minute, or rather, the whole complex of purposes" (Follett, 1940/1973, p. 226). Furthermore, in order to maintain coordination within the organization, the chief executive must work to foster cooperation rather than obedience. He or she needs to recognize that employees are working with, not under, him or her (Davis, 1997).

The second aspect of leadership, leadership of personality, Follett believed to be the least important. This is based on the idea that leaders have inherent traits, such as assertiveness, that predetermine them to rise to leadership positions. Instead, Follett argued that knowledge is significantly more important in leadership than personality (Follett, 1940/1973) and thus believed that the third aspect of leadership, leadership of function, is the most important.

When leadership arises as a result of function, the person with the most knowledge naturally ascends to the role of leader. "Different situations require different kinds of knowledge, and the man possessing the knowledge demanded by a certain situation tends in the best managed businesses, and other things being equal, to become the leader at that moment" (Follett, 1940/1973, p. 242). Follett describes an interesting example of the leadership of function concerning the undersecretaries in England. Although members of the Cabinet are appointed with each new administration, the undersecretaries to these members are permanent officials. Thus, the undersecretaries often have more knowledge of their offices and affairs than the Cabinet members, and therefore, they often determine important decisions.

Follett (1940/1973) suggested that in many respects the success of a business depends upon its organization's being flexible and coordinated enough that the leadership of function can operate freely. This allows those people with the knowledge of a particular situation to control the situation. Thus, the job is accomplished in the best possible way, and the organization as a whole benefits.

Contemporary Scholarship

An example of an empowering organization, as Mary Parker Follett envisioned, can be found in the plants of W. L. Gore & Associates. Rather than the traditional pyramid structure used by the majority of organizations, Bill Gore has established a "lattice organization." "As he defines it, a lattice organization means 'one-on-one communication' with whomever you need to talk to in order to get a job done" (Pacanowsky, 1988, p. 357). There is no fixed authority; instead, leadership evolves over time and adapts to meet specific problems. Tasks come about through personally developed commitments rather than through formal job descriptions and assignments.

Pacanowsky (1988) gives an example of the decentralized nature of Gore's practices. The committee in charge of the associate stock ownership plan (ASOP) had issued a memo to all associates announcing a change in the operating practice of the ASOP. Because a majority of associates did not understand the memo, a group of associates formed an ad hoc committee to determine how the details of the ASOP could be better communicated.

At their first meeting, Pacanowsky (1988) proposed that the group ask associates precisely what they wanted to know before going to the ASOP committee to determine exactly what they were trying to explain. The group agreed and quickly developed a plan to establish focus groups of associates to determine what needed to be communicated. Within two weeks, the ad hoc committee was able to go to the ASOP committee to obtain the answers associates were seeking.

This demonstrates the freedom that associates have to solve the problems they encounter in the organization. While working in a traditional hierarchical organization, Gore observed that the majority of workplace communication took place through informal channels. Therefore, when establishing his own organization, he decided to "free up the informal system as much as possible by doing away with the formal system. Thus the lattice" (Pacanowsky, 1988, p. 364). When an associate perceives a problem, he or she is free to communicate with other associates about the problem. They can then choose to form a group to address the problem in the most effective way. This group exemplifies Follett's idea of leadership of function. The person who is most capable of addressing the given problem will naturally rise to the role of leader.

W. L. Gore & Associates also embraces Follett's idea of collective responsibility. One of the company's principles is the "waterline." The waterline is a metaphor that imagines the company as if it were a ship in the ocean and the level where the water reaches the ship is the waterline. If someone drills a hole in the ship and it is above the waterline, then the ship is not in danger, but if a hole is drilled below the waterline, then the ship could sink. Gore encourages his employees to take chances with new ideas, new innovations, but he cautions them to stay above the waterline; that is, they should not let their idea cost too much money or expend so many resources that it might jeopardize the safety of the company. Following this line of thinking, the company policy suggests that "Each of us will consult with appropriate Associates who will share the responsibility of taking any action that has the potential of serious harm to the reputation, success, or survival of the Enterprise" (Pacanowsky, 1988, p. 358). Thus there is the tenet that a crucial decision will not rest upon an individual but instead will be made collectively.

Organizational democracy according to Follett is best achieved through the development of groups that interact, participate, and communicate. At a lecture given in 1928, she said:

> You may wonder why I have talked of government, and of the League of Nations, instead of spending all of my hour on leadership in industry. I have done it deliberately, because it seems to me a fact of very great significance that we are finding the same trend in all these different fields. It reinforces us in our conviction that we are moving in harmony with the deeper and more vital forces of human progress. (Rowntree Lecture Conference, Balliol College, reprinted in Fox & Urwick, 1973, p. xxi)

A contemporary scholar, Jürgen Habermas, who was born the year following Follett's 1928 speech, has devoted his career to promoting an egalitarian workplace. His theory of communication action and the ideal speech act calls for a morally responsible and ethically genuine participative society. Habermas (1984) suggests that "communicants (1) engage each other as persons in some understood relationship (claim of rightness), (2) claim that their assertions are true (claim of truth), and (3) profess truthfulness in their intentions" (p. 99). In short, communicators make assertions, engage each other relationally, and express their feelings. For the ideal speech act to occur, the communicants must be free to engage (equal), capable of making their claims (communicatively competent), and honest in their speech actions (sincere). If dishonesty or inequality prevails, then a true democracy cannot be achieved. Habermas suggests that too often privileged parties (whether they be capitalists, industrialists, or politicians) distort communication, which then closes off real dialogue. Habermas has been named one of the 100 most influential people of the twentieth century by *Time* magazine (Gitlin, 2004). After living through World War II, he has devoted himself to finding ways to end distorted communication, domination, and oppression of people. Like Follett, when invited to speak at Purdue University in October 2004, the Kyoto prize winner chose to speak about the League of Nations. Habermas (2004) began by setting the stage for the birth of the League of Nations as a Kantian project.

The American and French revolutions gave Kant the idea for his "republic of republics." It was too often interpreted as a world republic, but this did not have to be the end condition: "People can be citizens of their own states and members of an international community. Kant never renounced the idea of the World Republic; he was convinced that there would be progress," Habermas explained. Although Kant realized that "the nations were not sufficiently mature," he nevertheless called for a "voluntary federation of states committed to peace," Habermas told the audience.

Approximately 125 years after Kant, the League of Nations was born. Based on Kant's assumptions of a "peaceful character," "free trade," and an ability to "mobilize citizens all over the world" for the protection of one another, the League of Nations set out to negotiate disputes, Habermas said. For Kant, "peace is an implication of legal freedom," yet he was "troubled by the fear, a kind of Foucauldian fear, of normalization." With respect to a world republic, the League of Nations might have calmed that fear because it provided an "alternative to the World Republic," Habermas proposed. That is to say, a world republic could be construed as all countries' having to live under the rule of one world order, whereas a league of nations implied that countries could remain independent yet work in solidarity to achieve peace. The latter seems more acceptable; however, the former has strengths. For instance, if a leading nation refused to participate in the league, the strength of the alliance would be severely damaged, as was the case in the 1940s.

Because the League of Nations lacked the core elements of a fixed nation-state it could not survive the loss of strong members. In large part weakened by the U.S. Senate's refusal to support President Wilson's plan, the League of Nations was dissolved in 1946. Meanwhile reinvigorated as the United Nations at the end of World War II in 1945, the idea of world peace entered international discussions once again. The United Nations set goals to negotiate disputes, "that no one ever be permitted to use war as a means to settle disputes," "fulfill human rights," and address "global problems through compromise."

World Wars I and II were watershed moments in history. The development of the League of Nations and the United Nations, the cold war, and the collapse of the Soviet Union "inspired hope in a New World order." The League of Nations "translated a philosophic idea into a practice. Nineteen-eighteen intellectuals immediately recognized Kant's idea within the League of Nations," but it did not have the strength to withstand the powers of "Italy, Germany, and Japan," nor was it prepared for the horror of the "annihilation of the Jews, . . . their own population and other populations." The international laws that followed World War II "demanded responsibility" and would not tolerate "ambivalence." An international criminal court was established, yet it is "still not recognized by the U.S. and states like Libya," Habermas said wryly, and some audience members laughed or shook their heads at the not so subtle irony.

Habermas spoke of the strength of the United Nations and the advances that it had made over the years, including between 1990 and 1994 when the Security Council authorized "sanctions and peace-keeping interventions in eight cases. Plus, the U.N. has authorized military intervention from Sierra Leone to Afghanistan. There has been a 'materialization of international law,' and those states that violate the international law should [meet sanctions]."

"Don't forget NGOs are playing an important role in these assessments," Habermas said. These assessments are crucial to issues of human rights, ecology, and globalism. "Interventions that don't take place or take place too late . . . [or demonstrate] shameful selectivity" do not meet the goals of the Kantian project. "There are obligations . . . that apply . . . especially to the West due to its colonial history and . . . globalization," Habermas said. He continued, "The U.N. is encountering increasing complications . . . human rights violations. . . . The U.N. can act, but these rights are overshadowed by the armed forces of a particular state," Habermas paused. "Can there still be hope for the constitution of international law? Or does this mark the beginning of the end of international relations, the project of cosmopolitan law?"

Habermas admitted that the "United Nations is in need of reform" and that there are "complex empirical issues" as well as "actual inefficiencies," but he also pointed out that the United States of America is a superpower. With that status, "The U.S., the oldest democracy could—I say *could*—inspire a different [kind of] of ideological hegemony." This would be an order that addresses "international security and human rights, a cosmopolitan order." For this to happen, serious attention must be given to "the global market." Following Kantian morality the markets should be used for good. "Peace cannot be granted by [law or even by right], but through the market. International terrorism cannot be prevented through wars of state." In an aside, Habermas commented that "reducing terrorism to a nuisance" was one of the most intelligent comments he had heard during the 2004 U.S. presidential campaign. Then he continued to argue that military action is not the answer to terrorism and that the markets must meet the people halfway. Habermas is suggesting that markets might provide people with useful life-affirming commodities, such as education or medicine.

"Even if we start from a best-case scenario and describe the purest motives," we have "a well-intended hegemony . . . a government [that] can never be sure [if it acts on] its own interests or [universal] interests." This is "presumptive." Instead, we need "impartial decisions. . . . These are the presuppositions of any legal system—not just the U.N." Habermas called on his audience to be aware of the cognitive dissonance that is posed when democracy is forced on a people. He reiterated that "This cannot be made good just because hegemony has a democracy at home."

Why had Jürgen Habermas chosen to speak on the Kantian project and the League of Nations? Perhaps he provided this lecture to chastise the U.S. for being delinquent in the goals of peace and prosperity and to remind the audience of what Follett had suggested was her reason for speaking of the League of Nations, to reinforce "our conviction that we are moving in harmony with the deeper and more vital forces of human progress" (Follett, 1928/1973, p. xxi). Perhaps Habermas, like Follett, was trying to reach to humanity, for humanity, by reminding people of peace—its worthiness in everyday actions, in organizations, in society, and around the world. Perhaps, each scholar was reminding us of why we work.

Mary Parker Follett's education in economics and philosophy and her early experiences in politics and social work greatly colored her view of the managerial world. While those around her were focused on transforming people into efficient machines, Follett saw the importance and possibilities of treating people as individuals. Sethi observed that in 1962 her theories are "as much true today as they were novel when they first appeared" (p. 221), and Fox and Urwick (1973) conclude that "her work still remains a unique contribution to our knowledge of how human beings can participate more effectively in the systems of human collective action which our advancing technologies are making more and more complex" (p. xxxii).

Part Three

The Meaning of Work

Chapter Thirteen

Why Work?

Concluding Remarks

Why work? To some people this is a silly rhetorical question that deserves either no reply at all or the obvious answer, to survive, of course. However, the question, *why work?* is entangled with other questions about *how we work,* and that means a simple query like why work? becomes a philosophical, psychological, sociological, political, economical, and cultural question. The rhetoric surrounding the question and its various answers is deserving of serious consideration.

The previous chapters of this book have provided a general historical overview of work and biographies of some of the most intriguing historical figures who have contributed to the subject of work, along with summaries of their philosophies and discussions of how contemporary scholars have drawn from historical writings to explore the modern work world. Yet it has only touched the tip of the proverbial iceberg regarding philosophers, rhetoricians, and activists who have set forth opinions on why and how we work. Nevertheless, these chapters seem typical of the range of perspectives that have been asserted over the years, each adding to a grand debate.

Lyotard (1984) discussed the concept of the grand narrative, an overarching way of viewing the world that has been constructed through discourse. Having a grand narrative suggests that the social arrangement of society becomes reified; people come to think of it as the only way society can be organized. The more myopic one's world view, the more likely that the organizational system in place will seem like the only way or, at the very least, the only logical way to organize. Yet this book provides an overview of the varied philosophies of work, suggesting that rhetorical debate allows different world views to emerge concerning work. Rarely have the grand narratives been challenged; however, on those rare occasions when alternatives are raised, individuals are asked to question their taken-for-granted world view. More often than not, the challenges have been sequestered when they should be highlighted, and individuals do not realize that alternative ways of viewing the world exist. Highlighting the various philosophies and challenges to the status quo allows consideration and critique of the current system.

The Early Debates

Plato and Aristotle used their privileged positions as citizens and philosophers to educate, make assertions, and debate. They set forth differing positions on the way that work should be arranged in society. Although they agreed in general that slavery was a normal practice, they disagreed as to whether class constituted the criteria for job placement. Specifically, they argued about the work role of individuals based on their skills and intellect. They further debated the pros and cons of communal or private distribution and ways of living. They discussed the roles of women and children and came to distinctly different conclusions. Perhaps Plato was more open to the talents of women because his own mentor, Socrates, was taught by a woman, Aspasia, the partner of Pericles (see Bizzell & Herzberg, 2001 for a biography of Aspasia). Aspasia the Milesian wrote some of Pericles' speeches, entertained dignitaries and met with diplomats and philosophers. For a woman, and also in this case a foreigner, to speak on political matters without offending men would surely have required dialogic talent. Aspasia more than likely put strong opinions into the form of questions, guiding men to reach the conclusion she supported, perhaps influencing the *Socratic method*, as well. Plato tells us in the *Dialogues* that Socrates learned much from Aspasia, due to the times he swore those he told to secrecy as the following quotes attest:

> MEXENUS: Truly Socrates I marvel that Aspasia, who is only a woman, should be able to compose such a speech; she must be a rare one.
>
> SOCRATES: Well, if you are incredulous, you may come with me and hear her.
>
> MEXENUS: I have often met Aspasia and know what she is like.
>
> SOCRATES: Well, and do you not admire her, and are you not grateful for her speech?
>
> MEXENUS: Yes, Socrates, I am very grateful to her or to him who told you, · and still more to you who have told me.
>
> SOCRATES: Very good. But you must take care not to tell of me, and then at some other time I will repeat to you many more excellent speeches of her.
>
> MEXENUS: Fear not; only tell me, and I will keep the secret.
>
> SOCRATES: Then I will keep my promise.
>
> (*From Mexenenus*, as cited by Bizzell & Herzberg, 2001, p. 63)

Aristotle, on the other hand, never promoted the talents of women even if they held an upper-class status. Although Aristotle's world view was more restrictive, Plato's vision of a guardian society allowed those of superior intellect to join the privileged class once trained. Yet neither philosopher actually challenged the idea that some men should guide society and all others should follow their lead. Their rhetoric on the topic of work supported a class-based society. Thus, they debated with each other without attacking certain assumptions about the society in which they lived.

Confucius and St. Benedict could not have directly debated one another because they lived in different places during different eras. Yet their methods of arranging work and people in organizations and providing detailed models for the way in which people should behave had more in common than not. They each implied that hierarchy must be maintained for order to succeed. Confucius may be best known for establishing relationship rules to promote harmony. Although he wanted his students to be critical thinkers, strict adherence to relationship rules may well have restricted questioning certain forms of organizing, including hierarchy. Each partner in the hierarchical relationship had a certain decorum to follow and an ethical responsibility to the other person. This arrangement promoted harmony in a violent era. Indeed the Confucian way spread throughout China and remained a primary philosophy until Mao's cultural revolution instituted, in large part by force, an alternative philosophy and organization of labor. Generally speaking, hierarchy inherently promotes status differentiation and supports the concept of class, but Confucius's form of hierarchy called for these roles to be carried out with care. Benedict accepted hierarchy as a given in the Catholic Church, but the Pope's infallibility and the role of the Bishops had only recently been established. In an era of violence and a time when even the Catholic Church was divided (i.e., the schism between the Roman papacy and the Bishop of Constantinople was taking place at this time) hierarchy may have been a welcome relief to some. Thus, it is not surprising to learn that Benedict did not question the hierarchy of bishops or the infallibility of the reigning Pope. Yet Benedict called for meetings where every monk's voice could be heard with respect and without regard to age or class. Benedict challenged the view that with age comes wisdom, asserting that the young monks might very well make worthy contributions. He further challenged the notion of privilege based on wealth or political influence. His positions forced new arguments to be considered within the rhetorical debate about the organization of work. However, he is probably most famous for his rule concerning what counts as valuable work, that which is done with the hands. This rule, intended to require hard labor from all members of the monastic community including wealthy noble Romans who had sought refuge in the monasteries, may have provided the earliest treatise in Europe that demanded work equality and challenged the privileged status of the wealthy. The practice of slavery, which had been so common during antiquity, disappeared with the fall of Rome.

In order to survive, religious authorities encouraged Benedict's rule for centuries. However, during the dark ages peasant's contributions, including those of women and children fell primarily under the economic practice of feudalism, with its contract base, which was more in keeping with Confucian principles than with the work arrangements in the monasteries. Yet, the monasteries and the feudal kingdoms were intertwined in a unique economic and social relationship. Whether one highlights the philosophy of Confucius or of Benedict, it is clear that both men provided a rhetoric of work grounded in a pragmatic philosophy that strove for harmony.

Catholic rhetoric concerning the organization of society flourished across Europe, and for centuries the rule of the regal authority was synonymous with the rule of the Catholic Church. The rhetoric of the church with regard to work was powerful. Not until the invention of the printing press, the protestant reformation, the rise of mercantilism, the development of a merchant class, the spread of universities, and the exploration and exploitation of the Americas and Africa did the economic situation and philosophy of work change.

Challenging the political and economic policies of the era, Adam Smith regarded mercantilism and the monarchies' devotion to building armadas and armies, as a threat to economic development. Unconcerned about the exploitation of Native Americans or Africans, Smith was dedicated to reinforcing trade, banking, interest, entrepreneurship and production. Adam Smith not only saw capitalism as the most natural means of organization, but he also assumed that if left to its own resources it would flourish. He believed that all people held self interests and that most people longed to be idle. Furthermore, he based his theory on the assumption of rights, but rights were not bestowed equally. He agreed with earlier philosophers who suggested that classes did indeed exist due to natural forces and that laws would be necessary to protect the wealthy from the poor.

However, van Staveren (2001) argues that embedded within Adam Smith's writing, especially *Moral Sentiments*, is the notion of selflessness:

> How selfish soever man may be supposed, there are evidently some principles in his nature which interest him in the fortune of others, and render their happiness necessary to him, though he derives nothing from it except the pleasure of seeing it. (Smith, 1759, part I:I.i: 9, as cited in van Staveren, p. 82)

Furthermore, Smith's early work speaks of community, according to van Staveren:

> All the members of human society stand in need of each other's assistance, and are likewise exposed to mutual injuries. Where the necessary assistance is reciprocally afforded from love, from gratitude, from friendship, and esteem, the society flourishes and is happy. (Smith, 1759, part II:II.ii: 85, as cited in van Staveren, p. 83)

Finally, van Staveren notes that Smith called for liberty and justice for those who engaged in the "lowest species of common labour, [to] be able to earn something more than what is precisely necessary for their maintenance" (Smith 1776: Book I:VIII: 85–86, as cited in van Staveren, p. 76). However, it should be noted that these passages are few and far between and Smith seemingly did little to promote the concept of care when compared to promoting the concept of capital. Indeed, the notion that people are also generous and sympathetic may be crucial to the maintenance of capitalism. Today, churches as well as nonprofit organizations thrive as a result of people's generosity. Without these secondary resources, which might also include government assistance through welfare programs meant to help the sick, the poor, the jobless and the needy, capitalism may have faced stronger opposition. Smith challenged aspects of the mercantilist system that promoted regal wealth at the expense of trade and open commerce, but he did little to challenge the uneven distribution of wealth within a nation. However, according to Smith, capitalism does not enforce class restrictions; to the contrary, it suggests that even the simple weaver can expand his/her interests. Yet for the system to function, low-paid workers are required, and Adam Smith recommends that business owners follow the path to cheap labor without worrying about either the laborers who will lose their jobs or the new workers' exploitation. Some of the cheapest labor to be found in Adam Smith's day included slaves, indentured servants, paupers, criminals, women, and children, whose work and life situations are nearly invisible in his writings.

Nevertheless, van Staveren (2001) traces the concept of ethics from Adam Smith back to Aristotle to argue that modern economics is about more than the freedom of the individual to exchange; it is also a matter of justice. In addition van Staveren includes in her triumvirate of values the feminist ethic of care as developed by Charlotte Perkins Gilman and suggests that the dualism of modern economics, which separates capitalism from care, can be replaced by a new theory of economics. Aristotle's rule of values is invoked in order to bring freedom, justice, and care into an alternative model of economics. For Adam Smith generosity was an unintended consequence; for van Staveren it is a crucial underlying value of justice that, when balanced with freedom and care, bring rational meaning to economics.

Although van Steveren traced values to Aristotle, the role of exposing social injustice fell to Karl Marx. Marx contested the uneven distribution of wealth, the exploitation of workers, and the alienation of human beings. He argued that society had taken capitalism as natural, the only way of organizing. He argued that the history of the world could be discussed in light of varying socioeconomic modes (i.e., historical materialism) and, therefore, capitalism was not the one and only means to organizing labor. Marx launched a direct attack on Smith's rhetorical claims. He suggested that Smith's ideas were just that, arguments, not facts. Capitalist claims are not truth; they are only appearances of truth, Marx argued. Furthermore, he proclaimed instead that he had found the truth.

Perleman and Olbrechts-Tyteca (1958/1969) suggest that challenging an argument based on the *fact* that the opponents' argument provides appearances rather than truth allows the challengers to suggest that they know the truth. However, this also opens the gates to the possibility that their truth also is mere appearance. This thinking set the stage for postmodernism. Postmodernists could point out that neither Smith nor Marx held the tenets of Truth; instead, both Smith and Marx argued for a truth through lectures, pamphlets, and books like *The Wealth of Nations* and *Das Kapital*. Their rhetorical claims held powerful sway. Subsequently, two main schools of thought emerged, two grand narratives—capitalism and communism.

Unable to break out of this mindset, philosophers, rhetoricians, and activists, for the most part, challenged aspects of one system or the other but rarely challenged the limitation of only having two systems to choose from. For instance, Booker T. Washington found ways to work within the capitalist system, whereas W. E. B. Du Bois favored a socialist form of communism. Nevertheless, these men raised the issue of race from the unspeakable to the public podium. The exploitation of the darker races, as Du Bois put it, had received little attention in economic theory. These men, each in his own way, made race central. As Cornell West (1993) points out, *race matters*. But race is not the only reason their contributions should be considered among philosophies of work. Washington purposefully tried to raise the stature of physical labor from the demeaned position held since the time of antiquity to one that would engender pride. His thinking in this regard was novel. Du Bois also contributed to the rhetoric of labor and thus the meaning of work by asserting that economic practices of the imperializing nations had been at the expense of the darker peoples of the world. His travels across Europe and to Russia led him to the conclusion that Marxist revolution may have been the way to change class conflict in Russia, but the solution was not appropriate for the wider exploitation of people. His work on cooperatives and his credo that called for a simpler life achieved through nonviolence stood in stark contrast to either Adam Smith or Karl Marx.

Although Mother Jones rallied the workers for better conditions, she did little to challenge the grand narrative. Yet she did realize that women's and children's participation in the existing system was not a right that should be advocated. The system was flawed and she refused to support a liberal feminist agenda that argued for the rights of women to work alongside men. It seemed ludicrous to argue for the right to engage in such deplorable conditions. Her efforts to help establish a strong union system in the United States were invaluable and beyond measure. Unions born in the nineteenth century thrived through the twentieth century giving birth to such terms as *organized labor*, *sit-down strikes*, and *child labor*. The idea that working-class children should not be exploited brought a new set of terms to the world of work, making way for new *terministic screens*, which would allow society to percieve, to engage, and to change the way people work. Likewise, Emma Goldman discouraged women from participating in the movement for enfranchisement on the grounds that they would be participating in a system that did little to promote human equality or self-actualization. She railed against capitalism and communism, calling for anarchy, freedom, and liberty. Anarchists may have been the first to see that the philosophies of the past, capitalism and communism, failed to materialize in the way that their proponents dreamed. Neither system provided the freedom that Goldman sought for herself and others, especially women. Pleas for anarchy, however, fell on deaf ears; that philosophy disappeared literally from America through the deportation of anarchists; it disappeared from Russia before it even began; and it fell under the firm militaristic hand of fascism in Europe. Anarchy has since been rhetorically and connotatively constructed as violent chaos; its original Greek meaning, without leadership or the absence of government, has been forced into the shadows of the dominant paradigms. In fact, taken at face value, the term *anarchy* suggests living without imposed rule. Emma Goldman attacked laws that imposed nationalism (e.g., mandatory draft) and patriarchy (e.g., laws that undermined sexual education and made birth control illegal). She attempted to undo one law at a time; thus, her form of anarchy could be considered a work in progress. Anarchy itself as enacted by Goldman could be defined as a process rather than an outcome. Her adherence to the right to dance, to laugh, to drink, and to enjoy the arts gave anarchy a new meaning, especially as it related to work. In short Goldman provided a unique form of anarchy that quite likely would have led to unique definitions of work. However, her imprisonment and deportation and the imprisonment and deportation of other anarchists assured a capitalist mode of production in the United States that defined itself in direct contrast to the communism of Russia.

Allowing a bifurcated system (capitalism vs. communism) to flourish both materialistically and discursively constrained the ways in which work could be seen. Certainly there were socialist modifications to each economic order, but for the most part the two systems remained obstinately opposed. To frame the debates about work under a bifurcated *terministic screen* means that the questions asked and the answers found are restricted by assumptions of one or the other model of organizing. As Langer (1951) notes, assumptions frame the questions that are asked. For example, a question like how can managers get workers to work more efficiently and effectively? assumes and therefore accepts that a working class, as well as a managing class, exists. The system becomes reified. It further assumes that efficiency is a high priority and that effectiveness is the only goal. Turning the question around to *how can workers better manage themselves* may reduce the implications of capitalism's class structure, but it does not question the goals of efficiency and effectiveness. Asking certain questions, then, can further support the existence of certain dominant paradigms. A question like *why work when production far exceeds demand*—a question asserted by Emma Goldman—challenges the assumptions of capitalism and quite possibly of contemporary Chinese communism.

Returning to Adam Smith's writings, an answer to such a question about production is so that production *can* exceed demand, so that stock will be secured and supplies replenished, so that capitalism can flourish and nations become wealthy. Of course, this thinking did not set well with Marx, who challenged Smith, arguing that production exceeds demand because artificial needs have been created that exacerbate the artificial necessity to work.

Influenced by Darwin's theory of evolution, Marx suggested that a natural progression, one that included revolution, would move society from capitalism to communism. Communism would be the utopia that so many radical thinkers of the nineteenth century were seeking. Yet Emma Goldman hoped that communism would be but the stepping stone to anarchism—the model of society that required no authoritarian leadership, no centralized government, and no coercive or hegemonic control. This, of course, was not to be the case, and her disillusionment with Russian communism was no secret. Goldman's questioning of capitalism and communism provided the means to break the frame that forced a bifurcated choice. However, as previously suggested, anarchy nearly disappeared, and for the most part, the thinkers of the early twentieth century constrained their questions within the rhetorical limits of the grand narratives.

The Continuing Debates

At the turn of the nineteenth century, Weber wondered what, besides economic and political systems, contributed to our industriousness. Although Marx had argued earlier that religion is the *opiate of the masses*, Weber explored individual religions for their impact on industriousness and argued that Calvinism especially propagated the belief that work *paves the way to heaven*. He dismissed *Eastern* cultures (and presumably African, Native American, and any other non-European based culture) and numerous religions (including Catholicism) as inadequate to have developed a fully functioning form of capitalism. His thesis came under attack by various scholars who debated whether Protestants alone could promote the industriousness needed to develop capitalism. Those kinds of challenges stay within the system. That is, they do not question capitalism; instead, they question which cultures and religions are best suited to support capitalism. Weber's writings have led to interesting questions, especially about how people perceive work as a calling, but they do not challenge the system or extend the current debate beyond the bifurcated rhetorical frame. More recently, Scott (2007) has explored the discourses that surround the construction of work. She explores work as a calling from both religious and entrepreneurial positions. Passion, as a part of why we work, drives her own research, and she shares these feelings with her students. This is an area worthy of further investigation especially in light of whether these discourses promote a sincere sense of calling or whether the meaning of a calling is corrupted by business to encourage the industriousness of workers.

One argument that steps outside the boundaries of which religion or culture, if any, promotes the most industrious workers is that set forth by Bertrand Russell (1932), who questioned the very concept of the work ethic and reintroduced the question that Emma Goldman raised. Russell suggests

> that a great deal of harm is being done in the modern world by the belief in the virtuousness of WORK, and that the road to happiness and prosperity lies in an organized diminution of work. If an ordinary wage-earner worked four hours a day, there would be enough for everybody, and no unemployment—assuming a certain very moderate amount of sensible organization. . . . only a foolish asceticism, usually vicarious, makes us continue to insist on work in excessive quantities now that the need no longer exists. (as cited in Thomas, 1999, p. 567)

Russell's essay, "In Praise of Idleness," addresses the exploitation of the working class. Russell argues that the system of mass production as promoted by capitalism where some workers are laid off while others are overworked is irrational, especially when all could work a four-hour day.

Factory worker Mike LeFevre, who was interviewed by Studs Terkel (1972), fully agreed that four hours of work a day would more than supply the needs of demand. He discounted the idea of foolish asceticism as the source of this demanding work and believed that fear, the wealthy person's fear of the worker's leisure, drove this practice. No matter the reason, it would seem that people spend an inordinate amount of time creating a great deal of unnecessary things that then require the creation of desires for these things. Capitalism, as currently designed and perceived from this perspective, seems to be grounded in the irrational, a system of self-perpetuation creating mountains of unnecessary, meaningless work along with meaningless products that often become obsolete before the last person can buy the first version of the product.

Weber suggested that when encountering irrational practices, *verstehen*— looking at the seemingly irrational practice from the perspective of those who support it—will help bring understanding. Stepping into the shoes of the venture capitalist or the business owner, for example, might show that Adam Smith's theory of self-interest promotes this irrational practice for a logical reason— accumulation of wealth, a better life for the owner who is willing to participate. However, only a critical skeptic would stop at this point in an attempt to explain the practice, for the creative spirit of inventors should not be dismissed too quickly. Capitalism does provide an opportunity for inventors whose contributions to society have been stunning. Nor should we dismiss the altruistic spirit that drives certain people to reach for solutions to society's problems (e.g., cures for disease or designs for structural safety). Although capitalism does provide a haven for altruistic individuals, it does not promote dispensing those individuals' discoveries to others with much generosity. This results in a paradox for altruistic individuals, once again raising the question about how people participate in what for them becomes an irrational system. Capitalism rewards the owners, not necessarily the inventors, the artists, or the altruistic workers of society. The capitalist has a logical reason to support the seemingly irrational system. But if that is the case, then how do we explain the participation of the artists, the inventors, the altruistic individuals, the workers, or the managers in a capitalist society?

Marx argued that workers participate for several reasons, most of which are supported through the superstructure, the cultural and political institutions of society. Religions encourage work; parents encourage work; schools encourage work; democracy encourages work. Questions like when are you going to get a real job? encourage work and particular work arrangements. Freedom to achieve the American Dream perpetuated the premise that hard work is not only virtuous but also pragmatic and meritorious for millions of immigrants to the United States, especially in the early 1900s but equally so today (Trujillo, 2003). Immigrants believed the promise that with hard work anyone can become rich. Most people had a better chance of doing so in a democracy than in the totalitarian regimes of Europe (depending on race, religion, and gender). Yet the capitalist system, grounded in competition even among workers, made the dream nearly impossible for most to reach in the late 1800s and early 1900s. George Orwell's (1933/1961, 1937/1958) description of life in *Down and Out in Paris and London* or in *The Road to Wigan Pier* speaks not only of the oppressive work conditions worldwide but also of the degradation of unemployment. The poverty that engulfed America was no different from that which washed over Europe at the time. Depression, unemployment, or underemployment were common in America, and immigrants watched helplessly as the homes they dreamed of owning were foreclosed by banks. Upton Sinclair's (1906/2001) book *The Jungle* tells the story all too well.

Moving toward the Contemporary Debates

Communism, which accepted hierarchy, centralization, and the scientific approach to society, had trouble sustaining an egalitarian system. Taylor's promotion of scientifically arranging the workplace was quickly accepted by communists and capitalists alike, and those scholars who had seen the two systems as diametrically opposed were forced to face a new set of questions. Could the economic systems with such disparate philosophies depend on the same systems of management? By the mid-1900s, Kenneth Burke (1950/1962) argued that hierarchy is inherent in human nature, and thus society could not or, more accurately, would not exist without it, even though he supported a socialist perspective. He argued that hierarchy actually *goaded* people to create certain kinds of organization, and those organizations in turn contributed to "a *hierarchic psychosis*, prevailing in all nations" (p. 281). No matter whether capitalism or communism prevailed, hierarchy would exist, which in turn would manifest itself in *mysteriousness* as well as a variety of *psychoses*—inferiority complexes, sadomasochism, delusions of grandeur. All of this came out of our natural propensity to classify, according to Burke.

Classification, whether by race, religion, gender, or work status, creates categories, and categories create dialectical relations, which create tension. As a "symbol-using, symbol-making, and symbol-misusing animal," humankind created groups through rhetorical constructions, and those symbolic exchanges developed into material relations (Burke, 1966, p. 6). Burke (1950/1962) suggested with respect to class tensions that each class would be mysterious to the other, that identification with each other would be difficult, and that alienation would follow. He believed hierarchy could explain every aberration that Freud explained via sexuality. This inherited hierarchy existed everywhere. Following Burke, postmodernists eventually would discuss classification systems as discursive systems that create reality rather than reflect it (see Foucault, 1966/1973).

By the mid 1970s, feminists argued that hierarchy is not inherent to human nature, and models of work centering around feminist notions of consensus began to appear (for an overview of feminist literature in organizational studies, see Calás & Smircich, 1996; for an overview of feminist organizational communication, see Buzzanell, 2000). Although few feminists mention the work of Mary Parker Follett, her notion of allowing the commands to arise out of the situation surfaced again with a new vitality and a new twist. Follett called for work to be organized around the idea that when given the chance humans are motivated by responsibility. An organization that desires a collective sense of responsibility needs to allow independence and individual authority to flourish. Is such a system possible in America, in light of the sociopolitical order of democracy and the economic arrangement of capitalism? Is it possible for a communist society like China, still steeped with hierarchy in personal relationships and centralization in its socioeconomic relations, to allow self-authority? Are organizational systems trapped by the ills of hierarchy as Burke argued, or are they ripe for equality as Follett suggested? Questions like these step out of the bifurcated frame to address the grand narratives that currently guide human organizing. Encouraging debates, dialogue, and questions about the grand scale of organizing may in a certain way dwarf the questions related to the individual's reason to work.

Reasons to Work

As some philosophers and rhetoricians grappled with the larger issue of the work system, others explored the seemingly more individual issue of why people work. Of course it is important to note that why people work and how they work are inseparable. The psychological, sociological, cultural, economic, and political issues are braided together in a complex way through rhetoric, philosophy, and the everyday practices in which people engage.

For instance, philosophers assumed that the desperate economic situations of the nineteenth century explained why people worked; that is, the reason they worked seemed obvious. The possibility of starvation was never far from thought. But as a new and healthy economy blossomed following World War II, the question of why people work took a different direction. Rebuilding nations and lives was the priority of the day. The generation that followed, that is the baby boomers, built a managerial society. Nearly 25 percent of boomers attended college, perhaps the largest percentage in American history up to that point. They tackled giants with their creative business energy. For example, organizations like Apple Computer challenged IBM with their creative, youthful, energetic thinking. Somewhere along the way, young managers took over the roles of church and state, instilling the same work ethic in a new way in their employees. However, no matter how creative the managers, no matter how innovative the workplace design, computer chips still required assembly-line production. Owners still needed workers, and they needed managers to manage the workers.

Anthony (1977) suggested that the managerial class had been assigned the work of instilling an industrious work ethic in workers. Managers attempted to hire the best people, to support them with ongoing training, to prompt them with artificial awards (e.g., employee of the month, perfect attendance awards, quality circles, team philosophies), and generally to supply a work ideology that was once supplied by religious, educational, and family institutions. According to Anthony, workers were not duped by these contrived awards; they could see their work for the *meaninglessness* that it had become, but that did not mean that they could live without the wages.

Ironically, managers may have been the ones most duped by the system. Managers who were assigned to carry out the downsizing of organizations via firing employees found themselves faced with a new trend in the 1990s; they were being laid off. Mary Scott Nabers writing for the *Dallas Business Review* in 1996 reported that AT&T's lay off of 40,000 workers would include 24,000 employees from management's ranks. This practice persists. According to Kennedy (1999), "organizations are continually thinning out management ranks of older workers" (p. 2). In addition, Kennedy (1999) discovered that managers of earlier generations were motivated to work for money, promotion, public and peer recognition, and other incentives. Today's young professionals are motivated by time off and personal goals (Kennedy, 1999). Has work, in the organizational context, lost its meaning? Are young people finding their sense of accomplishment elsewhere? What impact will this have on work as a calling, as a virtue, or as *a real job*?

For many people times have changed. For others not much has changed at all. In *Nickel and Dimed*, Barbara Ehrenreich (2001) provides a glimpse into the lives of people living on minimum wage in America. Their reason to work fits our earliest answer, *to survive, of course*. Paying the rent requires that many of these individuals live in substandard housing or work two jobs. Going to college or getting ahead, which had been considered part of the American Dream, has become quite nearly *the impossible dream* for minimum-wage workers. The cost of living today far exceeds the pay of a minimum-wage worker. I recently spoke with a secretary, a single mother with two children; she was happy at first to have found a job, one that pays $10.00 an hour, well over minimum wage, only to realize that she made more money on unemployment. That is enough to make any person in the same situation ask, *why work?*

But she does work.

Booker T. Washington realized that work gives people a sense of pride through accomplishment, that slavery did an injustice not only to Africans but also to the meaning and practice of work. He understood the complexities of work, how it is entangled with political issues. Subsequently, he tried to keep recently freed slaves from being duplicitously led into political positions. Fearful that unscrupulous politicians would place naive individuals in political positions and then manipulate them as new minority marionettes, Washington worked tirelessly to bring freed slaves under his protection to learn to respect work, to develop skills, and to move forward. Du Bois, who already had the skills that Washington struggled to impart in others, moved ahead, and in so doing he found that capitalism and racism denied individuals the opportunity to reach their full humanity. It is capitalism, not work, that creates alienation, he argued, agreeing with Marx.

As long as slavery or oppressive work practices existed, work as defined by Marxism, as the extension of self, the creative act, could not exist. Yet Anthony (1977) challenged Marx's definition of work and his philosophy on the grounds that the Marxist theory of work is dependent on individuals' having a previous ideology of work. Anthony held that workers could not be alienated from their work through capitalism unless they already considered work a fulfilling activity. This explains why Booker T. Washington's job was so difficult. Slaves saw work as deplorable. He had to instill a new ideology of work. Anthony's point is that no ideology of work is natural. Perhaps the earlier chapters of this book help to make that point clear.

The debate on what the work ideology should be can be traced as far back as antiquity to Plato and Aristotle. Instilling a particular work ideology was clearly the goal of men like Confucius and St. Benedict. Adam Smith felt that workers would avoid monotonous work through invention but are never really intended to escape from it entirely, and Karl Marx defined labor as an inherent expression of self that workers should try to reclaim at all costs. Booker T. Washington attempted to instill a new ideology of work for freed slaves, and W. E. B. Du Bois begged them to question the system that he felt they were supporting by blindly following capitalism's lead. Mother Jones accepted the necessity of work but called for better working conditions. Emma Goldman questioned the systems but to no avail, and like most anarchists she equated capitalist production with war. Max Weber explored one ideology among many, and Emile

Durkheim questioned whether another system—the law—could regulate the economic system of capitalism. Frederick Winslow Taylor supported rigid scientific methods, whereas Mary Parker Follett argued for corporatists to loosen their grip and instate democracy in the workplace.

Economics Aside

Weber, Durkheim, Taylor, and Follett each argued in his or her own way that perhaps economics should not arrange work. Weber concluded that certain religions promoted certain economic styles and that rigid bureaucratic organization could offer a solution for greed as it was evidenced through nepotism and corruption. Durkheim, in spite of his limited thinking with respect to his racial and cultural prejudices, rejected a social system designed purely on economics. The division of labor and resulting economies could sustain themselves only if the law bound people together and carefully addressed their obligations to one another. But today, especially in the United States, the law has been co-opted by corporations that/who have legally gained the status of a person with limited liability for their actions (a law once intended to protect freed slaves from exploitation; Achbar, Abbott, & Bakan, 2004). As Meyers (2000) explains it, the Fourteenth Amendment to the U.S. Constitution (ratified in 1868) was intended to protect freed slaves who were free but had not been granted the status of citizens so that unscrupulous whites could take their land or possessions at will. The Fourteenth Amendment defined all persons born or naturalized in the U.S. as citizens whose life, liberty, or property could not be taken without due process of law. This particular time in U.S. history was rife with greed as exemplified through carpet baggers and industrial barons. Originally corporations were established by states to perform work for the good of society (e.g., build railroads, undertake waterworks) and were dissolved upon completion of the work, but corporate lawyers saw this amendment as their chance to solidify the corporations' power. Railroad magnates led the way. In the case of Santa Clara v. Southern Pacific Railroad (1886), the judge in an offhand comment (although this set a precedent, it also created controversy because it was not the specific ruling of that particular case) suggested that corporations could be equated with personhood. Personhood, in turn, was protected by the Fourteenth Amendment, and corporations used this status to increase their holdings and protect their wealth. Supreme Court Judge Hugo Black pointed out that less than .5% of the cases related to the Fourteenth Amendment were brought to court by African Americans, whereas more than 50% were brought by corporations. Today much controversy surrounds the status of corporations. In the case of United Airlines, which/who filed for Chapter 11 bankruptcy (protection from debtors' claims), the law left something to be desired for thousands of workers. When the company emerged from bankruptcy in 2006, instead of restoring the jobs to those who had been laid off, the money to those workers who had taken pay cuts, or the pensions to those who had retired without funds, the top executives gave themselves bonuses in the millions of dollars. In short, the personhood of corporations seems to have trumped the personhood of people, who in this case were unable to collect what the corporation owed them. Should such complete disregard for workers be written off as mere capitalist norms? Should the laws be improved to ensure a moral obligation to workers? Durkheim pointed out the role of the law to organize work relations, control capitalism, and regulate exploitive practices; yet his contributions are rarely if ever mentioned in organizational textbooks for young people to read and consider. Instead, newscasters report immoral outrages, the government continues to provide bail-out for many corporations, and students walk blindly into their futures. Organizational trust has been severely marred by recent incidents, leaving employees to ask questions such as can companies be trusted; can security and satisfaction be found elsewhere?

Young professionals today are motivated to work for organizations so that they can acquire skills and prepare for self-employment, among other motivators (Kennedy, 1999). What kind of organizations will they promote? Are we more likely to see Taylor's scientific method or Follett's democratic approach in the future? The very fact that young people are preparing for entrepreneurship sets them apart from yesteryear's *organization man* as discussed by Whyte (1956), the individual who was loyal to his organization, sometimes naively so. Perhaps young people are not walking so blindly into the future after all. But what of the nonprofessional working class; how are they preparing for the future?

In the past, union activists, such as Mother Jones, sought to protect workers from unsafe conditions and the greed of management. Yet unions, according to Anthony (1977), do not address the work that people are assigned; rather, they address the amount of money that people will receive from that work. Today students across U.S. campuses have campaigned for improved working conditions and a living wage for workers in underdeveloped countries (see Featherstone, 2002). Young women working in textile factories sew tiny emblems to sweatshirts until their fingers are raw, and they receive little pay for doing so. Unions address the raw fingers and the meager wages but never question the practice of sewing little emblems to university sweatshirts. Yesenia Bonilla of Honduras described her working conditions as unbearable. She reports that her supervisor "insulted me, made me cry, and hit me. . . . We endured a lot of abuse. We started at 7 in the morning and wouldn't finish until late at night . . . the water was really dirty" (p. 76). Does that mean that management should attempt to redesign the job (e.g., job rotation, flexible hours) or provide clean water, safe conditions, reasonable hours, and a living wage? Meeting safety standards and minimum pay does not change the job. Improving safety and pay, rotating jobs, and providing flexible hours makes life easier for the workers, but it does little to satisfy their emotional hunger for a better a life. And so we should not be surprised when the question is raised, *why work?* On the other hand, Yenny Perez, a factory worker from the Dominican Republic who lost her job for union organizing told me that she was good at her job, proud of her skills and feared that the only other options for her might be domestic work or prostitution. Some of her laid off co-workers had already turned to prostitution in order to support their families. Like many of them, Yenny is also a single mother (Clair, 2007).

A Hunger for Work

Some workers have a hunger that cannot be satisfied by the work that they do unless they create fantasy images. Their imaginations know no bounds, stretching from how their work is an art form to how heroic their accomplishments might be. For example, a waitress sees herself as a ballerina (Terkel, 1972), and a factory worker playfully fantasizes about being the Olympic champion of riveting just to get through the day (Hamper, 1986). The meaningfulness of much work exists only in fantasies, one of which is that what we do contributes to society.

Contribution to society is not entirely grounded in a religious ethic. Indeed, Marxist thinking advocates a concern for the community, for the people, yet Marx certainly did not advocate religion. He promoted this ethic based on the benefits of communal living, and he was not the first to do so. As suggested earlier, the debates over private property versus communal living date back to antiquity, with Plato encouraging a communal existence and Aristotle advocating the personal, or private, approach. These debates reached their apex with Karl Marx and Adam Smith, whose arguments covered the span of over one hundred years and others continue those debates today. Communal living was considered the epitome of caring for one another. Private property was considered selfish yet human.

W. E. B. Du Bois pointed out that the desire for wealth and private property led to the oppression of the darker races and asked his students to relinquish any desires for wealth, to seek work not for money but as an avenue to happiness. His developing food cooperative was quickly closed down by the government; communal activities can be frightening to those who advocate a different path. Similarly, Emma Goldman pointed out that private property, especially when women are conceived of as property, contributes to the poverty and exploitation of women and girls. The work traditionally assigned to females (and males of racial minorities) has been demeaned and continues to be so today. Even when the work that had been restricted to the domestic, private realm became public (e.g., child daycare, cleaning services, food services) the work continued to be marginalized through low pay and little respect (Clair & Thompson, 1996). When men's domestic labor (e.g., plumbing, car mechanic maintenance, landscaping, garbage removal) gravitated to the public arena, it may have received varying levels of respect, but it certainly enjoyed better pay than traditional women's work.

Although communism hoped to end the oppression of workers as well as both racial minorities and women, it was unable to establish itself without violence, censorship, and sustained corruption. Capitalism called for a laissez-faire policy, asserting that left to its own the system would allow the best to surface at the top. Somehow, the top positions have tended to be filled with white men. Neither men of color nor women of any race could break through the barriers when capitalism was left to its own devices. The "invisible hand" that Adam Smith suggested would raise the standard of living for all people has limitations. And pure capitalism does not exist, as pointed out by John Stewart (2007) during his interview with recently retired Chairman of the Federal Reserve Board Alan Greenspan. Stewart asked Greenspan why we needed the Federal Reserve to regulate interest rates if the "invisible hand" can guide capitalism; Stewart further suggested that perhaps the invisible hand is actually a "benevolent hand." Without regulation the pendulum between depression/recession and inflationary periods can become dangerously one-sided. Greenspan (2007) explains that "a worldwide entrepreneurial stirring . . . has led to the creation of institutions that now anonymously guide an ever-increasing share of human activity—an international version of Adam Smith's 'invisible hand'" (p. 15). Pure communism existed only in theory—just a dream as Lukes (1995) portrays it in his innovative novel about utopian societies. Communism has all but collapsed in Russia leaving only traces behind, and communism in China is fast incorporating capitalism. We must be wary of the greed, poverty, and prejudice that can prevail in both systems—capitalism and communism.

Poverty and prejudice can be debilitating. Neither capitalism nor communism has been able to end oppression or poverty. Muirhead (2004) suggests that "work may be necessary, but our organization of it is not; as such, it invites evaluation and justification" (p. 6). Neither capitalism nor communism has given a wholly suitable means for organizing socioeconomic systems. Neither has given us a truly satisfactory definition of work or a satisfactory answer to the question *why work?*

Nor can I give an answer that will be completely free of ideology. Any response that I provide would be riddled with tenets of belief systems that have been handed down to me through the ages. I cannot pretend to be unbiased. However, I struggle not to be a cliché, a product of my times, yet to pretend to have escaped the multiple ideologies that permeate society would be naive. Nevertheless, in the epilogue I will struggle not to provide answers but instead to provide questions that will allow us to critique the world of work and ask the question—*Why work?*

Chapter Fourteen

Why Work

An Epilogue

Why work? I want to answer with extremes: what seems natural to me and what seems most unnatural to me. I have argued elsewhere that nothing is natural (Clair & Kunkel, 1998). Yet some things, some feelings seem natural, a part of nature itself. Work is one such behavior that seems natural. Watch a woodpecker peck the bark of a tree, systematically working up and down the tree trunk, gathering insects, eating, surviving naturally. And yet the mere mention of work as natural brings a flood of examples that support the contrary notion that work is far from natural. Would Captain John Smith have had to threaten colonists with taking their food away for not working if work were natural? Perhaps work is both natural and unnatural. Hannah Arendt (1958) distinguished labor as hardship and work as lasting achievement, but sometimes, for some people or in certain situations, the distinction is crossed or blurred. Weren't there days when Shakespeare's work might have felt like labor or days when a waitress's labor might have seemed to her like a work of art? And who is to determine what counts as a lasting achievement? The results of good parenting may stretch into future generations, and the value of certain great works of art will always be debated. If this is the case, then multiple, varying, and even contradictory reasons for work seem not only to be possible but to exist simultaneously.

The story that Adam Smith told of a young lad whose job it was to open and close a valve in order for the steam engine to function was meant to promote the idea that monotonous work leads to invention. The job was extremely boring. After some time, the boy realized that he could rig the valve so that he could do one motion and the valve would do the other, thus, relieving him of work.

To the contrary, I recently met Curtis, a young man who suffers from extreme cerebral palsy. Unable to control his muscles beyond large gross motor movement, Curtis was confined to a wheel chair, unable to speak without assistance, and certainly unable to do any job that required dexterity. Physically but not mentally challenged, Curtis attends community college part-time. He also spends much of his time at a center for people with disabilities. The center has a job shop where mentally challenged individuals insert rivets into long thin strips of metal. They pop the rivets in place, one after another. Curtis's disability kept him from being able to perform this simple task. Yet with an indomitable spirit, he managed to communicate an idea that he had to staff members. Following his instructions, they wrapped a piece of duct tape around his forearm so that the sticky part of the tape was on the outside and then they wheeled him into the job shop. There, Curtis used broad jerking motions of his forearm to catch the rivets one at a time on the duct tape and then push them downward into the holes. A final jerking motion upward left the rivet in place and Curtis's arm free to catch another rivet. Curtis overcame great obstacles and invented a means to rivet so that he could work.

These two stories demonstrate the dialectic of work. One boy used his talents to gain a moment of relief, some time for idleness, and an escape from alienation; the other boy used his ingenuity to gain a moment of community, esprit de corps, and a paycheck. One boy strove to end monotonous work; the other boy strove to do monotonous work. Work exists as both pleasure and pain, as both expression and alienation, as individuality and cooperation, as choice and as hegemonic practice. The reasons why we work are complex to say the least.

Both boys were hungry for something—something that work both provided and thwarted. Their stories embody opposites. Each one used his creative energy; each one worked. Each one used his muscles and brawn; each one labored. And they did so in opposite directions—toward work and away from work.

In the novella *Life in the Iron Mills*, Rebecca Harding Davis (1861/1985) tells the story of a young man, destitute and working in the mines. This worker, who tended the furnace, spent time at the end of each day sculpting the korl,—a waxy, flesh-colored substance left behind after the iron is run through the furnace; refuse from the ore—inside the mine until at long last he had finished a sculpture of a woman, a brawny, working-class woman. Life–size, the figure reached out with her arms. When the mine owner brought an entourage of professional men into his mines for a tour, they stepped back, frightened at first by the figure they saw in the dark. They had the furnace tender bring a torch closer so that they might get a better look at the sculpture.

> "What does the fellow intend by the figure? I cannot catch the meaning," one of the men asked. After much conversation and speculation from the upper-class gentlemen, the artist replied, "She be hungry."

"Oh-h! But what a mistake you have made, my fine fellow! You have given no sign of starvation to the body. It is strong,—terribly strong. . . . It has the mad, half-despairing gesture of drowning . . ."

"Not hungry for meat," the furnace-tender said at last.

"What then? Whiskey?" jeered Kirby, with a coarse laugh. . . .

"I dunno," he said, with a bewildered look. "It mebbe. Summat to make her live, I think,—like you." (p. 33)

Davis captured the soul of one working man, and that man, the artist, captured the hunger of the working class. The idea that the artist or talented person is wasting away at hard labor addresses more than the evils of capitalism or communism. It highlights the hunger of all humanity.

Hunger comes in many forms. My students have demonstrated hunger for knowledge. When I provided a lecture on Weber's concept of bureaucracy and Ferguson's challenge to it, it was easy to use the university as the example of a bureaucracy. Students understood what it meant to become a number, to be alienated by the large lecture classes, to fight the system so filled with paperwork, to endure the frustration of arriving at one place only be to told that somebody else handles that problem and does so in a completely different location. They also understood the need for impersonalization, the problems that nepotism could cause and that bureaucracy could alleviate, and the need for the written word and written rules. At the end of the lecture, I read the description of the first university as provided by Burke (1985). He describes how the young people of Bologna came together during the twelfth century, pooling their money in order to hire professors so that education would not be restricted to the rich. "By 1189 there were strict guidelines for fixing the rents of students who were not native to the city" (p. 48). Back then, the students hired and fired the professors and determined the daily schedule as well as vacations and holidays. After the students laugh at the idea that out-of-state tuition is centuries old and discuss the shift in power as compared to universities today, I challenge them to discover whether Burke is correct to claim that "Bologna became the seat of the world's first university, a unique medieval foundation" (p. 47). Their answer is expected at the next class meeting.

Throughout the 1990s, my students returned to class with only two other possibilities: the University of Paris and Oxford University. They were, of course, stunned when I suggested that perhaps Timbuktu had a university with as rich a background and intellectual heritage as any of the European universities. Education flourished in Africa around the same time that Bologna was admitting its students. One semester an African-American student sat shyly in the last seat in the corner of the room, and when he heard me acknowledge the University of Timbuktu and then provide support of its existence, he leaned forward and said, "Yes!"

As the student population became more international, as the American students became more aware of international issues, and as computer access became more common, the answers they brought began to change. Over the last few years I have received the following answers: Salerno, Nalanda, Takshila, Fez, Al-Azher, and others that made me seek a world map. However, I have yet to hear my students discover Timbuktu as one of the earliest universities on their own. Why is it that they have never heard of Timbuktu in any other fashion than its representing the farthest spot in the parking lot—*I had to park all the way out in Timbuktu*. The discussion that follows includes how portraying Africans as inferior, especially intellectually, assisted the practice of slavery. Why it continues today and what it has to do with work, although some public school textbooks are demonstrating enlightenment and including Timbuktu in their discussions of world civilizations, is the theme of the day. By the end of the class period, they start to realize that their world has been confined, at best, and they hunger for more knowledge.

Once, after I lectured on scientific management, a student majoring in engineering sarcastically asked, "What else is there to learn?" He was surprised that the history of work and the various organizational systems did not begin and end with Frederick Taylor's style of management. On another occasion, after I explained that the Hawthorne studies of the famous experiment concerning worker motivation may have been seriously flawed due to research bias, a skeptical student set straight away for the library in search of answers. In the experiment the workers were set to perform a task. The lighting in the room was continually lowered, and production was measured. Production went up no matter how brightly or how dimly the researchers illuminated the room. The researchers concluded that workers produce at high levels when working under dimness equal to moonlight because they are receiving attention. Thus, the human relations movement was born. According to this philosophy, workers do not need more money; they need attention. Yet, as I told the students earlier, the studies are flawed. Researchers dismissed anyone who was not working up to speed. They threatened them with the loss of their jobs and prodded people to work harder (Carey, 1967; Franke & Kaul, 1978). The student who made a bee-line to the library returned to class the following week and told me that she thought I had lied to them and that she went to the library to find out for herself. She apologized and added that in the business school they had only told one part of the story.

Numerous stories about work are sequestered. Certain philosophers, rhetoricians, and activists' positions never make it into the general textbooks about work. Bringing them into the light of day provides an alternative view of how and why people work the way they do. History communicates when it is shared. I hope that this book has provided a few of the stories and philosophies that have been quite nearly lost throughout the long history of work. Taken together these chapters create a dialogue, sometimes contentious, concerning work. The theories and assumptions nearly speak to or debate with each other. Words, phrases, and philosophies wash over society, sometimes providing insights, other times providing challenges to the concepts and practices of work. Sometimes, the arguments are audible and other times they are silenced; sometimes, they are visible and sometimes they are hidden in plain sight, embedded within everyday talk. The concept of work is challenged when questions like *what constitutes a real job* or *what are the reasons people work* are proposed and addressed with serious interrogation (see Clair, 1996). Furthermore, the taken-for-granted concept of work is challenged when the marginalized voices of the past are juxtaposed with the traditional voices of yesteryear, offering a rhetoric of possibilities. These less frequently told stories have been presented along with those stories that have been highlighted in the past so that students can consider work from more than one perspective, so that they can enter the debate. In so doing, they have a better chance of answering the question *why work?* for themselves and for future generations.

References

About Mother Jones (2002). Retrieved October 7, 2002, from http://motherjones.com/
   about/index.html.

Achbar, M., Abbott, J., & Bakan, J. (2004). *The corporation*. Zeitgeist Films.

The Analects (Lunyu) of Confucius (1956) (A. Waley, Trans.) London: Allen & Unwin.

Anthony, P. D. (1977). *The ideology of work*. London: Tavistock Publications.

Arendt, H. (1958). *The human condition*. Chicago: The University of Chicago Press.

Aristotle (1969). *The Politics of Aristotle*. (Ernest Barker, Trans.) New York: Oxford
   University Press.

Barker, J. R. (1993). Tightening the iron cage: Concertive control in self-managing teams.
   Administrative Science Quarterly, 38, 408–437.

Barker, J. R., & Cheney, G. (1994). The concept and the practices of discipline in contemporary organizational life. *Communication Monographs, 61*, 21–41.

Barthes, R. (1972). *Mythologies*. London: Cape.

Beissinger, M. R. (1988). *Scientific management, socialist discipline, and Soviet power*.
   Cambridge, MA: Harvard University Press.

Benedictine Monks of St. Meinrad's Abbey (Eds.) (1937). *The Holy Rule of our most holy
   father Saint Benedict*. St. Meinrad, IN: Grail Publication.

Benians, E. A. (1925). Adam Smith's project of an empire. *Cambridge Historical Journal, 1*, 249–283.

Bizzell, P., & Herzberg, B. (2001). The rhetorical tradition: Readings from classical times
   to the present. Boston and New York: Bedford/St. Martin's.

Blake, W. O. (1860). *The history of slavery and the slave trade, ancient and modern. The
   forms of slavery that prevailed in ancient nations, particularly in Greece and Rome.
   The African slave trade and the political history of slavery in the United States*. Co-
   lumbus, OH: H. Miller.

Booker T. Washington (2005). Retrieved November 1, 2007, from http://www.spartacus
   .schoolnet.co.uk/USAbooker.htm.

Burke, J. (1985). *The day the universe changed*. Boston: Little, Brown and Company.

Burke, K. (1935). *Permanence and change: An anatomy of purpose* (3rd ed.). Berkeley:
   University of California Press.

Burke, K. (1962). *A rhetoric of motives.* Cleveland and New York: Meridian Books—The World Publishing Company. (Original work published in 1950)

Burke, K. (1968). *Language as symbolic action: Essays on life, literature, and method.* Berkeley: University of California Press.

Butler, G. R. (1991). Frederick Winslow Taylor: The father of scientific management and his philosophy revisited. *Industrial Management, 33,* 23–24.

Buzzanell, P. (Ed.) (2000). *Rethinking organizational & managerial communication from a feminist perspective.* Thousand Oaks, CA: Sage.

Calás, M. B., & Smircich, L. (1996). From the woman's point of view: Feminist approaches to organization studies. In S. R. Clegg, C. Hardy & W. Nord (Eds.), *Handbook of organization studies* (pp. 218–258). London: Sage.

Carey, A. (1967). The Hawthorne studies: A radical criticism. *American Sociological Review, 30,* 403–416.

Chai C., & Chai, W. (1965). *The sacred books of Confucius and other Confucian classics.* New York: University Books.

Chamberlin, J. (Ed.) (1982). *The rule of St. Benedict: The Abingdon copy.* Toronto: Pontifical Institute of Mediaeval Studies.

Chandler, A. (1991). Industrial revolution. *American History Files.* Retrieved October 7, 2002, from http://www.myhistory.org/historytopics/articles/industrial_revolution .html.

Chapman, D. J. (1971). *Saint Benedict and the sixth century.* Westport, CT: Greenwood Press.

Cheney, G. (1991). *Rhetoric in an organizational society: Managing multiple identities.* Columbia: University of South Carolina Press.

Cheney, G., Christensen, L.T., Zorn Jr., T.E., & Ganesh, S. (2004). *Organizational Communication in an Age of Globalization.* Prospect Heights, IL: Waveland Press.

Chilton, K. (1993, Nov/Dec). Lincoln Electric's incentive system. Can it be transferred overseas? *Compensation & Benefits Review, 25,* 21–30.

Ciulla, J. B. (2000). *The working life: The promise and betrayal of modern work.* New York: Times Books.

Clair, R. P. (1994). Hegemony and harassment: A discursive practice. In S. Bingham (Ed.), *Conceptualizing sexual harassment as a discursive practice* (pp. 59–70). Westport, CT: Praeger.

Clair, R. P. (1992, November). *Discursive practices surrounding the socialization and legitimation of work: Hegemony of a "real job."* Paper presented at the annual meeting of the Speech Communication Association, Chicago.

Clair, R. P. (1996). The political nature of the colloquialism, "a real job": Implications for organizational socialization. *Communication Monographs, 63,* 249–267.

Clair, R. P. (1998). *Organizing silence: A world of possibilities.* Albany: State University of New York Press.

Clair, R. P. (1999a). Ways of seeing: A review of Kramer and Miller's manuscript. *Communication Monographs, 66,* 374–381.

Clair, R. P. (1999b). Standing still in an ancient field: A contemporary look at the organizational communication discipline. *Management Communication Quarterly, 13,* 283–293.

Clair, R. P. (2007). Organizations as arguments: A case of monitoring sweatships. Paper presented at the Annual Meeting of the National Communication Association, Chicago, Ill., November 2007.

Clair, R. P. (2007). Interview with Yenny Perez detailed in "From hunger strikes to yellow roses: The story of Purdue University students' hunger strike" A working paper.

Clair, R. P., & Kunkel, A. W. (1998). "Unrealistic realities": Child abuse and the aesthetic resolution. *Communication Monographs, 65,* 24–46.

Clair R. P., & Thompson, K. (1996). Pay discrimination as a discursive and material practice: A case concerning extended housework. *Journal of Applied Communication Research, 24,* 1–20.

Clegg, S. R. (1989). *Frameworks of power.* London: Sage.

Conrad, C, & Poole, M. S. (2005). *Strategic organizational communication in a global economy* (6th ed.) Belmon, CA: Thomson /Wadsworth.

Coser, L. A. (1977). *Masters of sociological thought: Ideas in historical and social context.* New York: Harcourt Brace Jovanovich.

Coser, L. A. (1984). Introduction: *The division of labor in society* (pp. ix–xxiv). New York: The Free Press.

Critchley, J. S. (1978). *Feudalism.* London: George Allen & Unwin.

Culpepper Clark, E., & McKerrow, R. E. (1998). The rhetorical construction of history. In K. J. Turner (Ed.), *Doing rhetorical history: Concepts and cases* (pp. 33–46). Tuscaloosa: The University of Alabama Press.

Dalby, M. T., & Werthman, M. S. (Eds.) (1971). *Bureaucracy in historical perspective.* Glenview, IL: Scott, Foresman, and Company.

Daniels, T. D., & Spiker, B. K. (1987). *Perspectives on organizational communication.* Dubuque, IA: Wm. C. Brown.

Davis, A. M. (1997). Liquid leadership: The wisdom of Mary Parker Follett. *A Leadership Journal: Women in Leadership—Sharing the Vision, 2.* Retrieved February 4, 2003, from http://sunsite.utk.edu/FINS/Mary_Parker_Follett/Fins-MPF–03.txt.

De Certeau, M. (1984). *The practice of everyday life.* Berkeley: University of California Press.

Deetz, S. A. (1992). *Democracy in an age of corporate colonization: Developments in communication and the politics of everyday life.* Albany: State University of New York Press.

Derrida J. (1973). *Speech and phenomena and other essays on Husserl's theory of signs* (D. B. Allison, Trans.). Evanston, IL: Northwestern University Press. (Original work published 1967)

Derrida, J. (1976). *Of grammatology* (G. Spivak, Trans.) Baltimore and London: Johns Hopkins University Press. (Original work published 1967)

Du Bois, W. E. B (1968). *The autobiography of W. E. B. DuBois: A soliloquy on viewing life from the last decade of its first century.* New York: International.

Du Bois, W. E. B. (1940). *Dusk of dawn.* New York: Harcourt, Brace & Co.

Du Bois, W. E. B. (1967). *Darkwater: Voices from within the veil.* New York: Humanity Books. (Original published in 1920)

Dupré, L. (1966). *The philosophical foundations of Marxism.* New York: Harcourt, Brace, & World.

Durkheim, E. (1984). *The division of labor in society* (W. D. Halls, Trans.). New York: The Free Press. (Original work published in 1893 and original English translation published in 1933)

Durkheim, E. (1957). *Professional ethics and civil morals.* London: Routledge.

Durkheim's Anomie. (n.d.). Retrieved April 11, 2003, from http://www.hewett.norfold.sch.uk.

Dyer, C. (1983). English diet in the later Middle Ages. In T. H. Aston, P. R. Coss, C. Dyer, & J. Thirsk (Eds.), *Social relations and ideas: Essays in honour of R. H. Hilton* (pp. 191–216). Cambridge: Cambridge University Press.

Edwards, P. (1967). Emile Durkheim. *The encyclopedia of philosophy* (Vol. 2, pp. 437–439). New York & London: The Free Press.

Ehrenreich, B. (2001). *Nickel and dimed: On (not) getting by in America.* New York: Henry Holt and Company.

Eisenberg, E.M., Goodall, Jr., H.L. & Trethewey, A. (2007). *Organizational Communication: Balancing Creativity and Constraint* (5th ed.). Boston/New York: Bedford's/St. Martin's Press.

Elwell, F. (1996). *The Sociology of Max Weber.* Retrieved 26 April, 2003, from http://www.faculty.rsu.edu/~felwell/Theorists/Weber/Whome.htm#words.

Emile Durkheim: The Division of Labor. (n.d.). Retrieved April 15, 2003, from http://durkheim.itgo.com/.

Emile Durkheim: The Emile Durkheim Archive. (n.d.). Retrieved April 11, 2003, from http://durkheim.itgo.com.

Emile Durkheim: The Person. (n.d.). Retrieved April 11, 2003, from http://www.hewett.norfolk.sch.uk.

Emile Durkheim: The Work. (n.d.). Retrieved April 11, 2003, from http://www.hewett.norfolk.sch.uk.

Esbenshade, J. & Bonacich, E. (1999, July/August). Can conduct codes and monitoring combat America's sweatshops? *Working USA,* pp. 21–33.

Evensky, J. (1993). Retrospectives: Ethics and the invisible hand. *The Journal of Economic Perspectives, 7,* 197–205.

Featherstone, L. and United Students Against Sweatshops. (2002). *Students against sweatshops.* London & New York: Verso.

Ferguson, K. E. (1984). *The feminist case against bureaucracy.* Philadelphia: Temple University Press.

Ferguson, K. E. (1994). On bringing more theory, more voices and more politics to the study of organization. *Organization, 1,* 81–99.

Follett, M. P. (1973). *Dynamic administration: The collected papers of Mary Parker Follett* (E. M. Fox, & L. Urwick, Eds.). London: Pitman Publishing. (Original work published 1940)

Foucault, M. (1973). *The order of things: An archeology of the human sciences.* New York: Vintage Books (original work published 1966).

Foucault, M. (1979). *Discipline and punish: The birth of the prison* (A. Sheridan, Trans.). New York: Vintage Books. (Original work published in 1975, English translation in 1977)

Foucault, M. (1990). *The history of sexuality: An introduction* (Vol. 1; R. Hurley, Trans.). New York: Vintage Books. (Original work published 1976, English translation 1978)

Fox, E. M., & Urwick, L. (1973). Introduction to the second edition: *Dynamic administration: The collected papers of Mary Parker Follett.* New York: Hippocrene Books.

Fox, R. (2005, November). *Emma Goldman: Issues of credibility and birth control education.* Paper presented at the annual meeting of the National Communication Association, Boston.

Franke, R. H., & Kaul, J. D. (1978). The Hawthorne experiments: First statistical reinterpretation. *American Sociological Review, 43,* 623–643.

Frederick Taylor, Early Century Management Consultant. (1997, June 13). *The Wall Street Journal Bookshelf,* p. A17.

Frederick Winslow Taylor. (n.d.). Retrieved February 11, 2003, from http://www.accel -team.com.

Frederick Winslow Taylor. (n.d.). Retrieved February 18, 2003, from http://www.north star.k12.ak.us.

Freeman, M. (1996). Scientific management: 100 years old; poised for the next century . *SAM Advanced Management Journal, 20,* 35–37.

Friedan, B. (1963). *The feminine mystique.* New York: Norton.

Fu, P., & Yukl, G. (2000). Perceived effectiveness of influence tactics in the United States and China. *Leadership Quarterly, 11,* 251–266.

F.W. Taylor, Expert in Efficiency, Dies. (March 22, 1915). *New York Times* archives retrieved from www.nytimes.com/books/97/06/15/reviews/taylor-obituary.html.

Gaarder, J. (1996). *Sophie's world: A novel about the history of philosophy.* (P. Moller, Trans.) New York: Berkley Books. (Original work published in 1991)

Galestock, K. (1999, July/August). Sweatshops: Labor standards and codes of conduct. *The College Store.* Retrieved August 26, 1999, from http://www.nacs.org/info/cs/ 99-mj/advance_look.asp.

Ganguli, B. N. (1979). *Emma Goldman: Portrait of a rebel woman.* Bombay: Allied Publisher.

Gibbs, M. (1953). *Feudal order.* New York: Henry Schuman.

Gibson, M. K. & Papa, M. J. (2000). The mud, the blood, and the beer guys: Organizational osmosis in blue-collar work. *Journal of Applied Communication Research, 28,* 68–88.

Giddens, A. (1979). *Central problems in social theory.* Berkeley: University of California Press.

Giddens, A. (1992). Introduction. In Weber, M. *The Protestant ethic and the spirit of capitalism.* (T. Parsons Trans.) (pp. vii-xxvi). London & New York: Routledge. (Original Introduction written in 1976)

Gitlin, T. (April 26, 2004). Jürgen Habermas: The sage of reason. *Time,* p. 109.

Goldman, E. (1910). *Anarchism and other essays.* Port Washington, NY: Kennikat Press.

Goldman, E. (1923). *My disillusionment in Russia.* Garden City, NY: Doubleday, Page & Company.

Goldman, E. (1931). *Living my life.* Garden City, NY: Garden City Publishing-Alfred Knopf.

Gorn, E. J. (2001a). *Mother Jones: The most dangerous woman in America.* New York: Hill and Wang.

Gorn, E. J. (2001b, May/June). Mother Jones: The woman. *Mother Jones*, retrieved November 1, 2007, from http://www.motherjones.com/news/special_reports/2001/05/motherjones_gorn.html.

Grampp, W. D. (2000). What did Adam Smith mean by the invisible hand? *Journal of Political Economy, 108*, 441–465.

Greco, J. (1999). Frederick Winslow Taylor (1856–1915): The science of business. *Journal of Business Strategy, 20*, 26–28.

Greenspan, A. (2007). *The age of turbulence: Adventures in a new world.* New York: Penguin Press

Gronbeck, B. E. (1998). The rhetorics of the past: History, argument, and collective memory. In K. J. Turner (Ed.), *Doing rhetorical history: Concepts and cases* (pp. 47–60). Tuscaloosa and London: The University of Alabama Press.

Habermas, J. (1979). *Communication and the evolution of society* (T. McCarthy, Trans.) Boston: Beacon Press.

Habermas, J. (1984). *The theory of communicative action: Vol. 1. Reason and the rationalization of society* (T. McCarthy, Trans.) . Boston, Beacon Press.

Habermas, J. (2004, October). *The Kantian project of cosmopolitan law.* Lecture presented at Purdue University, West Lafayette, IN. (The first author of this book attended the lecture, took notes and transcribed portions of the lecture from a tape provided by the Department of Philosophy at Purdue University.)

Hall, S. (1992). The question of cultural identity. In S. Hall, D. Held, & T. McGrew (eds.). *Modernity and Its Futures* (pp. 273–316). Cambridge, MA: Polity.

Hall, S. (1985). Signification, representation, ideology: Althusser and the post-structuralist debates. *Critical Studies in Mass Communication, 2,* 91–114.

Hamper, B. (1986). *Rivethead: Tales from the assembly line.* New York: Time Warner.

Harding Davis, R. (1985). *Life in the iron mills and other stories.* New York: The Feminist Press. (Original work published in 1861)

Hare, R. M. (1996). *Plato.* New York: Oxford University Press.

Heilbroner, R. L. (1986). *The essential Adam Smith.* New York: Norton and Company.

Henderson, D. R. (2002). Biography of Adam Smith (1723–1790). *The Concise Encyclopedia of Economics.* Retrieved from: http://www.econlib.org.

Hendry, J. (2001). After Durkheim: An agenda for the sociology of business ethics. *Journal of Business Ethics, 34*, 209–218.

Hilbert, R. A. (1987). Bureaucracy as belief, rationalization and repair: Max Weber in a post-functionalist age. *Sociological Theory, 5*, 70–86.

Hill, R. B. (1996). *History of Work Ethic.* Retrieved January 23, 2003, from http://www.coe.uga.edu/~rhill/workethic/hist.htm.

Hochschild, A. R. (1983). *The managed heart.* Berkeley: University of California Press.

Hofstede, G. (1983). The cultural relativity of organizational practices and theories. *Journal of International Business Studies, 14*, 75–89.

Hofstede, G. (2001). *Culture's consequences: Comparing values, behaviors, institutions, and organizations across nations* (2nd ed.). Thousand Oaks, CA: Sage.

Hofstede, G., & Bond, M. H. (1988). The Confucius connection: From cultural roots to economic growth. *Organizational Dynamics, 16(4),* 4–21.

Hollingdale, R. J. (1973). *Nietzsche.* London and Boston: Routledge & Kegan Paul.

Hooker, R. (1996). Greek philosophy: Aristotle. Retrieved January 23, 2003, from http://www.wsu.edu/~dee/GREECE/ARIST.HTM.

Hooker, R. (1996). Greek philosophy: Plato. Retrieved January 23, 2003, from http://www.wsu.edu:8080/~dee/GREECE/PLATO.HTM.

Horne, J. F. (1997). *Mary Parker Follett: Visionary genius finds her own time.* Retrieved February 2, 2003, from http://www.auntl.org/mary.htm.

Hynes, G. C. (n.d.). *A biographical sketch of W. E. B. Du Bois.* Retrieved 2005 from http://www.duboislc.org/html/DuBoisBio.html.

Jablin, F. M. (2001). Organizational entry, assimilation, and disengagement/exit. In F. M. Jablin & L. L. Putnam (Eds.), *The new handbook of organizational communication: Advances in theory, research, and methods* (pp. 732–818). Thousand Oaks, CA: Sage.

Jersey, B., & Schwarz, M. (Producers). (1994–2003). *Stopwatch: Frederick Winslow Taylor and the "Taylorization" of America* [Television broadcast based on the book *The One Best Way: Frederick Winslow Taylor and the enigma of efficiency* by Robert Kanigel]. San Francisco KQED.

Jones, A. H. M. (1957). *Athenian democracy.* Baltimore, MD: Johns Hopkins University Press.

Jones, M. (1969). *Autobiography of Mother Jones: American labor: From conspiracy to collective bargaining.* New York: Arno & The New York Times. (Original work published in 1925)

Jones, R. A. (1986). *Emile Durkheim: An introduction to four major works.* Beverly Hills, CA: Sage Publications.

Josephy, A. M. (1994). *500 Nations: An illustrated history of North American Indians.* New York: Alfred A. Knopf.

Kaelber, L. (2003). Max Weber's dissertation. *History of the Human Sciences, 16.* Retrieved April, 26, 2003 from http://www.uvm.edu/~lkaelber/research/weber2.html.

Kamenka, E. (1983). *The portable Karl Marx.* New York: Viking/Penguin.

Kanigel, R. (1996). Frederick Taylor's apprenticeship. *The Wilson Quarterly, 20* (Summer), 44.

Kennedy, M. M. (1999). *An eye on "Trend spotting."* Retrieved from www.law.berkely.edu/administration/hr/worklife/trendspotting/pdf.

Kerr, R. L. (2002). Impartial spectator in the marketplace of ideas: The principles of Adam Smith as an ethical basis for regulation of corporate speech. *Journalism and Mass Communication Quarterly, 79,* 394–415.

Krone, K. J., Chen, L., & Xia, H. (1997). Approaches to managerial influence in the People's Republic of China. *Journal of Business Communication, 34,* 289–315.

Krone, K. J., Garret, M., & Chen, L. (1992). Managing communication practices in Chinese factories: A preliminary investigation. *Journal of Business Communication, 29,* 229–252.

Laclau, E., & Mouffe, C. (1985). *Hegemony and socialist strategy.* London: Verso.

Landry, P. (2002). *Adam Smith biography.* Retrieved September 18, 2002, from: http://www.blupete.com.

Langer, S. (1951). *Philosophy in a new key.* Cambridge, MA: Harvard University Press.

Lefkowitz, M. R., & Fant, M. B. (1982). *Women's life in Greece and Rome.* Baltimore: Johns Hopkins University Press.

Lerner, M. (1937). Introduction. In Smith, A. (1937). *An inquiry into the nature and causes of the wealth of nations.* New York: The Modern Library.

Lester, J. (Ed.). (1971). *The seventh son: The thoughts and writings of W. E. B. Du Bois,* (Vol. 1). New York: Vintage Books.

Levine, A. (2001). Fairness to idleness: Is there a right to work? In K. Schaff (Ed.), *Philosophy and the problems of work: A reader* (pp. 317–335). Lanham, MD: Rowman & Littlefield.

Lin, C. (2003). *Mao Zedong Thought and Organizational Communication Practices in China.* Unpublished dissertation. Lafayette, IN: Purdue University.

Lin, C., & Clair, R. P. (2007). Measuring Mao Zedung Thought and interpreting organizational communication in China. *Management Communication Quarterly, 20,* 395-429.

Lukes, S. (1995). *The curious enlightenment of professor Caritat.* London & New York: Verso.

Lyotard, J.-F. (1984). *The postmodern condition: A report on knowledge* (G. Bennington & B. Massumi, Trans.). Minneapolis: University of Minnesota Press. (Original work published 1979)

Mahowald, M. B. (Ed.). (1983). *Philosophy of woman: An anthology of classic and current concepts* (2nd ed.). Indianapolis, IN: Hackett Publishing.

Manton, E. J., & English, D. E. (1988). The ability of first semester college freshmen to identify the founding fathers of capitalism and communism. *The College Student Journal,* 363–366.

Marx, K. & Engels, F. (1964). *The communist manifesto* (S. Moore & Ed. J. Katz, Trans.). New York: Pocket Books, Simon and Schuster. (Original work published in 1848).

Marx, K. (1983). *Das Kapital* (Capital) Commodities. In E. Kamenka (Ed. & Trans.), *The portable Karl Marx* (pp. 437–461). New York: Penguin. (Original work published in 1867)

Marx, K. (1983). From Economico-philosophical manuscript of 1844—from the first manuscript 'Alienated labour.' In E. Kamenka (Ed. & Trans.), *The portable Karl Marx* (pp. 131–145). New York: Penguin. (Original work published in 1844)

Marx, K. (1983). On the Jewish Question. In E. Kamenka (Ed. & Trans.), *The portable Karl Marx* (pp. 96–114). New York: Penguin. (Original work published in 1844)

McLellan, D. (1971). *Karl Marx: Early texts.* New York: Barnes & Noble.

McLellan, D. (1977). *Karl Marx: Selected writings.* New York: Oxford University Press.

McSweeney, B. (2002a). Hofstede's model of national cultural differences and their consequences: A triumph of faith—a failure of analysis. *Human Relations, 55,* 89–118.

McSweeney, B. (2002b). The essentials of scholarship: A reply to Geert Hofstede. *Human Relations, 55,* 1363–1372.

Medved, C. E., Brogan, S. M., McClanahan, A. M., Morris, J. F., & Shepherd, G. J. (2006). Family and work socializing communication: Messages, gender, and ideological implications. *The Journal of Family Communication, 6,* 161–180.

Medved, C. E. & Kirby, E. L. (2005). Family CEOs: A feminist analysis of corporate mothering discourses. *Management Communication Quarterly, 18,* 435–478.

Meyers, W. (November 13, 2000). *The Santa Clara blues: Corporate personhood versus democracy.* Retrieved at www. mcn. org/e/iii/afd/sanatclara.html.

Miller, K. (2003). Organizational communication: Approaches and processes (3rd ed.). Belmont, CA: Wadsworth/Thomson.

Moore, J. D. (1997). *Visions of culture: An introduction to anthropological theories and theorists.* Walnut Creek, CA: Alta Mira Press.

Morgan, G. (1997). *Images of organization.* Thousand Oaks, CA: Sage.

Morgan, G. (1998). *Images of organization: The executive edition.* San Francisco: Berrett-Koehler and Thousand Oaks, CA: Sage.

Morrow, G. R. (1939). Plato and Greek slavery. *Mind, 48,* 186–201.

Morrow, G. R. (1927). Adam Smith: Moralist and philosopher. *The Journal of Political Economy, 35,* 321–342.

Muirhead, R. (2004). *Just work.* Cambridge: Harvard University Press.

Mumby, D. K., & Putnam, L. L. (1992). The politics of emotion: A feminist reading of bounded rationality. *Academy of Management Review, 17,* 465–486.

Murrel, G. (1984). W. E. B. Du Bois. In A. Commire (Ed.), *Historic World Leaders* (pp. 233–237). Detroit-Washington-London: Gale Research.

Nabers, M. S. (1996). Many workers will be laid off. *Dallas Business Review,* 7–15.

Nau, H. H., & Steiner, P. (2002). Schmoller, Durkheim, and Old European institutionalist economics. *Journal of Economic Issues, 36,* 1005–1020.

Nehrt, L. C., Truitt, J. F., & Wright, R. W. (1970). *International business research: Past, present, and future.* Bloomington, IN: Indiana University Bureau of Business Research.

Nietzsche, F. (1954). The birth of tragedy from the spirit of music (P. Fadiman, Trans.). In *The Philosophy of Nietzsche* (pp. 947–1088). New York: Random House. (Original work published 1872)

Nkomo, S. M., & Cox, Jr., T. (1996). Diverse identities in organizations. In S. R. Clegg, C. Hardy, & W. R. Nord (Eds.), *Handbook of organization studies* (pp. 338–356). London: Sage.

Okrent, M. (2001). Work, play and technology. In K. Schaff (Ed.), *Philosophy and the problems of work: A reader* (pp. 73–91). Lanham, MD: Rowman & Littlefield.

Orwell, G. (1961). *Down and out in Paris and London.* New York: Harcourt Brace Jovanovich. (Original work publish in 1933)

Orwell, G. (1958). *The road to wigan pier.* San Diego: Harvest Books. (Original work published in 1937)

Otteson, J. R. (2000). Adam Smith on the emergence of morals: A reply to Eugene Heath. *British Journal for the History of Philosophy, 8,* 545–551.

Oz, F. (1996). Whatever happened to "Red Emma"? Emma Goldman, from alien rebel to American icon. *The Journal of American History, 83,* 903–943.

Pacanowsky, M. (1988). Communicating in the empowering organization. In J. A. Anderson (Ed.) *Communication Yearbook,* 11 (pp. 356–379). New Brunswick, N. J.: International Communication Association.

Papesh, M. E. (n.d.). *Frederick Winslow Taylor.* Retrieved February 11, 2003, from http://www.stfrancis.edu.

Parker, B. (1996). Evolution and revolution: From international business to globalization. In S. R. Clegg, C. Hardy, & W. R. Nord (Eds.), *Handbook of organization studies* (pp. 484–506). London, Thousand Oaks, New Deli: Sage.

Parker, L. D. (1984). Control in organizational life: The contribution of Mary Parker Follett. *The Academy of Management Review, 9,* 736–745.

Perelman, C., & Olbrechts-Tyteca, L. (1969). *The new rhetoric* (J. Wilkinson & P. Weaver, Trans.). Notre Dame, IN: University of Notre Dame Press. (Original work published 1958)

Perrow, C. (1986). *Complex organizations* (3rd ed.). New York: Random House.

Plato (1974). *Plato's Republic.* (G. M. A. Grube, Trans.). Indianapolis, IN: Hackett Publishing Co.

Pomery, J. G. (Personal communication, August 18, 2006).

Poulakos, J., & Poulakos, T. (1999). *Classical rhetorical theory.* Boston and New York: Houghton Mifflin.

Quesnay, F. (1970). Oeconomical table: An attempt towards ascertaining and exhibiting the source, progress, and employment of riches, with explanations by the friend of mankind, the celebrated Marquis de Mirabeau. London: Printed for W. Owen. New York: Bergman (original work published 1766).

Randall, F. B. (1964). Introduction: Marx the romantic. In J. Katz (Ed.) *The communist manifesto* (pp. 7–44). New York: Pocket Books, Simon and Schuster.

Rawls, A. W. (1998). Rawls, Durkheim, and causality: A critical discussion. *American Journal of Sociology, 104,* 872–901.

Riba (July 30, 2007). Retrieved August 27, 2007, from http://en.wikipedia.org/wiki/Riba.

Riegel, J. K. (2002). *Confucius.* Retrieved November 1, 2007, from http://plato.stanford.edu/entries/confucius/.

Ritzer, G. (2004). *The McDonaldization of society* (Rev. new century ed.). Thousand Oaks, CA: Sage.

Robins, G. (1994). Dial-an-interview. *Stores, 76,* 34–35.

Rogers, E., & Agarwala-Rogers, R. (1976). *Communication in organizations.* New York: Free Press.

Ross, I. S. (1995). *The Life of Adam Smith.* Oxford: Oxford University Press.

Rothschild, E. (1994). Adam Smith and the invisible hand. *The American Economic Review, 84,* 319–322.

Russel, B. (1946). *History of western philosophy.* London: Allen and Unwin.

Russell, B. (1932). *In praise of idleness.* Retrieved November 1, 2007, from http://www.zpub.com/notes/idle.html.

Samosky, B. (2001). Living conditions in the southern West Virginia coalfields: The underlying cause of the West Virginia mine wars. *MU Online Historical Journal.* Retrieved October 7, 2002, from http://www.marshall.edu/pat/journal/samosky.htm.

Schafer, R. (1980). Narration in psychoanalytic dialogue. *Critical Inquiry, 7,* 29–54.

Scott, J. (2007). Our callings, our selves: Re-positioning religious and entrepreneurial discourses in career theory and practice. *Communication Studies, 58,* 261–279.

Senge, P. (1990). *The fifth dimension.* New York: Doubleday.

Sethi, N. K. (1962). Mary Parker Follett: Pioneer in management theory. *The Journal of the Academy of Management, 5,* 214–221.

Shapiro, M. (1997). *Sketch biography of author Mary Parker Follett.* Retrieved February 4, 2003, from http://sunsite.utk.edu/FINS/Mary_Parker_Follett/Fins-MPF-02.txt.

Shepherd, G. (1983). Poverty in *Piers Plowman.* In T. H. Aston, P. R. Cross, C. Dyer, & J. Thirsk (Eds.), *Social relations and ideas: Essays in honour of R. H. Hilton* (pp. 169–189). Cambridge: Cambridge University Press.

Shockley-Zalabak, P. S. (2006). *Fundamentals of organizational communication* (6th ed). Boston: Pearson.

Sinclair, U. (2001). *The jungle.* Mineola, NY: Dover Publications. (Original work published in 1906)

Singer, M. G., & Ammarman, R. R. (Eds.). (1962). *Introductory readings in philosophy.* New York: Charles Scribner's Sons.

Singer, P. (1980). *Marx.* New York: Hill & Wang.

Skrabec, Jr., R. Q. (2003). *St. Benedict's Rule for business success.* West Lafayette, IN: Purdue University Press.

Smith, A. (1937). *An inquiry into the nature and causes of the wealth of nations.* New York: Modern Library/Random House. (Original work published 1776)

Smith, A. (1759). *The theory of moral sentiments.* London: W. Strahan and F. Rivington, T. Longman, and T. Cadell 1781 version in special archives at Purdue University. Also available at http://www.adamsmith.org/smith/tms-p6-s3-c3.htm Adam Smith Institute 2001.

Smith, R. C. (1990/1993). *In pursuit of synthesis: Activity as a primary framework for organizational communication.* Unpublished doctoral dissertation. University of Southern California, Los Angeles. (The 1993 version is an unpublished summary of the dissertation.)

Smith, R. C. (1993, May). *Images of organizational communication: Root metaphors of the organization-communication relation.* Paper presented at the annual meeting of the International Communication Association, Washington D.C.

Solomon, M. (1988). Ideology as rhetorical constraint: The anarchist agitation of "Red Emma" Goldman. *Quarterly Journal of Speech, 74,* 184–200.

Sorg, D. R. (1953). *Holy work: Towards a Benedictine theology of manual labor.* Saint Louis, MO: Pio Decimo.

Specher, H. P. (1962). Introduction. In M. Weber, *Basic concepts in sociology* (H. P. Specher, Trans.). (pp. 7–23). New York: Philosophical Library.

Stewart, C. J. (1991). The internal rhetoric of the Knights of Labor. *Communication Studies, 42,* 67–82.

Stohl, C. (2001). Globalizing organizational communication. In F. M. Jablin & L. L. Putnam (Eds.), *The new handbook of organizational communication* (pp. 323–375). Thousand Oaks, CA: Sage.

Taylor, A. E. (1955). *Aristotle.* New York: Dover Publications, Inc.

Taylor, F. W. (1911). *The Principles of Scientific Management.* New York and London: Harper & Brothers Publishers. (Republished in 1934)

Terkel, S. (1972). *Working: People talk about what they do all day and how they feel about what they do.* New York: Pantheon Books.

Thomas, K. (Ed.) (1999). *The Oxford book of work.* Oxford: Oxford University Press.

Tilman, R. (2002). Durkheim and Veblen on the social nature of individualism. *Journal of Economic Issues, 36,* 1104–1110.

Tjosvold, D., & Sun, H. F. (2003). Openness among Chinese in conflict: Effects of direct discussion and warmth on integrated decision making. *Journal of Applied Social Psychology, 33,* 1878–1897.

Tjosvold, D., Hui, C., & Sun, H. (2000). Social faces and open-mindedness: Constructive conflict in Asia. In C. M. Lau, K. S. Law, D. K. Tse, & C. S. Wong (Eds.), *Asian management matters: Regional relevance and global impact* (pp. 4–16). London: Imperial College Press.

Tjosvold, D., Nibler, R., & Wan, P. (2001). Motivation for conflict among Chinese: Effects of other's expertise and confidence on choosing disagreement. *Journal of Social Psychology, 141,* 353–365.

Tonn, M. (1996). Militant motherhood: Labor's Mary Harris "Mother" Jones. *The Quarterly Journal of Speech, 82,* 1–21.

Toole, J. K. (1980). A confederacy of dunces. Baton Rouge: Louisiana State University Press.

Triandis, H. C. (1994). Theoretical and methodological approaches to the study of collectivism and individualism. In U. Kim, H. C. Triandis, C. Kagitcibasi, S.-C. Choi, & G. Yoon (Eds.), *Individualism and collectivism: Theory, methods, and applications.* London: Sage.

Trujillo, M. H. (2003). *The confluent space of dreams: Columbians' visions of the American dream in light of hegemonic discourses.* Unpublished master's thesis. Purdue University, West Lafayette, IN.

Turner, J. (1990). Emile Durkheim's theory of social organization. *Social Forces, 68,* 1089–1103.

Turner, K. J. (1998). Introduction: Rhetorical history as social construction. In K. J. Turner (Ed.). *Doing rhetorical history: Concepts and cases* (pp. 1–15). Tuscaloosa: The University of Alabama Press.

Turner, V. (1980). Social dramas and stories about them. *Critical Inquiry, 7,* 141–168.

Van Hook, L. R. (1923). *Greek life and thought.* New York: Columbia University Press.

van Staveren, I. (2001). *The value of economics: An Aristotelian perspective.* London & New York: Routledge.

Washington, B. T. (1902). *Up from slavery: An autobiography.* New York: Doubleday, Page & Co.

Weber, M. (1968). *Economy and society: An outline of interpretive sociology* (E. Fischoff, H. Gerth, A. M. Henderson, F. Kolegar, C. W. Mills, T. Parsons, and others, Trans.; G. Roth, & C. Wittich, Eds.). New York: Bedminster Press.

Weber, M. (1978). *Max Weber: Selections* (E. Matthews, Trans.). W. G. Runciman (Ed.). Cambridge: Cambridge University Press.

Weber, M. (1992). *The Protestant ethic and the spirit of capitalism.* (T. Parsons, Trans.). London & New York: Routledge. (Original book version published in 1930; original articles published in 1904–5)

Weisbord, M. R. (1987). *Productive workplaces.* San Francisco: Jossey-Bass.

West, C. (1993). *Race matters.* Boston: Beacon Press.

Wexler, A. (1984). *Emma Goldman: An intimate life.* New York: Pantheon.

White, H. (1980). The value of narrativity in the representation of reality. *Critical Inquiry, 7,* 5–28.

Whyte, Jr., W. H. (1956). *The organization man.* New York: Simon and Schuster.

Willis, P. (1977). *Learning to labor: How working class kids get working class jobs.* New York: Columbia University Press.

Wrege, C.D., & Greenwood, R.G. (1991). *Frederick W. Taylor: The father of scientific management, myth and reality.* Homewood, IL: Business One Irwin.

Wrong, D. (Ed.). (1970). *Max Weber.* Englewood Cliffs, New Jersey: Prentice-Hall.

Zarefsky, D. (1998). Four senses of rhetorical history. In K. J. Turner (Ed.). *Doing rhetorical history: Concepts and cases* (pp. 19–32). Tuscaloosa: The University of Alabama Press.

Zinn, H. (1995). *A people's history of the United States: 1492–present.* New York: Harper Perennial.

Index